Decolonial Love

Decolonial Love

SALVATION IN COLONIAL MODERNITY

JOSEPH DREXLER-DREIS

FORDHAM UNIVERSITY PRESS

New York 2019

Library of Congress Cataloging-in-Publication Data

Names: Drexler-Dreis, Joseph, author.
Title: Decolonial love : salvation in colonial modernity / Joseph
    Drexler-Dreis.
Description: First edition. | New York, NY : Fordham University Press, 2019.
    | Includes bibliographical references and index.
Identifiers: LCCN 2018024884| ISBN 9780823281886 (cloth : alk. paper) | ISBN
    9780823281879 (pbk. : alk. paper)
Subjects: LCSH: Liberation theology. | Love—Religious aspects—Christianity.
    | Baldwin, James, 1924–1987. | Fanon, Frantz, 1925–1961. | Postcolonial
    theology.
Classification: LCC BT83.57 .D74 2019 | DDC 261.8—dc23
LC record available at https://lccn.loc.gov/2018024884

Printed in the United States of America
21 20 19   5 4 3 2 1
First edition

for LaToya and Malcolm

CONTENTS

Decolonial Love

What Is Decolonial Love?

At the end of the fifteenth century, within contexts of commercial exchange, conquest, and colonization, Europe began to position itself as the center of the world. Europe became central not only as a physical referent in a political and economic sense, but also as a narrative or epistemological referent—that is, as the locus from which to make sense of reality. The political process of colonialism became constitutive of Western modernity. Within this form of modernity, which decolonial thinkers refer to as colonial modernity, colonial categories cease historical motion. They freeze relationships into hierarchical patterns of domination that continue after political decolonization. This process of solidification reifies the hierarchies within ways of being, thinking, and imagining crucial to political colonialism such that they outlast colonialism as a historical era of political domination.

The US empire, including both its conservative and liberal ideologies, has given evidence to this attempt to maintain historical and epistemological stasis within colonial modernity. Culturally dominant imaginaries, including ways of understanding the human person, knowledge, and the eschaton sustain colonial relations of power, often under the guise of "freedom." A

Christian imagination has in large part grounded this institution of freedom as a good.[1] There is a difference—a "colonial difference," Sylvester A.
Johnson argues—between reforming and civilizing missions of "progress"
and "betterment" that exist within the ideological "sign of Christian freedom" and its secular correlates, on the one hand, and the brutality that has
structured the colonial encounter between Europeans and non-Europeans,
on the other.[2] That is, that which has been naturalized within the white settler colonialism that grounds the US project and that which is experienced
as freedom by those committed to the project of Western modernity has a
shadow side.[3] This is the "colonial difference." Walter D. Mignolo clarifies
that, starting in the middle of the twentieth century, the colonial difference
became a reality that was no longer only in the "periphery" of the modern/
colonial world-system, or "out there, away from the center," but "all over,
in the peripheries of the center and in the centers of the periphery."[4] Sites
such as inner cities in the United States bear witness to the colonial difference both because they witness the brutality of the creation of a modern/
colonial world and because they are a "space where the restitution of subaltern knowledge is taking place."[5] Colonial modernity conceals both the
ways the colonial difference is constitutive of Western modernity and the
epistemic potential of the colonial difference.

Decolonial thinkers have identified the North Atlantic context as one
shaped by Europe's modernity and the colonial relations of power that
are constitutive of that modernity—that is, by the colonial difference—
during the last five hundred years. The colonial structures that constitute
the North Atlantic context demand a wide-ranging response, even if there
is no solution to the problems that stem from them. I opt for a form of
theological reflection as one response. As a response to a historical situation, theological reflection can expose idols, or human constructions pur-
porting to be ultimate, and hold up alternatives beyond the constraints
of market-driven rationalities that create idols within colonial modernity.
Theological reflection can offer a pathway toward a response because it
can re-situate commitments within reality.

Setting forth Christian theological reflection as one possible avenue of
responding to the long historical context of colonial modernity raises two
fundamental questions. First, can theology, as a discipline formed out of
experiences and intellectual traditions emanating from the Mediterranean
world and then, subsequently, Western Europe, adequately respond to historical contexts on the colonial underside of a matrix shaped by precisely
those traditions? In other words, can theology, as a mode of critical reflection that employs core concepts and images with lineages grounded in the

European experience, contribute to the task of decolonization? Second, if a positive response to this question were offered, what would the content of that response look like?

A negative reply to the first question regarding a potentially constructive link between theology and decolonization might claim that theology is irredeemably Eurocentric: theology as an academic discipline maintains reference points to an intellectual tradition developed within a social, cultural, and epistemological milieu that funded colonialism and on which colonial frameworks continue to draw. Theology is limited in addressing the oppressive social-political matrix of the current epoch that emerges from colonialism because its rationalities are confined to a local history with which decolonization is in conflict. While necessary to pursue such negative replies, it is also important to acknowledge that Christian communities and theologians have given positive answers to the basic question of the possibility of Christian theological reflection to move in liberating directions. Starting in the latter half of the twentieth century, theologians within what came to be known as "liberation theology" began to articulate the faith of communities whose primary project was not one of seeking inclusion into Western modernity. An important inroad that liberation theologians made has been their critical awareness of how their immediate historical situations related to global processes and their pursuit, through theological reflection, to establish different relationships to Western modernity than the relationship imposed by the dominant paradigm of assimilation. Continuing in this tradition, this book pursues a positive response to the question of whether theology can adequately respond to persisting colonial relations of power by continuing to develop a style of theological reflection that searches for new ways of relating to Western modernity.

In response to the second question regarding the content of a theological response to colonial modernity, I focus on the theological image of salvation. Gustavo Gutiérrez describes salvation as an "intrahistorical reality."[6] This description presupposes a unity within history between divine and human realities. Gutiérrez grounds this claim of the oneness of history that makes for both an "already" and a "not yet" in two biblical themes that he centralizes: creation/salvation and eschatological or messianic promises.

Gutiérrez develops an understanding of salvation grounded in faith in creation "as a part of the salvific process."[7] Creation itself grounds the gratuitous nature of God's salvation. God's creative act is linked to the liberative acts of Yahweh in history, or with the active political liberation of Israel: God both calls and actualizes liberation in history.[8] Salvation as an

"encounter with God" is the "deepest meaning" of the instances of political liberation in Israel's history.[9] As such, salvation, as God's self-offer to
creation that takes the form of love, is always encountered and experienced
in history, through processes of political liberation. Faith in the Hebrew
God demands taking on this specificity when understanding God's relationship to history.

The theme of creation/salvation, which has as its deepest meaning the
salvation given by God, coexists with God's eschatological promise that
unfolds and is revealed in history. Eschatological promises are "fulfilled
throughout history," even as they cannot "be identified clearly and completely with one or another social reality; their liberating effect goes far
beyond the foreseeable and opens up new and unsuspected possibilities."[10]
The eschatological promises to which Gutiérrez refers always include a
tension between "a concrete event, and *in* it to another fuller and more
comprehensive one to which history must be open."[11] There is thus both a
historical present and a future dimension to salvation as an eschatological
reality. Within the context of this tension, Gutiérrez affirms a "Christo-
finalized history," or a history in which there is an eschatological fullness
in the Christ event in history, but a fullness that depends on an orientation
toward an openness to the future.[12] Crucially, the eschatological reality is a
reality to which history is open or transparent.

Gutiérrez opens the historical present of salvation in reference to love.
Love is constitutive of God's creative act, as "God's gratuitous love" is "the
source of everything else and [is] a power that sweeps us along with it."[13]
Salvation is manifest in the freedom from that which motivates a turning
in on the self and freedom for communion with and participation in God's
gratuitous love. Historically, this participation appears as relationships of
love with the other, and specifically love concretized as solidarity with the
oppressed, and a praxis that moves toward liberation.

When I develop the content of a theological response to colonial modernity, I remain within this tradition of connecting salvation and love. I
do so while recognizing that love can be an amorphous concept—often
politically neutral, passive, nonviolent, and located within interior lives. It
is a particular form of love, of encounter with and participation in a divine
reality that grounds my theological response to colonial modernity—what
I call "decolonial love." With decolonial love, I refer to a way love is made
concrete in history within struggles to reveal and shatter the structures of
colonial modernity.

I specifically locate instances of decolonial love in the intellective and
political praxis of Frantz Fanon and James Baldwin. The commitments of

Fanon and Baldwin are not those to which many theologians are accustomed: they rarely use explicitly confessional language. Theologians can recognize Fanon and Baldwin within the negative (and often prophetic) tradition of exposing idols and revealing illusory notions of stasis. But—and this is the case not only for Fanon and Baldwin but also, though to a lesser extent, contemporary decolonial theorists—alternative commitments motivate these critiques. The critique of idolatry makes room for and implies a commitment to something else. Their rebuke of idols implies hope, and even faith, even as these terms are infrequently named or thematized. Decolonial love forwards visions of alternative possibilities grounded in commitments that are no longer shaped by an enchantment with Western modernity. Decolonial love is a mode of relating to concrete persons and communities—and necessarily the entire matrix of Western modernity—that takes shape in the recognition of not only the failure but also the destructiveness of Western modernity. I argue that Fanon and Baldwin operate out of orientations of decolonial love that break open cracks in Western modernity and make salvation present in history. Decolonial love thus becomes theologically pedagogic. Decolonial love offers one basis of theological reflection and one way of shaping the content of a decolonized image of salvation.

Mapping Decolonial Love

In the service of developing a way of thinking theologically within a decolonial perspective, Part I outlines an understanding of what decolonial theorists have called the "coloniality of power" as the dominant matrix that shapes the contemporary context. Decolonial perspectives raise the critical question of whether the academic discipline of Christian theology limits the footholds of rational argument and critical reflection to Eurocentric intellectual commitments and trajectories. To put this question toward theologians in a constructive way: Can communities that have been epistemically disenfranchised within and by Western modernity think theologically outside a Eurocentered epistemological framework? Underneath this question is the more basic question of whether a theological perspective has the capacity to link onto, in constructive ways, historical projects moving toward decolonization. This question has to be addressed before moving to more specific questions of what a decolonial theological project and a decolonized image of salvation might look like.

Gutiérrez has argued that Christian theologians have the task of critically reflecting on historical situations in light of faith in the divine reality incarnate and revealed in a particular way in Jesus of Nazareth.[14] This task of Christian theological reflection can be challenged, and subsequently deepened, by engaging perspectives within decolonial thought. The particularity of the Christian belief in the incarnation of divinity in Jesus is a significant interpretive locus for theologians in view of decolonial ways of thinking because incarnation grounds the Christian faith claim that God most fully reveals her or himself in history, among the oppressed, and as taking the side of the oppressed in their struggle for liberation, understood as the Reign of God. Liberation theologians refer to the particular nature of divine presence and revelation as God's "option for the poor."[15] The Christian understanding of the nature and locus of God's self-revelation prompts a critical reflection on human experience that works from the perspectives of communities on the undersides of history and within the ways they have made sense of the world. In this sense, the task of a Christian theologian is contiguous with a point of attention within decolonial projects. The recognition and affirmation that ways of thinking that have been rendered nonrational or nonproductive from the perspective of Western modernity provide crucial insight about the contemporary world grounds both Christian theology—or at least those theologies that prioritize a Christian commitment over a commitment to defend the benefits of Western modernity through a defense of Eurocentrism—and the task of creating decolonial futures.

While some similarities exist between theological and decolonial perspectives, Part I is more concerned with whether the differences between the two projects allow for a theological perspective to serve a decolonial project, not with merging the two intellectual trajectories. It does so by asking whether theology can meet the critiques that are present within the emerging field of decolonial thought. There are at least two basic reasons why addressing the challenges posed by decolonial perspectives to theology should serve as a prelude to theological reflection. First, theology is always a response to a particular historical situation, and articulating the relationship between Western modernity and its underside helps to analyze with increased precision and depth contemporary historical realities. The first chapter uses the concept of the "coloniality of power" from decolonial thought as a way of interpreting the contemporary historical situation. Specifically, it applies the interpretive lens of coloniality to ways of being, ways of knowing, and eschatological imaginaries. The second reason a decolonial challenge to theological ways of thinking should precede an assumption of the liberative role of theological reflection is the obvious entanglement between the epistemic structures produced within colonial modernity and the discipline of Christian theology, in terms of both causation and the continued distortion of rationalities that do not legitimize modern/colonial structures. Theologians have to address this connection if we seek to respond to the present global historical situation within ways of thinking shaped by convictions of Christian faith grounded in the option for the poor. Decolonial thought, therefore, can help to sustain the inner coherence of the theological task and force theology to more rigorously respond to a real historical situation.

The second chapter investigates the link between Christian thought and the historical matrix decolonial thinkers have theorized as the coloniality of power. In light of the historical theory of the coloniality of power and theology's entanglement in coloniality, this chapter opens up options for what decolonization might look like within theological reflection. Introducing these options leads to a threshold question for thinking from a Christian theological perspective within a decolonial project: Can members of communities who have been rendered nonpersons through various manifestations of the coloniality of power think and speak theologically on their own terms? The third chapter considers the possibilities within Latin American liberation theology for theological reflection to work together with a decolonial project in response to this threshold question. It specifically focuses on how the work of the liberation theologians Ignacio Ellacuría and Jon Sobrino points to the theoretical possibility of communities speaking theologically from epistemic loci located within the cracks of Western modernity.

Part II introduces two responses, from Frantz Fanon and James Baldwin, to the recognition that Western modernity both depends on and perpetuates a colonial underside. Ellacuría and Sobrino's theological approach, which opens the theoretical possibility of a decolonial theology and an opportunity to expand the sources that inform theological ways of thinking, motivates this move to the work of Fanon and Baldwin. This turn outward from the discipline of theology—that is, to two thinkers who neither identify as theologians nor explicitly engage theological traditions—is important in order to avoid a solipsistic tendency of theological discourse claiming for itself an epistemic privilege.[16] Turning to the work of Fanon and Baldwin as epistemic foundations that inform theological claims is one option for moving theological reflection out of a self-referential cycle on the level of concepts and ideas.

Orientations of decolonial love, which I uncover in and develop from the work of Fanon and Baldwin, establish starting points for theological reflection. As an eschatological reality, or a reality that opens up history to its depths, the occurrence of love in the world provides a site of divine revelation and salvation.[17] Recognizing the historical manifestations of the coloniality of power in the contemporary context leads me to specify love as decolonial—that is, a love that both affirms an ultimate reality and combats the modern world-system that creates idols that pose as ultimate realities. As an image, decolonial love brings together historical struggles against idols in a generative and unreconciled way, resisting attempts to bring historical conflict into a stasis. Reflective of the historical orientations that guide the work of Fanon and Baldwin, decolonial love is an open, unstable, and at times dialectical concept.

While some theorists have interpreted the work of Fanon using the category of love, it is not immediately clear that love is anything more than a peripheral concern for Fanon.[18] In chapter four, I read Fanon as a dialectical thinker who struggles to encounter an absolute reality within particular categories, such as race and nationalist struggle.[19] Within the context of his dialectics, I understand Fanon as a theorist of decolonial love. Decolonial love is one way of naming the orientation by which Fanon struggles to live into the motion of history. In his first book, *Black Skin, White Masks*, Fanon searches for "salvation," a term he uses outside a religious tradition's creedal statements. As he moved from Martinique to France and then to Algeria, and as he deepened his commitment within historical movements for decolonization and articulated the meaning of decolonization within these evolving commitments, Fanon developed an understanding of salvation as "the end of the world, of course."[20] Out of a love for those condemned by Western modernity, those whom he called "*les damnés*," Fanon worked to end the social, political, economic, and discursive world that Western modernity configures. He recognized Western modernity as a matrix that depends on a colonial underside, and took up a praxis of obliterating its idols.

Writing out of the experience of the colonial underside of the United States in a way that compliments Fanon's orientation of decolonial love, Baldwin worked out what salvation might mean from the experience of living within the center of the modern world-system as a result of colonialism in the Atlantic world. Baldwin criticized the projection of salvation in "the alabaster Christ and the bloody cross." This offer of salvation, Baldwin argued, perpetuates the signification of the black subject by the social imaginary of the United States as lacking any foundation outside acceptance of the alabaster Christ.[21] Baldwin reinterprets salvation as revelation. Salvation involves shattering, rather than accepting, the alabaster Christ in order to clear space for something else. The task of revealing the reality that exists underneath the way Western modernity configures reality is itself an actualization of salvation. As Baldwin presents it, salvation as revelation involves the tasks of both breaking down idols and unveiling the depth of reality that already exists, though concealed by a US imaginary and the alabaster Christ.

Love is a much more explicit, though still ambiguous, category in Baldwin's work. In a 1965 conversation with Colin MacInnes and James Mossman, MacInnes asks Baldwin whether he is "a religious writer" and a "believer." Baldwin responds that he believes "in love," which he recognizes "sounds very corny." He goes on:

> I believe we can save each other. In fact I think we must save each other. . . . I don't mean anything passive. I mean something active, something more like a fire, like the wind, something which can change you. I mean energy. I mean a passionate belief, a passionate knowledge of what a human being can do, and become, and what a human being can do to change the world in which he finds himself.[22]

Josiah Ulysses Young III interprets this statement as Baldwin's "credo,"[23] though what Baldwin means by love and the way it shapes his orientation within the world remains ambiguous. The fifth chapter explores the tensions in Baldwin's understanding of love, and demonstrates how love is, for Baldwin, an "energy" or at times a "force" that is both a critical and constructive orientation.

While the fourth and fifth chapters bring out differences in the way the image of love functions for Fanon and Baldwin, there are several points of connection that are crucial in my reading of Fanon and Baldwin as intellectuals who thought theologically. These points of connection, along with the ways differences are situated within these points of connection, shape the way I see the work of Fanon and Baldwin, and particularly the orientations of decolonial love that come through in their work, to be theologically pedagogic.

First, Fanon and Baldwin are both committed to exposing and naming idols. For Fanon, in a revolutionary struggle the "artificial sentinel" guarding "the Greco-Roman pedestal" in the back of the minds of colonized intellectuals "is smashed to smithereens."[24] Fanon's project is, in large part, an attempt to catalyze this process of smashing the guardians of the idols that emerge in Greco-Roman, Western European, and US traditions. Baldwin takes up this project in a US context, revealing the "lie" contained in the idea of the United States and seeking to destroy it:

All of the Western nations have been caught in a lie, the lie of their pretended humanism; this means that their history has no moral justification, and that the West has no moral authority. Malcolm, yet more concretely than Frantz Fanon—since Malcolm operated in the Afro-American idiom, and referred to the Afro-American situation—made the nature of this lie, and its implications, relevant and articulate to the people whom he served.[25]

Baldwin, like Fanon, works to "serve" as an intellectual in a similar way, by critiquing idolatry and clearing space for something else.

Second, in this process of exposing idols, both Fanon and Baldwin hold up some sort of positive ultimate reality; they are not merely critics. In some ways, both thinkers have humanist commitments. Fanon begins his first book by proclaiming: "Striving for a New Humanism. Understanding Mankind. Our Black Brothers. I believe in you, Man."[26] There is also an element in Baldwin's work that affirms salvation as a reality within and of humans themselves, as seen in what Young reads as Baldwin's "credo."[27] But, I read both Fanon and Baldwin as more than agnostic humanists. Both thinkers affirm a transcendent, irreducible reality, and they value the human person insofar as the human person is in relationship with a transcendent reality, or that which remains after exposing idols.[28] I use the image of decolonial love to refer to this transcendent reality.

Third, Fanon and Baldwin are both vigorously opposed to historical stasis. They demand historical movement, and see the praxis of catalyzing and authenticating historical movement to be part of their task as intellectuals. Like other interpreters of Fanon, I read him as a committed dialectical thinker. Fanon employs categories that might capture something of an absolute reality, such as blackness and national consciousness, but also quickly moves from these categories when they are in danger of solidifying. Although Baldwin is less explicitly dialectical, he more explicitly uses love as a force that prevents stasis. Love is for Baldwin the energy that releases "the white man" from "the tyranny of his mirror" and "takes off the masks that we fear we cannot live without and know we cannot live within."[29] Baldwin, like Fanon, relentlessly pushes for human encounters that destroy the possibility of stasis.

Through their work that responds to specific iterations of colonial modernity, Fanon and Baldwin give content to decolonial love. They show what it means to love in a decolonial way, and what it means to incorporate an orientation of decolonial love into intellective work. An orientation of decolonial love, they show, is concretized in history in at least three ways.

Decolonial love exposes the idolatry of Western modernity and creates space for an alternative. It situates the human person in relationship to a transcendent and irreducible, even if unnameable, reality. And, it commits to catalyzing and authenticating historical movement—that is, hastening the end of the modern world-system. In these three moments, decolonial love is a posture by which to face up to reality.

The political and intellective praxis of decolonial love that Fanon and Baldwin take up opens up options. Walter D. Mignolo has argued that a single system of knowledge "is pernicious to the well-being of the human species and to the life of the planet."[30] He distinguishes between "missions" and "options" as a way to avoid imposing a single thought system. Decolonial projects express their legitimacy within the arena of other options for imagining the world; decolonial projects are not "missions," or single systems of knowledge to which others need to be converted.[31] In light of this distinction, Mignolo is in general suspicious of the rhetoric of "salvation" as a mission-rhetoric that emerges from Western modernity. Whether it functions within the framework of Christianity, modernization, or development, salvation generally connotes a mission.[32] It commonly indicates a single position that demands a practice of conversion. To propose salvation as a decolonial option, as Fanon and Baldwin do, requires showing how salvation is a reality that underlies historical reality that opens up into possibilities. The orientations of decolonial love of Fanon and Baldwin open up into an unresolved, and unresolvable, mystery: their projects are concerned with neither nostalgia for a past to be reclaimed nor a linear movement toward a Eurocentered future. Their orientations of decolonial love open up into a set of possibilities for engaging with reality, for making space for the encounter with the mystery of reality's eschatological dimensions.

Part III offers a constructive proposal for a theological understanding of salvation from the epistemic sites of the decolonial love that Fanon and Baldwin offer. Both the content and approach to this constructive theological work emerge from the way Fanon and Baldwin develop orientations of decolonial love. Decolonial love provides an epistemic framework that can be what Marcella Althaus-Reid has called "theologically pedagogic."[33] I propose a way of doing theology as a decolonial option—that is, a form of critical reflection on historical situations in light of Christian faith that works toward unsettling colonial relations of power. Seeing decolonial love as having the capacity to inform the meaning of the theological image of salvation, I articulate a decolonized image of salvation by claiming decolonial love as an orientation and praxis that makes historically present the encounter with the divine mystery. I read Fanon and Baldwin to have thought theologically because they are committed to opening up space for the encounter with the mystery of an eschatological reality in history, or because they're concerned with salvation. Their orientations of decolonial love make a claim about a divine reality: that the sacred is historically present in the human relationship to history and in the forcing of historical motion.

Understanding how decolonial love is theologically pedagogic requires responding to at least two questions. First, it demands responding to the question of how the theological pedagogy of decolonial love is a (new) way of doing theology. Second, it requires bringing the content of the pedagogy into theological images and concepts. The sixth and seventh chapters each address both of these questions.

The sixth chapter addresses these two questions with respect to theological ways of thinking, broadly conceived. In doing so, it revisits what it means to think theologically while standing under the direction of the orientation of decolonial love in the work of Fanon and Baldwin. Asking this question leads to two central categories in a way of thinking theologically: revelation and history. I argue that the interaction of these two realities, which I define theologically from the work of Fanon and Baldwin, must ground theological images of salvation.

The seventh and final chapter addresses the two questions above with respect to the particular theological image of salvation. It responds to the first question, regarding a new way of envisioning salvation in light of decolonial love, by situating a decolonized image of salvation in relation to different ways liberation theologians have envisioned salvation. It responds to the second question, regarding bringing the content of decolonial love into a theological image of salvation, by arguing for decolonial love as a site of salvation, and embracing the tension such a site evinces between love and violence.

Through imagining a decolonial way of doing theology and decolonizing the theological image of salvation, this project demonstrates and then confronts the inconsistencies between, on the one hand, Christian faith claims of divinity as incarnate in Jesus of Nazareth, and on the other, many theologies' dependence on Eurocentered discourses to explain divinity. It does so by starting from the claim that the "irruption of the poor" that Gustavo Gutiérrez identified as a starting point for liberation theology, which is "a tough entry that asks permission of no one, and is sometimes violent,"[34] while recognizing that those who "irrupt" think on their own epistemic terms. Rather than an irruption that gets included and assimi-

lated into Western Christian traditions, the irruption can offer other options of epistemic loci. Ways of being, doing, and thinking that irrupt
within communities from the undersides of Western modernity have the
capacity to make theological claims, and specifically to shape a theological
image of salvation.

The Theological Pedagogy of Decolonial Love

Because Fanon and Baldwin engaged reality with commitments to exposing idols, to situating the human person in relationship to an irreducible
reality that transcended the confines of modern rationalities, and to hastening the end of the modern world-system, I read them as theologically
pedagogic. Gutiérrez quotes the Bolivian priest Luís Espinal Camps to
describe the role of contemplation and reflection within God-talk, which
always accompanies a prophetic commitment to the victims of social arrangements: "Train us, Lord, to fling ourselves upon the impossible, for
behind the impossible is your grace and your presence; we cannot fall into
emptiness."[35] Decolonial love, when understood as theologically pedagogic, both throws light on "the impossible"—that is, on that which is
outside the parameters of understanding within colonial modernity—and,
as a practice, is a way of "fling[ing] ourselves upon the impossible." Decolonial love is a modality of encounter with an eschatological reality in
history. The eschatological reality that decolonial love historicizes is full in
the sense of the commitment that decolonial love entails and is a foretaste
in the sense that decolonial love is constantly open to an infinite reality that
exceeds any particular praxis.

Frantz Fanon and James Baldwin both envision decolonial love as a form
of relation and a type of praxis that exists on the borders of the dominant
epistemic framework that conflates knowledge with the geopolitical site of
European modernity. Decolonial love exceeds the progressive and asymp-
totic assimilation to modern Western ideals. The ways of being, thinking,
and imagining that Fanon and Baldwin articulate provide a ground from
which to speak about a divine reality on epistemic terms that exist on the
borders of Western modernity. It's in this sense that decolonial love can
ground God-talk, and might offer a source that can inform how theologians articulate salvation.

PART I

Christian Theology in the Networks of Colonial Modernity

CHAPTER I

Colonial Modernity as a Historical Context

Theological reflection, even in Liberation Theology, becomes
a commodity. The doctrine of salvation as if it was a pound of
sugar reproduces endlessly the misery of the poor in abstract
discourses based on real material suffering. The poor person
as a theological author in her own right (the right of her
experience of sacralised forms of oppression such as sexism,
racism and classism) is thingified (reified) in the process, by the
intellectual producers who get their profit in terms of power.

—MARCELLA ALTHAUS-REID, *Indecent Theology: Theological Perversions*
in Sex, Gender and Politics (London: Routledge, 2000), 28

Marcella Althaus-Reid's concern that theological reflection that seeks to
address material situations of oppression often becomes a commodity and
"thingifies" the epistemic capacity of the poor person challenges any attempt at doing theology within an academic context in response to oppressive historical structures. Bringing in decolonial thought does not
in itself get around the problem to which Althaus-Reid draws attention.
The proliferation of concepts and neologisms in decolonial theory, often
developed in the contexts of academic conferences and elite universities,
can easily be seen as part of the problem of commodifying misery. There
are, however, some possibilities within decolonial thought that can help
to push theologians beyond the commodifying tendency within theological reflection that Althaus-Reid notes. First, decolonial thought situates
the contemporary context within a long history, and thus avoids forwarding superficial solutions to historical problems. Second, decolonial thinkers demonstrate how Christian thought has been and remains entangled
with discourses that legitimize "the misery of the poor" and "real material
suffering." As most thinkers within the emerging field of study of decolonial theory are not committed to Christian theology as a perspective,

decolonial thinkers have not been reluctant to criticize even those theologies that fashion themselves as liberative. Third, decolonial thinkers have been concerned with the project of struggling to see from the viewpoint of material situations of oppression, and intentionally seek to bring in the "authorship" of the oppressed. Engaging a decolonial perspective, I wager, can open up possibilities for avoiding what Althaus-Reid refers to as the thingification and reification of "the poor person as a theological author in her own right."

This chapter begins by describing the concept Aníbal Quijano has developed as the "coloniality of power," in view of how it might be useful for theologians. This is, I suggest, one way to conceptualize the present historical context to which theological reflection must respond. In the three subsequent sections, this chapter considers ways the historical situation to which Quijano refers with concept of the coloniality of power shapes understandings of the human person, ways of thinking, and eschatologies. In the process of offering an explanation of the present historical situation, the chapter draws on Quijano's work and on thinkers influenced by his work. This sets up the task of the following chapter, which considers the entanglement of Christian and theological thought in colonial structures, and pushes toward avenues of decolonization.

The Coloniality of Power

The theorization of coloniality and decoloniality within the work of the Peruvian sociologist Aníbal Quijano conceptualizes how a colonial structure of power persists beyond the end of political colonialism. The idea of coloniality had precedents in the Bandung conference in 1955,[1] and in thematic and theoretical underpinnings of the struggle for decolonization in the work of thinkers such as Aimé Césaire,[2] Frantz Fanon, and José Carlos Mariátegui.[3] As a concept, coloniality emerged in Latin America in the 1990s with the work of Quijano in response to the limitations of frameworks such as dependency theory in addressing the conditions of what came to be called the "Third World" during the Cold War. Quijano developed coloniality in conversation with other decolonial thinkers as a concept that articulates the historical relationships between what Immanuel Wallerstein refers to as the modern world-system and its concealed underside of coloniality, and the response of decoloniality.[4]

In Quijano's understanding of coloniality, political colonialism constructs hierarchical relations of power, and within this context, European forms of knowledge gain a privileged status. They become "seductive" insofar as they give "access to power."[5] With the end of European politi-cal colonialism in the mid-twentieth century, these hierarchies established through political domination don't come to an end; they are naturalized within labor relations and categorizations of the human person. The so-lidification of these modes of relation within Western modernity is what Quijano calls coloniality, which he argues is "still the most general form of domination in the world today."[6] The relations of power created within colonial domination, understood under the umbrella concept of colonial-ity, persist as the concealed underside of Western modernity.

In theorizing Western modernity, Quijano argues that a matrix of colo-niality is constitutive of the form of modernity emerging at the end of the fifteenth century, and that this form of modernity emerged as a specific and historically unique entity. European modernity is the first global net-work of power that controls all spheres of social existence, such that this network of power reproduces, from within its own systemic structure, dis-torted relations of power. Power, in Quijano's understanding, is a network of relations of exploitation, domination, and conflict configured within disputes over labor and the natural world, sex, authority, and subjectivity. Quijano is specific with respect to these four realms of power: capitalism controls labor and its products, as well as nature and its resources; the bourgeois family controls sex and its products; the nation-state controls authority and its instruments of coercion, which function to secure the continuation and flexibility of colonial relations; and Eurocentrism con-trols intersubjectivity and its products, which includes knowledge.[7] Modes of relation are thus central to Quijano's use of coloniality to conceptualize the contemporary world-system.

A core element of Quijano's use of the concept of the coloniality of power to explain relationships within the modern world-system is the role of labor, race, and gender within the historical establishment and unfold-ing of Europe's modernity, and the naturalization of forms of domination.[8] Quijano describes the control of labor through a capitalist system as the "primary factor" and "central condition" within the coloniality of power.[9] Unlike the way he understands Karl Marx to centralize labor in a deter-minative way, however, Quijano sees capitalist control and authority over labor as having *primacy*. Labor, in Quijano's work, does not act "as a de-terminant or basis of determinations in the sense of historical materialism, but rather strictly *as an axis or axes of articulating the whole*."[10] Quijano, in other words, allows other spheres of existence to reveal different forms of domination, irreducible to the mechanisms of capitalist exploitation of labor.[11]

In *Capital*, Marx cites a claim he made in *A Contribution to the Critique of Political Economy*, which indicates the base-superstructure model that Quijano refers to as a "reductionist" move in Marx's thought[12]:

> My view is that each particular mode of production, and the relations of production corresponding to it at each given moment, in short "the economic structure of society," is "the real foundation, on which arises a legal and political superstructure and to which correspond definite forms of social consciousness," and that "the mode of production of material life conditions the general process of social, political, and intellectual life."[13]

Marx could be read here as presenting an economic base that produces political and epistemological frameworks. Whereas much of Marx's work proceeds without assuming a causal relationship between an economic base and superstructure, but rather as indicating contradictions within the base that open up myriad possibilities in the superstructure, Quijano is allergic to any sense of reducing reality to a single "base." Irrespective of locating a "correct" reading of Marx, Quijano rejects a form of thinking—which he associates with Marxism—that presents a causal model in which a single moment is lifted up as that which propels the movement of history. Quijano adamantly affirms the heterogeneity of historical processes.

Related to the reductionism he associates with Marx's analysis, Quijano brings forth a concern with ways of understanding social classes centered within a European experience. In centralizing the roles people play in relation to capitalist control of labor and of its resources and products, the idea of social classes within Eurocentered thought operates within a duality between Europe and Europe's exteriority. This produces a distorted representation of the historical situation, which Quijano is working to avoid. This false duality between Europe and its exteriority implies "that much of that which was not Europe, even though it existed on the same temporal stage, actually corresponded to the past within a linear temporal framework whose point of origin was (is), obviously, Europe."[14] Rather than understanding relationships within the world-system, Eurocentered class-based analyses understand historical sites within a constructed linear progression. Within this reduction shaped by Eurocentered experience and liberal ideology, non-European forms of social classification are seen as "pre-capitalist"—that is, within a stage before capitalism but progressing toward a capitalist form of labor control—and as indicating natural differences in power between Europeans and non-Europeans.[15] This concealment and distortion of reality within Eurocentered analyses, which end up legitimizing the coloniality of power, calls for new ways of making sense of the modern world-system, which take into account the reality of the colonial undersides of Western modernity and think from such spaces.

Ultimately, Quijano identifies a limitation in the analytical options within the tradition of historical materialism that does not allow it to adequately address historical iterations of power in society. Historical materialism reduces the heterogeneity of historical processes to a single causal base and assumes Eurocentered experience as a global model. Quijano offers the coloniality of power as an alternative framework of analysis. In doing so, he makes the broad claim that, since the creation of "America," there have been three different lines, all articulated within the common global structure that he calls the coloniality of power, that order conflict and shape processes of social classification: labor, race, and gender.[16] Labor occupies "the central and permanent sphere," yet these three instances can neither be seen to be distinct nor in conflict with each other within a social analysis capable of providing an adequate ground to move toward liberation.[17]

Capitalism has organized the exploitation of labor and its resources and products. Quijano's view of capitalism as ordered by the coloniality of power includes primitive accumulation; he does not exclude what historical materialism generally refers to as "pre-capitalist" as a stage before capitalism. Whereas wage labor guides the relation between capital and work within the colonial center, and has become structurally dominant in the colonial periphery, other forms of the exploitation of labor, such as slavery, have been dominant when taking a long view of the last five hundred years. These other forms of the organization of labor play a crucial role within the coloniality of power, and bear an obvious link to capitalist production: they have been, "from the beginning, articulated under the domination of capital and for its benefit."[18] Race and gender are mechanisms of organizing labor and Eurocentered capitalism within the modern/colonial world-system that naturalize relationships of domination such that they can extend beyond physical domination.

Quijano argues that race was "the key element of the social classification of colonized and colonizers."[19] Forms of social classification based on race were used within the context of European colonial domination to order work within the world capitalist system between salaried labor and other forms of labor, including independent peasants, serfs, and slaves.[20] Establishing new labor relations within the modern/colonial model of power went hand in hand with establishing new intersubjective relations.[21] As race is a central part of the work of thinkers influenced by Quijano's articulation of the coloniality of power, including Sylvia Wynter and Nelson Maldonado-Torres, I will postpone a more thorough discussion of race within the coloniality of power until below, when I consider the relationship between the coloniality of power and being.

Quijano acknowledges that gender relations have also been ordered around the coloniality of power, insofar as sexual and gender norms, as well as patterns of family organization, have been ordered around European ideals.[22] María Lugones has shown, however, that Quijano understands the scope of gender much too narrowly. In Quijano's model of the coloniality of power, he limits his analysis of gender to the realm of power in which the bourgeois family controls sex and its resources, including both intimacy and offspring. Lugones claims that in limiting gender to this area of concern, Quijano takes on an "overly biologized" understanding of gender "as it presupposes sexual dimorphism, heterosexuality, patriarchal distribution of power, and so on."[23] Her argument for a broader understanding of gender within the modern/colonial world-system begins with the claim that sexual dimorphism is associated with what she calls the "light side" of the colonial/modern gender system. Western practices of surgically or hormonally "correcting" intersexed individuals "make very clear that 'gender' is antecedent to the 'biological' traits and gives them meaning."[24] Lugones thus argues that "[a]s global, Eurocentered capitalism was constituted through colonization, gender differentials were introduced where there were none."[25] Quijano misses this, taking gender to be a product of biological differences. Quijano's conception of gender purely within the lens of the coloniality of power hides the ways a particularly Eurocentered understanding of gender was used to disrupt non-European social life.

Lugones draws on Quijano's model of the coloniality of power along with work done by "Third World and women of color feminists" to bring forth a historical understanding of what she calls "the colonial/modern gender system."[26] She begins with the recognition that a new gender system created within colonialism introduces a particular conception of gender as a way of ordering broader cosmologies.[27] This gender system, Lugones argues, "was as constitutive of the coloniality of power as the coloniality of power was of it," such that "[t]he logic of the relation between them is of mutual constitution."[28] The control over the "areas of existence" that Quijano identifies—labor and nature, sex, authority, and subjectivity—"was itself gendered," such that seeing gender to be limited to the control over sex and its products is an ideological move complicit with gender domination.[29] Lugones thus places gender with race as mythical distortions that naturalize power within the modern/colonial world. Whereas Quijano makes a similar overarching claim, Lugones is not convinced that Quijano has understood the constitutive role of gender within the coloniality of power. Lugones's work provides a helpful corrective when moving to consider the impact of coloniality on human existence.

The coloniality of power, as a model of power that emerges with Europe's modernity as its concealed underside, is one way of understanding the long history that shapes the contemporary historical context to which theological reflection responds. To move toward a constructive theology —which, if using the hermeneutic Quijano develops, would be a decolonial theology—it remains necessary to concretize the ways the imposition of gender and racial systems, in the service of organizing labor within global capitalism, has shaped material realities within the modern/colonial world-system. Bringing forth three historical iterations of the coloniality of power, on the levels of being, knowledge, and eschatology, provides a more concrete understanding of the context of colonial modernity. These historical manifestations of the coloniality of power ultimately shape the central theological image of salvation, and indicate the historical structures that decolonial theological options and a decolonized image of salvation must unsettle.

Coloniality and Being

A primary way the coloniality of power shapes human communities and historical modes of relation is through defining the human person. Sylvia Wynter, a decolonial thinker working out of a Caribbean context, sees the mid-sixteenth century Valladolid debate between Bartolomé de Las Casas and Ginés de Sepúlveda to indicate in a decisive way the trajectory of modern/colonial understandings of the human person. She frames this debate as a contest between anthropologies. Las Casas's theological understanding of the human person grounded the evangelizing mission of the church, whereas Sepúlveda's humanist understanding of the person grounded the imperializing mission of the state.[30] Sepúlveda's humanist anthropology would win out within the broad imaginary of Western modernity, but while incorporating elements of the Christian anthropology on which Las Casas depended. Wynter describes this as a shift from a Christian, theocentric understanding of the human person to an understanding of the human person as a political subject. She calls the new descriptive statement of the human that emerges in the sixteenth century "Man," and draws out the first emergence of a humanist conception of the human person as a political subject. "Man" functions as the culturally dominant framework within which the coloniality of power shapes being.

The political subject on which Sepúlveda—and Western Europe more broadly—depends for this emerging anthropology is deeply connected to the emerging material reality of colonialism and the model of the coloniality of power. Enrique Dussel has elucidated the quality of being that Wynter refers to as Man, in its first secular iteration as a political subject, by describing a genre of the human emerging from what he calls the *ego conquiro*. The ego conquiro, or "I conquer" that shapes European notions of personhood beginning at the end of the fifteenth century introduces a new subjectivity more than a century before its expression as the ego cogito. Sepúlveda, as "the modern philosopher par excellence," justifies the violence of the modern subject as ego conquiro.[31] For Dussel, the modern / colonial situation that began with Europeans positioning themselves as the center of the world-system within the context of North Atlantic contacts comes forth "as a new paradigm of daily life and of historical, religious, and scientific understanding."[32] This new historical moment is, for Dussel and more explicitly for Wynter, grounded in a new understanding of being.

Wynter shows that religious thought is deeply entangled with this political and secular understanding of the human person as the conquering subject. Christopher Columbus's "discovery" is made possible by an "epochal shift" in subjective understanding, in which the state becomes the entity that effects redemption, now conceived of as "rational redemption."[33] Columbus introduces a conceptual framework that joins a theocentric understanding of the world with the humanistic principle that the whole earth needed Christian redemption.[34] This shift, in which the (conquering) human rather than God dominated the relationship between humans and the divine, allowed for those who fit into the category of "Man" to reorganize concepts around themselves. Willie James Jennings describes this process as one in which the European discovery of the Americas initiated a project of relating this discovery to Europe and its theological logic. In this process, there were a set of epistemological ruptures, the most fundamental of which "was a split between geography, philosophy, and theology."[35] Although Christian theology shaped secular ways of thinking, material realities, including human persons, were no longer tethered to Christian thought. The ego conquiro thus emerges as autonomous, though from a logic entangled with Christian theological ways of thinking.

This semi-autonomy of the ego conquiro that never quite gets out of frameworks of Christian thought is apparent in new forms of representing or classifying those who fall outside of Man. Wynter argues that Columbus named those he encountered and then conquered in the New World "idolaters," which allowed him to conceptually signify them within an ontological difference, and thus as exploitable within his new conceptual frameworks.[36] Within this form of classification introduced by Columbus, Wynter argues that race becomes a mode of representing the nonhomogeneity of the species.[37] Race allows for the classification of ontological distinctions.

Nelson Maldonado-Torres goes further by asking how the religious representation of people as "idolaters" moves into secular racial categories of Native/Indian, and then how Native/Indian moves into blackness as form of representation outside of Man.[38] Core to Maldonado-Torres's argument is that Columbus in fact saw the Indigenous peoples he encountered in the Americas not merely as "idolaters," but as "without religion."[39] Maldonado-Torres sees this new social category, introduced by the ego conquiro, as fundamental to the modern/colonial world.[40] The invention of new categories within the European encounter with the Americas, such as the category of the nonreligious tethered to an ontological difference, functioned to both confront a world that no longer fit with traditional philosophical-theological categories and to contain capitalist expansion within a Christian narrative. The new category of the "non-religious" produced not only a distinction within being (i.e., between Christians and idolaters), but a distinction between being and "the active negation of being," which Maldonado-Torres refers to as the "sub-ontological difference."[41] The sub-ontological difference, Maldonado-Torres argues, is the difference produced by the coloniality of power "and provides the basic coordinates for the production and always selective and complicated (re)generation of other forms of differences, including racial, gender, sexual, but also political and economic differences."[42] While both Wynter and Maldonado-Torres focus on race, their projects leave space open for the heterogeneity of the coloniality of power that Quijano and Lugones affirm.

The sub-ontological difference grounds the movement from the first iteration of the secular descriptive statement of the human into a second, bio-economic, definition of the human person, concretized in the eighteenth century. Like the first iteration of Man as a political subject, Man as a bio-economic subject develops within the humanist strategy of defining Man by returning to Greco-Roman thought, yet the current conception of the human as Man is discursively constituted in purely secular terms. This bio-economic conception of the human person is the discursive legitimization of an economic system that serves the interests of Man—that is, of the overrepresentation of the Western bourgeois understanding of the human person as the human person as such.[43] Race is a crucial term within this conception of Man "as a part of a totemic signifying complex" to legitimize a value difference between Man and its others.[44] The modern process of racialization within the coloniality of power has implications on the levels of being because it is "the moment when *race* comes to be the code through which one not simply *knows* what human being is, but *experiences* being."[45] When engaging the work of Fanon and Baldwin in the middle part of this book, I will bring to the forefront this particular way the coloniality of power impresses on being.

Coloniality and Knowledge

With the end of European political colonialism in the 1960s, the hegemony of forms of knowledge that travelled with the European bourgeois class did not come to an end; coloniality has remained not only on the level of being but also as a structure that orients ways of knowing. Colonial domination continues after political decolonization because of a relationship between Europeans and their others that consists, Quijano argues, "in the first place, of a colonization of the imagination of the dominated."[46] The "systemic repression" carried out by the modern/colonial European form of power fell not only on material resources and the products of labor but also on knowledge production, resulting in "the imposition of the use of the rulers' own patterns of expression, and of their beliefs and images with reference to the supernatural."[47] The repression of knowledge within political colonialism set up the structure for the possibility of the continuation of the specific form of power associated with European colonialism beyond its formal or political end.

Knowledge categorized as "Eurocentric" is, for Quijano, of a more specific category than simply all knowledge emanating from the history of Europe. Quijano uses the term Eurocentrism to refer to knowledge formations emerging with "the specific bourgeois secularization of European thought and with the experiences and necessities of the global model of capitalist (colonial/modern) and Eurocentered power established since the colonization of America."[48] Further, Eurocentrism "is not the cognitive perspective exclusively of Europeans, or only of those who dominate world capitalism, but also of the group educated under its hegemony."[49] For this reason, Ramón Grosfoguel distinguishes between an "epistemic location" and a "social location," and argues that "the success of the modern/colonial world-system consists in making subjects that are socially located in the oppressed side of the colonial difference, to think epistemically like the ones on the dominant positions."[50] Eurocentrism is thus the confluence of knowledge that shapes what Wynter describes as the secular humanist understanding of the human person in Europe. Like Wynter, Quijano acknowledges that the roots of this knowledge are much older than the fifteenth-century modern/colonial emergence of Europe, yet the reference point for Eurocentrism remains the perspective of knowledge that "was made globally hegemonic, traveling the same course as the dominion of the European bourgeois class."[51] The formal process of colonialism thus creates a colonial relation of power between cultures and ways of knowing that I will call, following Quijano, "Eurocentric."

Eurocentricity is a particular quality of knowledge shaped within the coloniality of power. While Eurocentric modes of knowledge can be seen as simply a limited way of thinking, Linda Martín Alcoff, in agreement with Quijano, argues that there is a historical foundation that shapes the limitation of Eurocentric thinking, and that it is necessary to interrogate this historical foundation. Alcoff suggests that "conquerors are in an epistemically poor cultural, intellectual, and political context for judgment."[52] There is a structure of knowledge shaped within the coloniality of power that is debilitating. Charles W. Mills refers to this as an "epistemology of ignorance"—that is, "a particular pattern of localized and global cognitive dysfunctions (which are psychologically and socially functional), producing the ironic outcome that whites will in general be unable to understand the world they themselves have made."[53] Responding critically to Eurocentrism, therefore, is not a form of what has been caricaturized as identity politics; the type of critical response Quijano develops involves intervening in the way an organized and institutionally supported identity politics of whiteness continues to produce an a-critical way of thinking. Decolonizing knowledge, as I will show in the next chapter, is a much more far-reaching project than diversifying knowledge or a project of inclusion; decolonizing knowledge is a project of unmooring knowledge from a-critical roots, from a cowardly retreat from Europe's exteriority that functions to maintain the coloniality of power.

Coloniality and Eschatology

The eschaton refers to a future reality of fullness that deeply shapes, and is even encountered in, the present. That is, reaching out toward the future can structure present life and becomes a part of present life. The coloniality of power turns the genre of the human that Wynter refers to as Man into an eschatological subject and Eurocentric rationalities into that which reveals the eschaton. Man becomes the subjectivity for which all should strive, and the Greco-Roman-Western European intellectual tradition becomes the end and criterion for all knowledge. The coloniality of power shapes eschatology by reifying a particular chronological telos of history, knowledge, and the human person. In this reification, only a particular set of geohistorical loci, epistemic sources, and modes of humanity are seen as capable of informing eschatological claims. Christian, civilizing, and modernizing missions are all a part of the modern/colonial eschatological imagination within the coloniality of power. Communities outside the physical and epistemic center of Western modernity enter into being and enter into rationality insofar as they enter into the progressive historical trajectory of Western modernity. In this framework, the modern/colonial matrix, and the ways of being human, ways of thinking, and cosmologies within this matrix become eschatological. Becoming modern is itself salvation.

In theological terms, Man replaces or supersedes biblical Israel as the point of connection between human experience and the transcendent. Willie James Jennings makes this point by arguing that the white European fills the space occupied by biblical Israel in the Christian imagination, and in doing so reconfigures Israel's election. The genre of the human person that Wynter describes as Man discerns God's grace and salvation.[54] A Christian spirituality becomes the center by which a modern/colonial white identity politics becomes eschatological. "Man" not only becomes the model of the human person and knowledge; Man also becomes the criterion of salvation.

Although neither Fanon nor Baldwin uses the language of coloniality developed within and in response to Quijano's work, they both point to the idea of colonial relations of power existing on the plane of eschatology. In his introduction to his first book, Fanon indicates that racial categories get incorporated into human ontology: "As painful as it is for us to have to say this: there is but one destiny for the black man. And it is white."[55] Because no adequate ground seemingly exists on which to stand as a human person and as rational except for what has been constructed within the coloniality of power, the ways coloniality shapes being and knowledge also shapes eschatology. Assimilation—that is, in entering into what Grosfoguel refers to as the "epistemic location" of European modernity—structures salvation. Recognizing the limitation of this destiny, and also its impossibility, prompted Fanon, who inhabited a context shaped by the relationship between Europe and its colonies, to forge his own ground. He sought to break into being within a "new world" and "new humanity" created out of a decolonial struggle. Fanon thus breaks open the ways the coloniality of power manifests within an eschatological imagination, and imagines salvation anew through breaking open the determination of being and knowledge by the coloniality of power.

Within a US context, Baldwin indicates how coloniality shapes eschatology by pointing to the inauthenticity of the culturally dominant understanding of salvation. Baldwin describes the "Negro story" as something "America" cannot hear. The estrangement between "America" and "the Negro" produces America's estrangement from itself, as "the Negro" is America's own creation, yet is also a signification that protects America against chaos. Baldwin argues that this "Negro story" is ultimately needed, however, because it reveals. It discloses a reality that America protects against and avoids in order to obscure the relationship between the United States as a social, political, and economic entity, and the ways it has produced and signified its colonial underside.[56] Taking on the persona of a white American, Baldwin claims: "the loss of our [American] identity is the price we pay for our annulment of his [i.e., the black subject]."[57]

Baldwin breaks open the idea of salvation by showing that black communities experience different histories, and that these experiences can forge a more authentic understanding of salvation. The United States, in a theological maneuver, invests black communities with a "shameful" past, in need of redemption by the alabaster Christ. Referring to a black subject, Baldwin describes this phenomenon:

> As he accepted the alabaster Christ and the bloody cross—in the bearing of which he would find his redemption, as, indeed, to our outraged astonishment he sometimes did—he must, henceforth, accept that image we then gave him of himself: having no other and standing, moreover, in danger of death should he fail to accept the dazzling light thus brought into such darkness.[58]

The signification of a nothingness and in need of the dazzling light presented by the US social imaginary is intertwined with the presentation of the alabaster Christ as a uniquely valid telos.

If Christian theology is, in Gustavo Gutiérrez's widely cited definition, "a critical reflection on Christian praxis in the light of the Word,"[59] what sort of theological reflection can engage with epistemic loci on the undersides of Western modernity, while seeing these loci as fundamental theological loci? And, if theology also entails a project of historical transformation,[60] what sort of theology can be a part of a larger praxis of unsettling colonial relations of power? In the service of responding to these questions, the following chapter questions how Christian theology is entangled with the historical matrix that Quijano understands as the coloniality of power. Recognizing how theology is related to this historical situation provides a basis for finding ways Christian theology can actualize its task of critical reflection.

CHAPTER 2

The Entanglement of Christian Theology and the Coloniality of Power: The Possibilities of a Response

Therefore, comrade, you will hold as enemies—loftily, lucidly, consistently—not only sadistic governors and greedy bankers, not only prefects who torture and colonists who flog, not only corrupt, check-licking politicians and subservient judges, but likewise and for the same reason, venomous journalists, goitrous academics, wreathed in dollars and stupidity, ethnographers who go in for metaphysics, presumptuous Belgian theologians . . . all of them tools of capitalism, all of them, openly or secretly, supporters of plundering colonialism, all of them responsible, all hateful, all slave-traders, all henceforth answerable for the violence of revolutionary action. And sweep out all the obscurers, all the inventors of subterfuges, the charlatans and tricksters, the dealers in gobbledygook. And do not seek to know whether personally these gentlemen are in good or bad faith, whether personally they have good or bad intentions. Whether personally—that is, in the private conscience of Peter or Paul—they are or are not colonialists, because the essential thing is that their highly problematical subjective good faith is entirely irrelevant to the objective social implications of the evil work they perform as watchdogs of colonialism.

—AIMÉ CÉSAIRE, *Discourse on Colonialism*, trans. John Pinkham
(New York: Monthly Review Press, 2000), 54–55

Western intellectual traditions, as Césaire bluntly charges, are entangled in the matrix that Quijano identifies as the coloniality of power. This chapter analyzes that historical entanglement with respect to Christian theology, and then opens up paths for decolonization. Both of these steps are necessary in order to get out of the "gobbledygook" in which Western academic disciplines—and perhaps foremost among them Christian theology—too often deals.

This chapter begins with the task of considering the place of Christian theology within the coloniality of power. It then moves to discerning decolonial options by engaging the three loci of historical manifestations of the coloniality of power set up in the first chapter: of being, knowledge, and eschatology. In conversation with decolonial theorists, this chapter offers possibilities for decolonizing descriptive statements of the human person, ways of knowing, and eschatological imaginations. These decolonial options lead to a threshold question for theology, or a question to which theologians must respond before proceeding in a constructive vein, raised in the third and final section of the chapter.

Christian Theological Reflection within the Coloniality of Power

The historical appearance of Western modernity with the form of colonialism emerging in the fifteenth century has had the effect of restricting the possible trajectories that intellectual work, and knowledge processes more broadly, can take. The coloniality of power as a historical matrix excludes the possibility of what Fanon describes as the necessary conditions for the colonized intellectual to adequately respond to a historical situation: "The colonized intellectual who wants to put his struggle on a legitimate footing, who is intent on providing proof and accepts to bare himself in order to better display the history of his body," he argues, "is fated to plunge into the very bowels of his people."[1] The process of moving into the bowels of a people condemned by Western modernity in order to reveal a history only makes sense as an intellectual task, however, when it is acknowledged that there is a way of being, knowing, and imagining among colonized peoples relevant beyond the world of the colonized. In other words, if the creative production of a colonized person is seen as limited to the domain of the particular experience of that person, then it doesn't make sense to do the work of entering into that creative production. The assumptions that the colonized person does not think in any adequate or relevant way and that Western traditions are uniquely capable of referring to an eschatological reality preclude the intellectual relevance of journeying into the "bowels" of a colonized people.

This negation demonstrates the license that those within the center of Western modernity and those who can afford to operate on the presumption that Western modernity is not constituted by a colonial underside can enjoy. Intellectuals who benefit from Western modernity can assume that communities outside colonial centers lack the ability to reason in a reciprocal way to ourselves, and thus we can avoid the work of this journey and ignore others who do this work, for reasons we perceive to be legitimate and rational. In relation to how philosophers have theorized this tactic of willed ignorance, I refer to the privilege of ignorance that those who benefit from Western modernity and who can coherently operate within ideologies that link progress and the solidification of Western modernity have.[2] The privilege of ignorance allows for a coherent structure to narratives within Western modernity that does not actually exist, by way of an ability or privilege to be ignorant of an exteriority. As long as this privilege persists, the motivation to do the type of intellectual work Fanon envisions—that is, intellectual work located in epistemologies of communities on the borders and exteriorities of Western modernity—remains limited. In constructing a theological perspective that brings the challenge Fanon poses to colonized intellectuals to all theologians, it is necessary to discern how the discipline of Christian theology is involved in the dynamics of the coloniality of power.

While theologians often critique "modernity," many of these critiques rely on the privilege of ignorance and thus fail to attack the basis of Western modernity, which decolonial theorists name as coloniality. Often, critiques coming from the discipline of theology depend on the ability to conceal that which seemingly exists outside the Western orbit, such that modernity, even when critiqued, continues to be understood as a phenomenon internal to Europe.[3] The privilege of ignorance appears in such engagements with modernity insofar as these critiques cling to the Eurocentricity of modernity as they critique modernity. Reflections on modernity from a postmodern perspective often fall victim to this tendency when they characterize modernity as a phenomenon internal to Europe, without accounting for subjectivities developed in and shaped by the historical acts of conquest. That is, they fail to see colonization as a historical act that was generative on the epistemological level. Reflections on modernity that see modernity as a secularization project, as a move away from a transcendent reality, are one example. Modernity, within such understandings, is the consequence of processes within European intellectual trajectories; European colonialism does not enter the picture as a set of historical processes that impacts the epistemologies of Western modernity in a fundamental way. The knowledge processes within Western modernity occur without relation to the historical establishment of Europe as the center of the world-system and the historical institution of the coloniality of power. In their Eurocentrism, without seeing how a colonial underside forms Western modernity, postmodern thinkers remain "modern" in a fundamental sense, refusing to see how the West is constituted by its exteriority. Thus, even in critiquing modernity's move toward absolute cognition, a postmodern critique maintains the intellectual arrogance fundamental to Western modernity. It maintains the ways the coloniality of power bears on knowledge: only the Western tradition itself has the capacity to affect

knowledge. Detaching the production of knowledge from historical processes conceals the Eurocentricity that is fundamental to the enterprise of
Western modernity and results in legitimizing the "Western" through a
partial critique of the "modern."

This type of Eurocentric analysis leads to two sets of problems. First,
it is an uncritical analysis insofar as it ignores the epistemic and material
foundations that the process of colonialism made possible. In this vein,
Dussel argues that the postmodern turn in general fails to think beyond
what he calls "the extinction of European-North American modernity
with its claims to 'sole' universality, beyond its present crisis, beyond its
limit, beyond modernity's 'post'-modern moment."[4] He addresses this
problem by interpreting Western modernity within a global perspective,
and seeing the movement of absolute cognition within Western modernity
to be tied to the conquest of the Americas. Second, a Eurocentric analysis
is inconsistent insofar as the analysis of modernity accounts for a shifted
current of thought while obscuring theorizations of the experience of modernity coming from its underside. Only thought narrated to be in continuity with Western intellectual traditions is taken to have the capacity to
challenge European thought on an intellectual level. In other words, there
is a reflexivity allowed for and valued at an intellectual level within Western traditions, for example in the form of a re-reading of its intellectual
predecessors, yet this reflexivity is not allowed from experiences of Western modernity as coloniality. These two sets of problems show how the
movement from modernity to "post"-modernity indicates a position that is
not only naively Eurocentric; it is also uncritical in that it cravenly retreats
from the appraisals made of Western modernity from its exteriority. This
type of position benefits from the privilege of ignorance, or the privilege
of living as if questions posed to Western modernity from its underside do
not come from sites valued as intellectually generative.

Philosophers concerned with the intersection of epistemology and ethics have developed responses to such positions that delegitimize (most often implicitly) ways of knowing that do not foster inclusion into the mod-
ern/colonial world-system in order to legitimize the continued reliance
on a European intellectual trajectory. Miranda Fricker has articulated the
ethical and political dimensions of epistemology in ways that can be helpful to uncover how Christian theology remains bound to the coloniality of
power, and how this is the case even in its moments of critiquing modernity. Fricker explores two forms of epistemic injustice. She identifies the
primary form of epistemic injustice as "testimonial injustice." Testimonial
injustice generally relies on prejudices against people belonging to particu-

lar social groups. It results in some speakers having a "credibility deficit."[5] The example Fricker gives of a testimonial injustice is a police officer not believing a black woman's story because she is black and a woman. This type of injustice wrongs the subject "in her capacity as a knower," and "[t]o be wronged in one's capacity as a knower is to be wronged in a capacity essential to human value," namely, the capacity to give knowledge and the capacity for reason.[6] One way this tendency infuses theological discourse is in how some theologians use the concept of "contextuality." Theologians often affirm that there is a general condition of all knowers, and different social positions lead to different perceptions of reality in particular situations.[7] Knowers have particular experiences, capabilities, and backgrounds that allow them to know in particular ways. But, theologians can often use this recognition of contextuality in perverse ways to justify remaining within Eurocentered ways of knowing. Being European or American, the claim goes, legitimizes a contextual theology that focuses exclusively on the European intellectual tradition. This type of justification relies on a naïve separation between modernity and coloniality, or on an understanding of modernity without reference to its underside or exteriority.

The second type of epistemic injustice Fricker identifies is "hermeneutical injustice," which exists prior to testimonial injustice and also shows how Christian theology is entangled with coloniality. Hermeneutical injustice comes out of an intentional gap in a society's interpretive tools that has unjust results for particular groups.[8] To illustrate hermeneutical injustice, Fricker gives the example of a woman who suffers from sexual harassment in a culture that still lacks the concept of sexual harassment. "Hermeneutical marginalization," or the unequal participation in practices that form social meaning, causes this type of injustice.[9] Hermeneutical injustice wrongs the subject insofar as "the concrete situation is such that the subject [i.e., the one marginalized by hermeneutical injustice] is rendered unable to make communicatively intelligible something which it is particularly in his or her interests to be able to render intelligible."[10] Hermeneutical and testimonial injustices together produce systemic epistemologies of ignorance. Ignorance here is not simply a lack; rather, something motivates ignorance. An investment in the modern/colonial matrix creates a positive interest to not interrogate the full implications of social injustice—that is, to not listen to people outside those benefiting from colonial modernity (testimonial injustice) and to block out conceptual categories that can make sense of the experiences of those outside the dominant group (hermeneutical injustice). Investment in colonial modernity affords the privilege for this ignorance.

These forms of epistemic injustice Fricker identifies are often present in Western European and US postmodern theologies when postmodernity is taken as a rupture with modernity, such that modernity is believed to be over. When postmodern theologies theorize a rupture, they conceal the ways the contemporary context in the West is in material and ideological continuity with the modern/colonial context. A postmodern use of contextuality, in other words, often avoids the concrete other and concrete forms of alterity that have been concealed within the modern/colonial project. It renders a hermeneutical injustice. Plurality exists as a raw material, but not in epistemologies. In other words, the raw material of society is recognized as plural, yet epistemologies remain Eurocentric. In this case, theology would fall into a solipsism, positing an idea of alterity to simulate a critical and forward movement, but limiting ways of thinking to those emanating from Europe. In this move, such theologians render a testimonial injustice.

Articulating the privilege of ignorance in terms that are more direct, Maldonado-Torres uses the term "epistemic racism" to name a phenomenon in which some people groups have the capacity to determine the content of knowledge as a general category based on their own limited knowledge frameworks, and to then use racial categories in order to legitimize this determination. Maldonado-Torres develops the concept of epistemic racism to refer to an interested blindness to the epistemic capacity of particular groups of people. He describes epistemic racism as an attitude necessary to maintain the structural apparatus of Western modernity, which holds that the logic of certain people groups must be negated in order to legitimize the endurance of the Western intellectual tradition as a criterion for rationality and intellectual relevance.[11] Forced ignorance, therefore, is a luxury of the subject within the center of Western modernity that can be legitimized by connecting epistemology to processes of social classification within the colonial moment that have yet to be decolonized. Although seemingly counterintuitive, forced ignorance is a form of what feminist philosophers have called "epistemic privilege."[12] It is a privileged position to be able to be ignorant when this ignorance allows one to discount the credibility of other ways of knowing in order to maintain the credibility of the ways a particular, local tradition has made sense of a historical situation from which one benefits. This points to a reality that demands something more than individual change; the systemic structures that communicate and (re-)produce knowledge have to be questioned and developed anew.

A Response to the Entanglement: Decoloniality

On a broad level, decolonization can be seen as a disruption and ultimate destruction of colonial relations of power. In this vein, Quijano claims the following:

> Today, the struggle against exploitation/domination implies, first and foremost, the struggle for the destruction of the coloniality of power, not only to end racism, but to end racism because of its status as the axis of articulating the universal matrix of Eurocentric capitalism. This struggle is part of the destruction of capitalist power, as it is today the living fabric of all historical forms of exploitation, domination, discrimination, both in material and subjective terms. The central place of corporeality in this situation leads to the need to think, to rethink, specific paths for its liberation—that is, for the liberation of the people, individually and in society, from power, from all power.[13]

This struggle for the destruction of the coloniality of power requires the confluence of the possibility to be, think, and imagine in ways that are not beholden to the confines of the coloniality of power. Liberation from the coloniality of power as an apparatus of social, political, economic, and historical structures is the condition for the possibility of decolonization. In order to specify decolonization, at least initially, I will consider how it can manifest on the interrelated levels of being, thinking, and imagining.

DECOLONIZING DESCRIPTIVE STATEMENTS OF THE HUMAN PERSON

Sylvia Wynter's work—like that of Fanon's and Baldwin's—is primarily concerned with what Quijano refers to as the "corporeality" of the coloniality of power, or with the matrix within which the human person lives. Her focus is on the ideologies that are impressed onto the human person in ways that concrete persons "live their inscriptions as the historically varying modes of our truth."[14] In broad terms, decolonizing descriptive statements of the human person implies a destruction of ideologies that shape the experience of our humanness.

A crucial step in this process of shattering ideologies in which the coloniality of power impresses on the material reality of the human person is to reveal such ideological structures. As seen in the first chapter, Wynter describes the discursive production of the human as the contemporary mechanism of control. This descriptive statement of the human person has shifted from a religious understanding of the human person to, in the fifteenth century, a political understanding of the human person, to, in the eighteenth century, a bio-economic understanding of the human person. This logic of Man has been invented by modern/colonial centers during the last five hundred years, yet Wynter also sees Man as a contested logic during the last half millennium. And, it has been contested from a particular space:

> that logic [of Man] is total now, because to be not-Man is to be not-quite-human. Yet that plot, that slave plot on which the slave grew food for his/her subsistence, carried over a millennially *other* conception of the human to that of Man's. . . . So that plot exists as a threat. It speaks to other possibilities. And it is out of that plot that the new and now planetary-wide and popular musical humanism of our times is emerging.[15]

Border thinking, or thought that emerges from the colonial difference as "musical humanism," provides a locus that offers the possibility of constituting another way of imagining the human focused on the well-being of the human species as such, rather than on the specific ethno-class held up by Western modernity.

In interviewing Wynter, David Scott makes an important intervention by noting attempts in Wynter's work to both historicize the way Europe's Man has been impressed onto the human person as a general category, and to reimagine the human person as such, from an ahistorical, ontological ground.[16] Wynter sees the secular, humanist break in the fifteenth century to offer a possibility to conceptualize this "unhistoricizable" mode of being human, which is one element of Western secularism that she sees to have some positive potential.[17] Wynter turns to human experience—a potentially universalizable site—as a place to construct, departing from the "half-starved" articulations of the human person from the natural sciences, "a new science."[18] Being—and particularly modes of being outside of Man and the purview of Man—is the ground from which Wynter finds a possibility of unsettling the coloniality of power. Wynter thus does not share the postmodern concern to reject master narratives. The problem is not tendencies toward totality in ways of knowing, but the way knowing is shaped by the coloniality of power. Decolonizing being, therefore, is profoundly related to decolonizing ways of knowing.

Decolonizing Ways of Knowing

At a minimum, decolonizing knowledge requires dislodging a single reference point of meaning. It requires liberating knowledge from the illusion of a central marker of meaning and rationality.[19] Decolonizing knowledge does not require the elimination of totality; rather, the project of decolonization seeks to dismantle the way Western modernity positions the other in relation to its perception of totality.[20]

Walter D. Mignolo has introduced the concept of the "colonial difference," which is organized around "the geopolitics of knowledge." These concepts help to locate options for a decolonial project that attempts to break the coloniality of power on the level of knowledge. The colonial difference is a concept that connects historical experiences of the coloniality of power.[21] It is shaped by the geopolitics of knowledge—that is, by the ways the spatial and embodied dimensions of all knowledge is formed within the modern/colonial world-system. The colonial difference points to the geopolitics of knowledge, and specifically to the difference, on the epistemological level, between a discourse that starts from concepts reified in colonial centers in the fifteenth and sixteenth centuries and a discourse that starts from the historical consequences of those concepts. The colonial difference indicates the limits of Western thought:

> It is no longer possible, or at least it is not unproblematic, to "think" from the canon of Western philosophy, even when part of the canon is critical of modernity. To do so means to reproduce the blind epistemic ethnocentrism that makes difficult, if not impossible, any political philosophy of inclusion. The limit of Western philosophy is the border where the colonial difference emerges, making visible the variety of local histories that Western thought, from the right and left, hid and suppressed.[22]

Thinking from the colonial difference is thus thinking from the "densities of the colonial experience" and building "on the ground of the silence of history."[23] This implies claiming an epistemic locus in tension with the epistemologically legitimate sites in the modern/colonial world-system.

With the concept of border thinking, Mignolo doesn't just claim that knowing is always situated; rather, he shows that there are specific epistemic potentials that pertain to border thinking, as a type of thinking born of the encounter between imperial and colonial differences, wherein "the imaginary of the modern world system cracks."[24] Because of Mignolo's focus on encounter, Alcoff has pointed out that decolonizing the representation of knowledge is not merely moving to a new space, but a transformation of the impermeability of epistemic boundaries controlled by the coloniality of power.[25]

Understanding Enrique Dussel's theorization of the "transmodern" strengthens the historical grounding for border thinking. Dussel's concept of the transmodern can respond to the forms of epistemic injustice that Fricker delineates, and it can be a way of advocating for giving up the privilege of ignorance that persists within the center of the modern world-system. Dussel starts with the positive potential of knowledges created outside the trajectories that inform, sustain, and proceed from the historical matrix of Western modernity. He attempts to retell the story of modernity as a global story delinked from Europe as the center, and uses the category of "exteriority" to indicate "a process that takes off, originates, and mobilizes itself from an 'other' place . . . than European and North American modernity."[26] Dussel develops a different meta-narrative of world history by proposing a decentered narrative. In doing this, Alcoff argues, Dussel doesn't ignore the postmodern critique of meta-narratives, but questions postmodernity's claim to articulate justice by arguing against meta-narratives. Further, the postmodern focus on the particularity of the local can be historically inaccurate, as this focus can deny the global networks through which local practices are constituted. Thus, Alcoff argues that Dussel does not develop a meta-narrative in the same way that modern European thinkers have developed them; transmodernity is a meta-narrative that has an intentionally decentered epistemology that can unite local praxes against oppressive aspects of Western modernity into a framework.[27] A transmodern framework can articulate the global networks within which local oppressions are couched, which allows for the possibility to pose constructive alternative futures. Moving to a transmodern perspective requires letting go of the constant attempt to defend and legitimize a Western trajectory of thought that allows for the privilege of ignorance.

Because of its development within imperial histories, and recently on the modern side of the colonial difference, Mignolo has strongly questioned the possibility for Christian theology to be border thinking, or to emerge from a transmodern space. He thus questions the possibility for a positive connection between Christian theology and decoloniality.[28] While there are a number of good reasons for making this argument, there are also opportunities for a potentially positive relation between border thinking, decoloniality, and Christian theology.

First, rejecting outright the possibility for Christian theology to be border thinking obscures the ways communities have confronted historical situations on their own epistemic terms, even while using Christian categories. Although the reality of the colonial difference should prompt a critical and suspicious relationship to Christian theology, it doesn't require doing away with theology couched in Christian terms. To throw out Christian theology would suggest that those who have employed its categories and frameworks from positions and experiences of being exiled from and by Western modernity were merely duped by Christianity and Christian missionaries. Appreciating the reality of the colonial difference, on the contrary, requires uncovering how some ways of claiming Christian perspectives gave Christian categories new meaning that allowed for living into a new way of being human, and forging new epistemologies and ways of imagining the eschaton, thereby occupying another epistemic locus, even while using Christian categories. Using Christian categories within border thinking remains a difficult task, however, and one that deserves constant suspicion. It's easy to simply interpellate those who have employed Christian categories as living out forms of Christianity in opposition to modernity, thereby returning the focus to "theology" as a discipline concretized in Europe rather than the actual praxis of border thinking.

Second, religious orientations and theological ways of thinking are one way of transforming epistemic frontiers used to maintain a coherent way of making sense of the world from perspectives of modernity. Mignolo presents border thinking as emerging out of the failures of the modern Western episteme, brought to light by particular encounters, rather than from "outside" the modern/colonial world-system.[29] Religious orientations have proven to be one way communities have lived, imagined, and thought in reference to a reality different than the modern/colonial world-system. When communities have lived in reference to a religious reality and in so doing have thought theologically, they have undone epistemic boundaries thought to be stable, for example, those between transcendence and immanence, salvation and liberation, or supernatural and natural ways of knowing. Breaking down these epistemic boundaries, which has at times been done using Christian theological perspectives, has allowed historical struggles, ways of loving, and political stances to take shape as eschatological orientations that break the constraints of modern rationalities.

Third, historically rooted theologies have at times come forth in the cracks of Western modernity as forms of border thinking that prioritize historical concreteness. In these cases, theologians have transcended typical starting points in textual or authorial subjects. Theological perspectives that have moved from the classical epistemic loci of the academy to the perspectives and historical praxes of those who address, on a historical level, the reality of exile from the modern/colonial world-system, can exist as decolonial options. While Mignolo affirms this aspect of border thinking on the abstract level,[30] it remains a task to develop such concrete ways of thinking as border thinking.[31] Theological work that responds to and is informed by a history potentially contributes toward border thinking. For many liberation theologians—and this was especially the case in the 1960s, 1970s, and 1980s—theological reflection emerges organically out of their immediate historical situations. Historical experiences of the colonial underside of Western modernity provide the light by which to see Christian faith, and the perspective from which to read texts.

Decolonizing Eschatological Imaginations

Decolonization requires affirming the "difference" of the colonial difference, while undoing the coloniality of power that is attached to the colonial difference.[32] Decolonizing is thus a fundamentally different project than "opening" particular disciplines or "diversifying" Western thought systems; the goal in projects of decolonization is to transcend Western thought systems. This requires a different eschatological imagination. Decolonization, rather than inclusion, becomes the desired end.

Quijano makes clear the need for a horizon that can allow for a historical and critical imaginary.[33] Such a horizon requires concrete, historical, and critical images. I propose decolonial love as an option for an image that can shape an understanding of an eschatological horizon. As an eschatological reality, decolonial love functions as a concrete image for a reality that remains fundamentally mystery. As an image, which both shapes and is shaped by a praxis, decolonial love can hold together a decolonial project on the intertwined levels of being, knowledge, and eschatology. There is an impossibility of love when that which the coloniality of power falsely presents as ultimate—creating what theologians call idols—is accepted or affirmed as an eschatological horizon. As such, the reality of love exists and is practiced in history when the modern/colonial system breaks—that is, love happens in decolonial spaces and possibilities, or in places where the idols of colonial modernity are destroyed. I thus concretize love as decolonial, even though, within a modern/colonial context, "decolonial love" is in some sense tautological.

Chela Sandoval first used the concept of decolonial love to imagine a way of being and acting in the world, and there are aspects of the way she uses the term that I carry forward here. Most fundamentally, Sandoval describes decolonial love as both a hermeneutic and a tool—that is, as a mode of consciousness that motivates "technologies of method and social movement."[34] While I start with Sandoval's basic connection between decolonial love as a framework and political tool, I depart from her use of decolonial love in two significant ways, which will become more apparent in the second and third parts of this book.

First, although I share Sandoval's interpretation of decolonial love as a hermeneutic or tool, I also posit decolonial love as an eschatological orientation. While these aren't necessarily opposed, my understanding of decolonial love pushes Sandoval's postmodern commitments.[35] Sandoval develops a five-fold "topography" of tactics of resistance that subordinated groups in the United States have employed.[36] Within the topology, there are four standard political programs—equal rights, revolutionary, supremacist, and separatist—that can be equally effective within what Sandoval refers to as US third world feminism.[37] Sandoval privileges the fifth political program, a "differential" mode of consciousness, in which one employs whatever modes of subjectivity are necessary without depending on any single ideology.[38] The "differential mode of consciousness functions like the clutch of an automobile, the mechanism that permits the driver to select, engage, and disengage gears in a system for the transmission of power."[39] This mode of consciousness functions on a different register, escaping any coherent ideology or political program. The differential mode of consciousness, and the "tactical subjectivity" that it implies, characterizes US third world feminists during the post-World War II period of social transformation. In this subjectivity, the status of truth claims is ultimately relativized.[40] Sandoval sees "love," which she ultimately concretizes as "decolonial love," "as a hermeneutic, as a set of practices and procedures that can transit all citizen-subjects, regardless of social class, toward a differential mode of consciousness and its accompanying technologies of method and social movement."[41] Love "guides" political movement insofar as it "represents a signifier without any set signifieds unless it is in direct political engagement through one of its specific tactics."[42]

I shift in focus from Sandoval's project and emphasize decolonial love as a method that is also a way of facing reality with a commitment to or faith in an eschatological reality. In line with the ways Paula M. L. Moya has critiqued Sandoval's reliance on postmodern assumptions,[43] I push for a way of understanding decolonial love as a struggle to perceive an opening in history toward its depths, the mystery of which is often eclipsed by constrained rationalities of the modern world-system. Decolonial love is the struggle to participate in this eschatological mystery—though never grasping or controlling it—and in this sense is a hermeneutic or tool.

Second, and relatedly, in understanding decolonial love in reference to an eschatological reality, and working off the ways Jorge Aquino has theorized love vis-à-vis revolution, I understand decolonial love as "ambivalent."[44]

Aquino argues that there is a limit in Sandoval's project with respect to seeing the ambivalences within decolonial love. Sandoval's conception of decolonial love produces a set of elisions that need to be overcome. Most basically, Sandoval's project conceals the violence that sustains and reinscribes capitalist hegemony, which ends up obscuring a fundamental ambivalence between love and violence when it is lived out in modern/colonial contexts.[45] Within this elision, Sandoval creates "U.S. third world feminists" as a subjectivity "outside" the coloniality of power and, as such, "a subjectivity *ready-made* to critique the intellectual and ideological productions of power."[46] This move "elide[s] the question of how this subjectivity was formed," allowing Sandoval to suggest that creating an alternative ideology "can be (or *is*) practiced by women of color *regardless of social location*."[47] Sandoval suggests that this subjectivity happens among US third world women, but then, as Aquino demonstrates, only shows how this subjectivity matures in elite intellectual circles. The distortion of the form of subjectivity on which Sandoval relies produces a final elision that Aquino identifies: there are similarities in methodology between strategies of differential consciousness and the oppressive strategies of late capitalism. Universities are institutions within late capitalism, membership in which requires that one must "have renounced violence as an option. Indeed, not only violence, but most forms of oppositional praxis that would discernibly threaten power relations within capitalist society."[48] The risk here involves "a subtle co-optation project" of "U.S. third world feminists" into an identity centered in academia.[49] While I will pursue Aquino's constructive account of decolonial love further in the second and third parts of the book, it's important to note now that I embrace what he identifies as the ambivalences of orientations of decolonial love that emerge from the colonial difference and are made concrete in history. Wrestling with the ambivalences of decolonial love in the way it stands in relation to the violence of colonial modernity and is practiced by subjects within this matrix forces decolonial love beyond static definitions.

As a way of facing up to reality within a commitment to the mystery of decolonial love, which is always historicized in ambivalent ways, I understand decolonial love as a historical—and always not-yet-full—participation in an eschatological reality. This understanding largely comes out of the role of love in the work of Fanon and Baldwin—generally only implicit in the former's work, and fairly explicit in the latter's—coupled with my reading of Fanon and Baldwin as theologically pedagogic. Employing the work of the work of Fanon and Baldwin, and relying on Sandoval's basic articulation of decolonial love and the ways Moya and Aquino have pushed

Sandoval's work in new directions, allows me to decolonize the theological image of salvation by presenting decolonial love as opening up the possibility for an encounter with the mystery of the eschaton, and thus for salvation.

A Threshold Question for Theology

The options for decolonization presented thus far are important for Christian theologians to engage in order to be more consistent with the faith claims that guide their projects, and to face up to the reality of the present historical situation. In understanding and reflecting on the world, theologians have too often relied on tactics of epistemic disenfranchisement and have taken advantage of the privilege of ignorance that the discipline of theology can afford. In doing so, theologians have often failed to uphold the task of theology as critical reflection on historical praxis. Concepts forged within the epistemic center of Western modernity do in fact bear a relation to coloniality, whether this is recognized or not. Theologians can only maintain the idea that ignoring their exteriority results in a contextual theology if they hold to a Eurocentric understanding of Western modernity, or to a view that modernity was and is an internal process. Addressing and debunking this pervasive claim within theological ways of thinking, and doing so in view of avenues of decolonization, offers a constructive way forward wherein theologians can actualize the task of critical reflection on historical situations in light of faith.

From a decolonial perspective, Mignolo is suspicious of moving from questions about Christian theology's implication and continued investment in the epistemological structures that inform and maintain colonial modernity to questions about the positive decolonial potential of Christian theology. Mignolo unpacks two perspectives from which to tell a historical narrative regarding Christianity's role during and since the colonial moment at the end of the fifteenth century. Those employing a perspective of coloniality see the role of Christianity within Western expansion from the experience of colonization. This perspective involves dwelling within the intellectual currents and memories that move among those whose lived experiences are shaped by coloniality and the need to offer a response to coloniality as a historical problem. One can alternatively narrate Christianity out of a perspective of modernity. A perspective of modernity assumes the normativity of the hegemonic epistemological position articulated within Western Europe and now the United States. This position gains the status of the only, or at least the most authoritative, locus of enunciation, and is thus the primary reference point when narrating the role of Christianity within the modern world-system. Mignolo uses Christian and Marxist analyses of a given event as examples of perspectives of modernity. A perspective of modernity, even if it is leftist or critical, remains centered within a Western European locus of enunciation.[50] Without first dealing with this issue of the geopolitics of knowledge, Mignolo claims, it is difficult to make any easy moves toward decolonial potentials within theology.

Mignolo does not distinguish between these two perspectives as a mirror imaging of the Western academy's blind privileging of European and North American epistemologies over all others, but rather as a way to show how loci of enunciation affect knowledge production. Mignolo avoids what Sandoval refers to as an ideological "apartheid of academic knowledges" in the distinction he makes between the perspectives of modernity and coloniality by grounding his analysis of the geopolitics of knowledge in his recognition of the constitutive relationship between coloniality and modernity.[51] Attempts to remain within a perspective of modernity in order to cure its ills often end up replicating the disease in concealed ways, and Mignolo's distinction tries to avoid this problem. While the dualistic separation sometimes falters, thinking from the perspective of coloniality—that is, thinking under the leadership of those who experience Western modernity as coloniality—is basic to Mignolo's response to the reproduction of modernity.[52] In other words, out of a need to transcend the internal critique and repetition of modernity into its various trajectories, a need motivated by a desire for the reproduction of coloniality, Mignolo strongly differentiates epistemic positions, and, in doing so, questions the utility of Christian theology for a decolonial project.

In Mignolo's analysis where Christian theology inevitably fails to become a perspective of coloniality is in the discipline's failure to change "the terms and not only the content of the conversation."[53] Mignolo argues that decolonizing epistemology requires undoing foundations on which knowledge and public discourse are built.[54] A decolonial way of thinking goes beyond changing the content within existing thought systems and confronts "the entire colonial matrix."[55] Mignolo uses theology as an example of a way of thinking that only succeeds in changing the content of current thought frameworks:

> While there is a history of theology obviously linked to imperial
> designs and interests, the papacy being an obvious example, there are
> theologies of liberation in South America, North America, and Africa,
> as well as a Jewish theology of liberation. My claim is that, as in the

disputes between (neo)liberalism and (neo)Marxism, both sides of the coin belong to the same bank: the disputes are entrenched within the same rules of the game, where the contenders defend different positions but do not question the terms of the conversation.[56]

Mignolo searches for a way of thinking that moves beyond the epistemic categories delineated by Europe, of which he sees the Jewish and Christian traditions to be an expression, rather than simply making a change in content. This shift can ground decolonial ways of being, thinking, and imagining, and thus, ultimately a decolonial praxis.

A "threshold question" that demands a response before undertaking a decolonial style of theological reflection arises here.[57] Gutiérrez defines theology as "a critical reflection on Christian praxis in light of the Word."[58] His understanding of "the Word" is heavily shaped by the option for the poor, which involves, Gutiérrez suggests, an epistemic turn: "This option involves a commitment that implies leaving the road one is on, as the parable of the Good Samaritan teaches, and entering the world of the other, of the 'insignificant' person, of the one excluded from dominant social sectors, communities, viewpoints, and ideas."[59] As such, Gutiérrez describes the dialogue partners of liberation theologians as "the poor, those who are 'nonpersons'—that is, those who are not considered to be human beings with full rights, beginning with the right to live and to freedom in various spheres."[60] This prompts Gutiérrez to phrase the central pastoral and theological question of liberation theology as, "How is it possible to tell the poor, who are forced to live in conditions that embody a denial of love, that God loves them?"[61] Reframing this question that Gutiérrez bases on internal criteria of Christian theology (i.e., faith convictions) in view of the external—though contiguous—concerns of decolonial thought, I ask whether members of communities that have been rendered nonpersons through various manifestations of the coloniality of power can think and speak theologically on their own terms. I concretize (and at the same time broaden) "thinking and speaking theologically" in terms of orientations of love. I thus ask: Can the ways of loving and orientations of love among those who have been relegated to a position below being inform God-talk? Without a positive response to this general question, theology as a mode of critical reflection remains mired in the coloniality of power and its manifestations in forms of epistemic injustice. For this reason, an argument for the theologically pedagogic nature of decolonial love is necessary.

In light of the connections between Christian thought and the coloniality of power, it is easier—or at least less ambiguous—to reject Christian theology and turn elsewhere than to develop a constructive, decolonial theology. The former approach is necessary and should not be discounted, as Christian theology does not monopolize the interpretation of the world. Articulating a decolonial theological response to the historical manifestations of coloniality remains important, however, for a number of reasons.

First, attention to the actual historical situation calls into question the absolute option to turn from Christian theological paradigms that Mignolo sets forth. Formerly colonized and enslaved peoples have adopted and appropriated the language of Christian faith to describe an experience of divinity. It's not just that some communities on the colonial undersides of Western modernity use Christian categories; they have claimed an experience of, or relationship with, a divine reality that they have understood in Christian terms. This demands a response to the question of how to take this experience seriously, and account for a theological framework that allows for creativity and fluidity such that faith in a divine reality does not get conflated with the idol of Eurocentrism. Denying the creativity of the various appropriations of Christian theology would give priority to an abstract notion of theoretical purity over ways people have responded and are responding to their historical situations and the worldviews they use.

Second, critical reflection on the historical situation in light of faith in divinity incarnate in Jesus of Nazareth and the understanding of this faith conviction as an ultimate reality remains a powerful way to contest social configurations. As a commitment that exceeds the secular world of colonial modernity, Christian faith offers a horizon of critical reflection and engagement with the world that is not necessarily confined to modern/colonial rationalities. The resources of religious thought, and particularly of Christian theology, should not be given up easily.

Third, Christian faith remains a dominant category by which communities continue to understand all of reality. As such, it is necessary to show how communities can move and have moved toward a praxis of decolonization not only without giving up this category but by embracing it more fully. Fourth, and relatedly, Christian theology has been deeply entangled with the coloniality of power. Continuing to reveal the nature of this entanglement—but also that Christian theological thought is not necessarily limited to the terms of this entanglement—continues to be an important task in itself. For these reasons, I take on the challenge of this threshold question.

CHAPTER 3

Decolonial Openings in Theologies of Liberation

Those who make themselves deaf and blind, because they
think that [the open wounds of injustice and suffering] is
not a religious problem, these are the lukewarm that God,
disgusted, has already vomited out of his mouth.

—IGNACIO ELLACURÍA, *Escritos teológicos, tomo II*
(San Salvador: UCA Editores, 2000), 135

The possibilities for decolonization introduced in the previous chapter center on a movement beyond Eurocentrism, understood as a historical and epistemological matrix introduced in the fifteenth century. Liberation theology centers much more immediately on an understanding of God and the historical mediation of God, the reign of God. Ignacio Ellacuría, a Basque Jesuit theologian who became a Salvadoran citizen and worked at the Universidad Centroamericana (UCA) in San Salvador before and during the Salvadoran Civil War, demonstrated in his life and in his work that standing with suffering peoples and committing to the struggle for liberation is not only a matter of loving other people; it is a matter of closeness to God and to the encounter with God and participation in God's life that salvation entails.[1] This chapter pursues this connection between commitments to God and liberation, which in the present historical context takes the form of decolonization.

There is a general suspicion as to whether the movement beyond Eurocentrism is possible within available forms of theological reflection. While decolonial theorists have articulated this suspicion, it has also been present among theologians themselves. From within theology, Marcella Althaus-Reid

has set forth one of the most substantial critiques of Latin American liberation theology as an extension of Eurocentric epistemologies. Althaus-Reid
has, for example, pointed to how Latin American liberation theologians
have "domesticated" liberation theology into "systematic Western patterns,"[2] dichotomized political and gender liberation,[3] and pushed classical
theological concepts onto liberation struggles, and have thereby maintained
the epistemic domination embedded within theological discourse.[4] Examining three early articulations of approaches to a theology of liberation from
theologians working in Latin America from Clodivis Boff, Ignacio Ellacuría,
and Jon Sobrino, this chapter demonstrates both the validity of such calls
for a yet-to-be-made epistemological shift within a liberation theological
project as well as the potential—though perhaps not yet realized—of making this shift within some available approaches to liberation theology.

There are other liberation theologians who are seemingly more natural
choices to begin with in a decolonial theological project, including Vine
Deloria Jr., Marcella Althaus-Reid, Ivan Petrella, Delores S. Williams,
Ivone Gebara, James A. Noel, Jawanza Eric Clark, Noel Leo Erskine, Ada
María Isasi-Díaz, Mayra Rivera, An Yountae, and Josiah Ulysses Young III.[5]
Not only are these theologians working on more contemporary questions
than Boff, Ellacuría, and Sobrino; they also use language more similar to
that of decolonial theorists, and most of these thinkers more intentionally rely on non-Eurocentric epistemic resources. The reason I turn to
three liberation theologians who were most formative of liberation theology in the 1970s and 1980s is that their theological approaches raise a basic
question of how a commitment to the victims of colonial modernity—
and within this general commitment, a specific attention to epistemologies within the undersides of Western modernity—should impact theological reflection. Whereas Boff maintains the Eurocentric boundaries of
theology, Ellacuría and Sobrino present a theological approach wherein
those outside Eurocentric commitments can shape theology on their own
epistemic terms. Ellacuría and Sobrino open up the methodological possibility to decolonize theological images and concepts, and in doing so offer the possibility for theological reflection to decolonize social-historical
structures. A decolonial option requires, but is also more than, a methodological shift that prioritizes the viewpoint of the poor as the starting point
in theological reflection. Investigating how Ellacuría and Sobrino are able
to open up the epistemic boundaries of theology is thus not an endpoint,
but can provide a way forward for a decolonial theology.

Boff works to develop a theological method that takes the material world
seriously, which leads him to argue for the necessity of the social sciences

for theological reflection and construction. Though this move is important, the method he develops indicates a broader problem within some forms of liberation theology: the historical situation is mediated or disciplined by Eurocentered theological and sociological concepts. Boff's method calls for ciphering the historical situation through European thought systems, such that only the product of this mediation by Eurocentered disciplines informs a theological perspective. The theological approach Ellacuría introduces and that Sobrino carries on also engages Eurocentered frameworks, yet in a way that does not preclude historical movements toward liberation, and the epistemologies that motivate these movements, from informing theological claims. Ellacuría's way of doing theology offers an option by which a theological approach might move beyond Eurocentric criteria and toward a decolonial project insofar as what he calls "the world of the poor" takes on the role of a formal object of theology and becomes in his theology the primary locus from which to encounter and speak about God. Because historical reality is the locus where the transcendent God is most fully present and encountered, the depth of an encounter with a particular reality—and because of Christian faith convictions, an encounter with the specific reality of the world of the poor—becomes the criterion for God-talk rather than disciplinary criteria.

This chapter begins by briefly articulating the relationship between the commitments of decolonial thinkers and the early generation of Latin American liberation theologians in order to establish the context out of which these different thinkers work. It then outlines how the specific moves Boff calls for end up limiting the possibility for theological reflection to open up methodological possibilities for decolonial avenues. In a third and final section, it shows that the theological approach Ellacuría and Sobrino develop, though it works through European sources, can offer a theoretical possibility of unsettling the coloniality of power. The rest of the book pursues this possibility.

Decolonial Theory and Latin American Liberation Theology

Decolonial theorists' suspicion of Latin American liberation theology might be expected based on the context from which liberation theology emerged in Latin America, which Enrique Dussel describes as the center of the modern world-system.[6] While this suspicion should be clarified and investigated, the reliance of theologies of liberation on Western intellectual traditions is not necessarily a reason to close the conversation between theologies of liberation and secular decolonial thought.

    A difference between decolonial thought and liberation theology can be discerned in the revised introduction to Gustavo Gutiérrez's classic, *A Theology of Liberation*, in which he describes the task of liberation theology by identifying three historical transformations "basic" to liberation theology.[7] These include recognizing and starting with the "irruption of the poor" into history in the latter half of the twentieth century, the "option for the poor" that ties Christian faith to living in solidarity with this irruption, and the connection between liberation struggles and the reign of God.[8] In Gutiérrez's articulation of the three basic points to liberation theology, it is clear that the historical phenomenon of the irruption of the poor into history—that is, the poor "mak[ing] a tough entry that asks permission of no one, and is sometimes violent"[9]—plays an absolutely central role in Latin American liberation theology. The irruption of the poor that is perceived as violent from those committed to the mission of Western modernity shapes the historical form that commitment to God takes. The option for the poor is a "theocentric" option insofar as it is grounded in a commitment to a God who fundamentally opts for the poor.[10] The historical mediation of God, the eschatological reign of God, concretizes this commitment.

    In view of Gutiérrez's understanding of liberation theology, different but related concerns are apparent among decolonial thinkers and liberation theologians. Decolonial thinkers develop an explicit concern with how ways of thinking have been suppressed within Western modernity and therefore argue for a need to decolonize epistemology by freeing thinking from its Eurocentrism. As a liberation theologian, Gutiérrez is more explicitly concerned with how to respond to concrete experiences of poverty through social transformation in view of the reign of God. Although Gutiérrez refers to undertaking a theological reflection in solidarity with the irruption of the poor into history, he is not concerned as explicitly as decolonial thinkers are with how Eurocentrism informs, and might thereby limit, a response. While Gutiérrez critiques the Eurocentricity of concerns within theology, he relies a great deal on ways European thinkers have developed theological tradition and draws on their insights in order to address the particular realities he is confronted with in Peru, and more broadly in Latin America.[11] In other words, whereas Mignolo focuses on how epistemology is used as a tool to maintain Western logics of modernity over logics from the underside of Western modernity, and thereby maintain the material effects of the coloniality of power, Gutiérrez is concerned with the failure of concepts within Western traditions to be adequately inflected by lived experiences of poverty, and thereby transformed in ways that address these experiences.

Acknowledging this basic difference, a significant convergence between decolonial and liberationist projects can generate constructive possibilities for these two intellectual traditions. The concerns of decolonial thought and liberation theology meet insofar as those working within each theoretical current respond to ways that Western modernity is constituted by a colonial underside. Because of this convergence, decolonial theorists' epistemological concerns can help liberation theologians to better address the tasks Gutiérrez articulates: living in solidarity with the irruption of the poor, committing to the life of the poor as a locus of critical theological reflection, and understanding the reign of God in light of how the irruption of the poor is embodied in the immediate situation. Ada María Isasi-Díaz is one of the relatively few theologians who has made initial moves to bring liberationist and decolonial thought together. Isasi-Díaz sees decolonial thought to highlight "the epistemological and hermeneutical privilege of the impoverished and the oppressed in ways that . . . liberation thought has not done. While liberation thought advocates for impoverished and the oppressed, it has not focused on their cosmologies and epistemologies."[12] While Isasi-Díaz gestures toward a generative collaboration between decolonial thinkers and liberation theologians, the task of discerning what forms this collaboration might take has yet to be taken up in a sustained way.

Although bringing the epistemological move decolonial theorists have made into theology can help theologians, decolonial theorists can also learn from liberation theologians. Specifically, theological ways of thinking can contribute toward a movement beyond the epistemic criterion of Eurocentricity through an orientation to an infinite, transcendent reality, even if such ways of thinking continue to struggle to make an adequate turn to non-Eurocentric epistemic sources. Whereas Boff's way of doing theology indicates a way liberation theologians have generally failed to focus on the "cosmologies and epistemologies" of the oppressed, Ignacio Ellacuría's approach to theology opens up decolonial options not typically offered by secular decolonial theorists.

Prioritizing Disciplinary Criteria: Clodovis Boff's Epistemology of Liberation Theology

Boff's articulation of the epistemology of liberation theology unwittingly shows how God-talk can become circumscribed within criteria of an academic discipline that have their points of reference in the stability of European intellectual trajectories, rather than in the irruption of the poor that Gutiérrez describes. When Boff was working out the epistemological foundations of liberation theology in the early 1970s, he did so in large part in response to various attacks on liberation theology from academic and institutional quarters.[13] In general, these attacks claimed that liberation theologians reduce faith to politics, or at least risk such a reduction, make uncritical use of Marxist analysis, and separate the "popular" church from the institutional church.[14] In short, critics of liberation theology argued that the form of social analysis liberation theologians wagered on, namely Marxist analysis, led to an ideologically constituted theology that replaced the (seemingly nonideological) tradition of the faith centered in Europe. Boff tries to clarify the methodology of liberation theology in order to both address the ideological constitution of European theology and avoid the ideological constitution of Latin American liberation theology. The epistemology of liberation theology he develops thus ends up being shaped, in large part, by attacks on liberation theology coming from ways of thinking committed to how the discipline of theology has been constructed in Europe.

One way to understand the epistemology of liberation theology that results from this project is as a way of thinking inscribed within the tendency of what Lewis R. Gordon calls "disciplinary decadence." Gordon argues for the prevalence of this tendency within theoretical discourse, and defines this academic posture as "the phenomenon of turning away from living thought, which engages reality and recognizes its own limitations, to a deontologized or absolute conception of disciplinary life. . . . Becoming 'right' is simply a matter of applying the method correctly. This is a form of decadence because of the set of considerations that fall to the wayside as the discipline turns into itself and eventually implodes."[15] By highlighting the tendency for a discipline to become solipsistic and thus "decadent," Gordon's work opens up a way of critiquing a theological approach that develops in order to sustain itself against internal critiques, yet which cannot adequately respond to external critiques. In other words, Gordon opens up a need for theology to be coherent with respect to lived experience, and not only coherent as a closed discourse. In developing an epistemology of liberation theology in primary reference to theologians' criticisms of liberation theology as ideological, Boff's method has the appearance of mistakenly understanding the discipline of theology as the world.[16]

To show that liberation theology is not ideological, Boff distinguishes two types of ideology that liberation theology must avoid. In one form, ideology appears as an uncritical acceptance of historical experience and phenomena as truth claims. In this case, the problem is with "error (mis)taking itself for truth."[17] Because of liberation theology's explicit rootedness in the historical situation, it is more vulnerable to this type of ideology. In a second form of ideology, theologies justify the status quo by concealing their own social engagement. In this form, ideology takes the form of the immoral or unjustifiable being dressed up in the moral or justifiable, even as it stands in complicity with violent historical structures.[18] European theology, which often uncritically presents itself as universal, is more vulnerable to this type of ideology.

To articulate a theology that avoids both of these types of ideology, Boff employs the French Marxist theorist Louis Althusser's articulation of the process of "theoretical practice."[19] Althusser describes a scientific or theoretical process by indicating specific, separate moments of that process, which he calls "generalities." The separation of a scientific process into generalities allows Boff to argue for an epistemology of liberation theology that avoids ideology. For Boff, theological reflection, like theoretical practice more broadly, begins with broad ideological notions that theorists find in their social world.[20] This "raw material" of ideological notions constitutes the "first generality" of theoretical practice. Theoretical inquiry of this body of material is necessary to prevent scientific inquiry from becoming ideological either by naively accepting these ideological notions or by ignoring them and completely removing itself from historical phenomena. A "second generality," or a set of concepts within a particular theoretical discipline, thus has to come in to interpret the first generality. This encounter produces knowledge, or a concrete scientific theory with new concepts, which is the third generality.[21] Althusser's demarcation of generalities within scientific discourse allows Boff to maintain the disciplinary construct of theology while opening a space for social analysis to inform theological reflection. He does this by positing three "mediations," or "means or instruments of theological construction,"[22] within liberation theology: the socio-analytic, hermeneutic, and practical. These three mediations organize Boff's presentation of theology as a process of scientific cognition, and act as tools to reflect on what Christians consider to be revelation.

In positing these three mediations within an epistemology of liberation theology, Boff situates Latin American liberation theologians' use of social analyses within a theological epistemology that avoids the ways critics of liberation theology charged it to be ideological.[23] Boff roots the turn to social analysis within a "scientific" understanding of an intellectual process, acceptable within a European intellectual tradition, to show that this turn is not ideological. He contrasts liberation theology's reliance on the social sciences with European theology's dependence on a philosophical mediation by arguing that the empirical analyses of the social sciences avoid the mystification of reality that philosophical speculation can create.[24] Theology that relies on philosophy to the exclusion of the social sciences, Boff argues, can become ideological by reducing concrete and particular political and economic situations to sets of common and universal traits.[25] While the theological gaze will enter in as a way to evaluate reality, Boff maintains that a philosophical or theological perspective cannot by itself appropriate reality in a nonideological way. Boff thus argues for a starting point in a set of concepts produced by the social sciences in order to bring forth nonideological knowledge of the historical situation on which theologians can work.

To show how the use of social analysis dispels accusations that liberation theology is ideological and instead allows for a scientific form of theological reflection requires an account of the relation between theology and the historical situation that the social sciences uncover. Boff provides this by delineating points where theology is either dependent on or independent of the political, social, and cultural matrix that exists outside theological epistemology. He describes an "internal regime of autonomy" and an "external regime of dependence" within theological discourse. When the liberation theologian reflects on historical praxis, her theological reflection functions within an autonomous, self-governed internal regime. The theological reflection can be judged as true "within its own epistemological perimeter," such that social analysis only has an instrumental role in liberation theology.[26] Social analysis, therefore, only functions as the material object of liberation theology—that is, as a raw material that needs to be reworked by proper theological ways of thinking—within its external regime of dependence. Social analysis occupies an intentionally limited place, only serving to interpret a social reality in a way that is "not-yet-theological" or "pretheological."[27] In distinguishing the product of the social sciences as the material object of theology, Boff prevents the social world, and particularly what Gutiérrez calls the irruption of the poor, from acting as an epistemological ground for theological reflection. When Boff mediates the historical situation through the European social sciences, and then makes the further move to distance the historical situation from proper theological articulation, liberation theology is deeply beholden to the criteria of Eurocentered discourses. The historical situation is necessarily mediated by the European social sciences and then, in a distinct and separate step, European theological traditions. Decolonial theorists' critique of the normativity of Eurocentered thought systems can bring out the need to push past Boff's liberationist thought in order to adequately uphold the irruption of the poor as a starting point and free theology from a Eurocentered framework.

Boff introduces a second, hermeneutic mediation as a purely theological mediation, separate from the material object of liberation theology that it garners from the social sciences. When Boff speaks of the purely theological, he refers to a set of Christian concepts based on God's self-revelation in Jesus Christ that have the capacity to evaluate analyses of the social world. In making a sharp distinction between theological categories (the formal object) and that which is "theologizable," or worked on by theology (the material object), Boff specifies—and, in a sense, contains—the role that the historical irruption of the poor plays within theology. Rather than this irruption making a claim about the divine reality and providing a theological perspective, as Gutiérrez suggests it does, Boff envisions theology in such a way that the discipline of theology makes a claim about the irruption. That is, Boff delineates these two moments in a dualistic fashion, such that the formal (theological) object is not only separate from the material (social scientific) object, but is also free from the material object in the sense of not being receptive to it. Theological concepts, and not the irruption of the poor, are thus primarily determinative in Boff's outline of an epistemology of liberation theology.

In order to demonstrate both the self-contained nature of theological reflection and the constitutive role of the social sciences in liberation theology, Boff distinguishes between "first theology" as a way of thinking that deals with concepts internal to the discipline of theology, and "second theology" as a way of thinking that brings "first theology" to bear on the political. The basic difference between first and second theology is that whereas the material object of first theology seemingly remains within the internal regime of theology, the material object of second theology is explicitly secular. Second theology, or liberation theology, reflects on themes within the external regime of theology. Although this process does lead to constructive theological positions, Boff's theological approach insulates the discipline of theology as a mode of thinking.[28] Boff demonstrates that while liberation theology makes use of social analysis, social analysis (and particularly Marxist analysis) does not contaminate theological concepts within theology's internal regime.

By demonstrating this constitutive relationship, Boff explicitly shows that second theology comes out of first theology, or that liberation theology is strongly rooted in the theology that came to Latin America from Europe. While this move addresses the Eurocentered critique of liberation theology as ideological, often a euphemism for it not being adequately invested in the way the discipline of theology has been organized in Europe, it opens Boff's approach up to a decolonial critique on two levels. At the same time, these critiques question the capacity of Boff's approach to theology to fit within Gutiérrez's claims about the liberationist aspects of liberation theology, thus indicating some points of connection between decolonial thought and a vision of liberation theology, such as Gutiérrez's. First, centralizing a constitutive relationship between first and second theology shows that liberation theology proceeds most fundamentally from the third generality of European theology, not the irruption of the poor into history.[29] Faith in theology as a discipline, particularly as the discipline has taken shape in Europe, takes on a normative position in Boff's theological epistemology. This leads to a second problem. Boff begins *Theology and Praxis* by describing Eurocentered theological concepts, which he sees to be grounded in a philosophical rather than social scientific mediation, as ideological.[30] This raises the question of why he prioritizes the task of showing that categories from first theology play a central role in the epistemology of liberation theology he develops.[31]

When Boff turns explicitly to the relationship between theology and praxis in what he calls the practical mediation, he continues to prioritize a response to Eurocentered, disciplinary concerns over a concern to respond to the irruption of the poor. To explain the relationship between theory and praxis, Boff acknowledges that each theologian is socially engaged in a particular way, standing with a particular people group and struggling for specific causes. This social commitment changes the "theoretical *expression* of revelation" in theological discourse, yet it does not change the content of revelation or theology. An "epistemological breach" separates social engagement and theological expression.[32] The historical loci that might inform theological reflection on the formal level (i.e., changing the content of revelation or theology), such as the irruption of the poor into history, are, according to Boff, ideological and not epistemological sites.[33] As such, Boff remains consistent in his distinction between the material and formal objects of theology, even as he opens the possibility for a relation between the two.

In his relegation of praxis and history to the external regime of theology, Boff does not allow a concrete historical situation to shape theological perspectives outside the way that context has been ciphered through the disciplinary norms of the social sciences. Historical praxis, in Boff's conception, does not generate theological discourse as much as it is the object of theological analysis.[34] As such, a critique of liberation theology as too indebted to its point of origin in the modern world-system is applicable to the internal level of Boff's epistemology of liberation theology.

Because liberation theology cannot distance itself from its Eurocentricity in Boff's method, it also cannot adequately allow the irruption of the poor into history to shape theological reflection. This problem motivates a turn to Ellacuría's approach, which was further developed by Jon Sobrino after Ellacuría was killed. Whereas Boff, Ellacuría, and Sobrino all identify as liberation theologians, Ellacuría and Sobrino's way of doing theology engages the irruption of the poor into history in a way that Boff's approach cannot. While Boff crucially shows the need to engage a historical situation within a theological reflection, in his way of articulating this engagement, he distances the historical situation and social-political movement, or the irruption of the poor, as the fundamental criterion and limits the capacity for historical praxis to be theologically pedagogic. Disciplinary criteria begin to displace the fundamental role that Gutiérrez argues the poor to have in Latin American liberation theology.

If the manifestation of the coloniality of power in the realm of epistemology is to be addressed, it is necessary to move beyond a theological framework in which theology as such maintains a disciplinary coherence, even as it can be applied to different historical situations. Theology as a discipline cannot operate as a world, in the mode of what Gordon describes as disciplinary decadence. Some forms of descent into what Audre Lorde calls "the chaos of knowledge" are necessary in order to return to a decolonial vision.[35] This implies an unsettling and opening up of theology on the formal level. Historical praxis cannot merely be raw material to be worked on by theology; it must also be theologically pedagogic. In this process, the strong entanglement between theology and the coloniality of power that conceals ways marginalized peoples speak theologically on their own epistemic terms begins to be unwound. Theology ceases to be a Eurocentered way of thinking applied to the peripheries of the modern/colonial world-system.

Prioritizing Encounters within Historical Reality: Theology as Intellectus Amoris

Ellacuría does not provide a direct response to decolonial thinkers' concerns about the problematic origin of liberation theology. Ellacuría continues to rely on European sources to develop a way of doing theology in a

Latin American context. His theological approach opens up the possibility of a response to the coloniality of power from within liberation theology, however, because it allows theological reflection to proceed from the historical situation that Gutiérrez calls the irruption of the poor. Ellacuría thus addresses some of the more fundamental concerns that decolonial theorists bring up, even as the field of decolonial studies emerged only after Ellacuría's death. Isasi-Díaz recognized the need for a decolonial turn within liberation theology,[36] and made passing references to how Ellacuría's theological approach influences her own emerging decolonial approach, although she did not substantially develop this connection.[37] It is necessary to eventually push past Ellacuría's way of doing theology and engage concrete ways of knowing and acting in the world that emerge out of the colonial undersides of Western modernity without relying on Euro-centered epistemologies as a legitimizing norm. Yet, I pursue Isasi-Díaz's intuition by arguing that Ellacuría's theological approach, though Euro-centered, can open up a theological framework that is receptive to—and which requires—a movement beyond Eurocentric epistemologies.

Despite his reliance on European sources—and I do not intend this as an apology for using European sources, but rather as opening up a theological approach that can ultimately transcend Eurocentricity—Ellacuría approaches theological reflection in a way that the historical irruption of the poor itself provides a theological perspective. This irruption from the underside of Western modernity informs theology, to go back to Boff's terminology, on the formal level. Whereas Boff's theological method is primarily concerned with legitimizing liberation theology as a discipline, Ellacuría's approach focuses on a posture of honesty toward reality that maintains the centrality of the historical irruption of the poor. To develop the potential of Ellacuría's liberationist method in view of the concerns of decolonial theory, which can push liberation theology to attend more faithfully to its own basic premises of liberation, I focus on two aspects of Ellacuría's theology. First, Ellacuría's approach to theology connects lived experience and the apprehension of reality to the formal theological project, which in turn requires that the liberation theologian face up to the irruption of the poor as a reality that shapes an understanding of divinity. Ellacuría's distinctive understanding of history and the way he confronts history grounds this claim. Second, Ellacuría and Sobrino make use of this understanding of historical reality in their christology, in which they articulate the divine reality by starting from the concrete ways the poor irrupt into history.

Ignacio Ellacuría's Theological Epistemology

Ellacuría develops a theological approach in response to the weight of the historical situation that presents itself, and in doing so focuses primarily on the importance of the site from which theological reflection proceeds, rather than the scientific character of theology. He argues for the importance of starting "by determining the sphere of reality, determining what theological activity should pursue, and determining the critical conditions necessary for theological activity to achieve its concrete ends."[38] When critically reflecting on God's self-communication in history, the content of the historical situation informs the theological method. A theological reflection thus cannot be delineated in an absolute sense, and cannot be developed primarily in reference to an academic debate. Theological reflection is a process of discerning the presence and manifestation of divinity in history, working toward historical transformation, and interpreting how this transformation is wrapped up with the Christian understanding of God, salvation, and the reign of God. Theological ways of thinking, as well as ways of doing and acting in reference to theological thought, are thus necessarily informed by and constantly receptive to a historical situation.

Ellacuría forwards a method of "historicization" as his way of facing up to reality.[39] The experience of transcendence within daily experience, of the divine transcending in intramundane reality and being encountered in history, fundamentally shapes Ellacuría's way of apprehending reality through the process of historicization. Sajid Alfredo Herrera indicates three elements of Ellacuría's method of historicization. First, historicization requires presenting concepts that show what reality gives of itself in particular historical situations. In this sense, concepts are historical rather than abstract. They emerge out of the unfolding of reality as a dynamic structure.[40] Concepts articulated within the method of historicization are thus opposed to constructions that serve to reify or freeze reality—for example, in categories that sustain colonial relations of power. Second, the method of historicization functions to "de-ideologize" and "un-veil what has been hidden out of interest."[41] Historicization opposes the form of ideology that Boff associates with European theology that justifies the unjustifiable. Third, historicization is a "theoretical labor" that "correctly situates those concepts . . . that have been stripped of what is true in them, of their real and historical truth."[42] Historicization is a method—and for Ellacuría, a theological method—that facilitates the critique of ideology and makes space for imagining alternatives.

To ground this understanding of reality that informs theological reflection, Ellacuría turns to philosophy. Nelson Maldonado-Torres articulates a form of philosophy as "post-continental philosophy" that aptly describes Ellacuría's earlier engagement with philosophy.[43] Unlike philosophical meanderings and arguments that function to justify "'the continent,' Europe or elsewhere, as the foundation for a form of being or thinking," post-continental philosophy responds to the existential situation shaped by the coloniality of power.[44] Post-continental philosophy thus takes decolonization, not a geographical space, as its fundamental point of reference.[45] Crucially, post-continental philosophy brackets "the assumed validity and general legitimacy of European traditions of thought and of European modernity as a project,"[46] and in doing so, analyzes how Western modernity is able to provoke "different modes of deception and self-deception in the underworld of coloniality."[47] Post-continental philosophy is thus a project of moving beyond disciplinary decadence in order to confront the modern/colonial world-system. While the discourse of decolonial theory was not current in Latin America when Ellacuría was writing, it's clear that Ellacuría was engaging in what Maldonado-Torres would later term post-continental philosophy. Ellacuría draws on philosophical concepts in order to respond to the irruption of the poor into history in light of his Christian faith.

Ellacuría specifically draws on philosophical categories because of their capacity to further reveal foundations of reality, which allows for more rigorously attending to the historical praxis of facing up to reality. A primary philosophical category Ellacuría uses to understand reality and its relationship to divinity is the concept of "historical reality." Ellacuría takes on this concept from the work of his mentor, the Basque philosopher Xavier Zubiri, who was critical of Western philosophy, yet did not reject the utility of philosophy in articulating a response to reality. Historical reality as a philosophical concept refers to the highest manifestation of the material dimensions of reality, and therefore articulates a basis for theological reflection. Andrew Prevot describes Zubiri as offering Ellacuría an analogical structure situated within the question of reality rather than the structure of being.[48] This shift allows Ellacuría to develop a theological perspective that balances a commitment to history and a commitment to a transcendent God.

Drawing on the work of Zubiri, Ellacuría argues that "'[h]istorical reality' is the 'ultimate object' of philosophy, understood as intramundane metaphysics, not only for its englobing and totalizing character, but as the supreme manifestation of reality."[49] Historical reality, as a philosophical

concept, is broader than the material dimensions of reality; it is a unified field where reality takes place.[50] Ellacuría develops historical reality
as a formal object of philosophy and theology because of what Zubiri describes as the "theologal" dimension of reality, and because of how Zubiri
and Ellacuría understand the human person to be situated within reality.[51]
The theologal dimension of reality is a structural element of reality without a concrete idea attached to it, which is accessible to analysis.[52] Zubiri
distinguishes the theologal from the theological by arguing that the theologal exists as a reality before the discourse of theology, and "refers to
a human dimension that formally and constitutively envelops (*envuelve*)
the problem of the divine reality, of Theos."[53] Ellacuría draws on Zubiri's
philosophical theology but, as Prevot argues, crucially brings it together
with a biblical theology. Whereas Zubiri develops an understanding of
the theologal structure of reality primarily within a metaphysical account
of reality, Ellacuría articulates the theologal structure of reality primarily
within "the properly Christian task of prayerfully interacting with God
precisely through the freedom of the economy of salvation."[54] By using
Zubiri's understanding of historical reality and the theologal character of
reality, which makes both a metaphysical and epistemological claim, Ellacuría understands reality and the human person situated in reality as itself
a formal theological ground. By bringing in a biblical understanding of
salvation, Ellacuría remains tethered to a Christian—and, in some sense
christocentric—understanding of the movement of history.

Zubiri elaborates on the theologal dimension of reality and its implications through an analysis of the human reality that connects divinity and
transcendence with the human experience of reality. In the encounter with
reality, Zubiri describes the human person as going through a process of
both "empowerment" (*apoderamiento*) and "religation" (*religación*). The human person is empowered in being dominated, moved, and fully grasped
by reality.[55] In this sense, the world is fundamentally part of the human
person—it is our ontological structure that empowers our existence. Religation, which Robert Lassalle-Klein translates as "bondedness,"[56] is this
process of empowering. We are empowered by being religated, or tied
back to the power of the real. Michael E. Lee notes a connection between
the process of religation and the way transcendence functions in Zubiri's
philosophy. As a description of the phenomenon of being tied back to
the empowering character of the real, religation evokes "a transcendence
that binds the human to reality in terms of depth."[57] Religation, therefore, redefines transcendence in terms of deepening our presence in reality. Transcendence is a drive into history rather than a movement out of

history. Religation is the experience of "the ultimacy of the real" that is encountered within this saturation in historical reality.[58] We are religated or "thrown" (*lanzado*) to a "fundament" (*fundamento*), the "precise internal structure" of the power of the real.[59] The theologal dimension of reality to which we are thrown is "a dimension that constitutively and formally involves an inexorable confrontation with the ultimacy of the real, that is, with that which, in a manner merely nominal and provisional, we can call God."[60] In describing the theologal dimension of reality as such, Zubiri develops a unified understanding of the human person, reality, and God. This unified understanding of our existence in reality and in relation to God drives Ellacuría's theological reflection inflected more explicitly by biblical themes, and allows Ellacuría to connect the process of entering more deeply into reality to the process of encountering divinity.

Ellacuría, like Gutiérrez, describes the starting point of liberation theology as its distinctive feature. This starting point is crucial for Ellacuría in discerning the salvific character of the struggle for liberation,[61] and indicates an implicit connection between Ellacuría's liberationist concerns and decolonial concerns. Ellacuría describes liberation theology as a response to "the Christian and epistemological locus in which the theologian is situated, from the theologian's preferential option for the poor."[62] He clarifies the nature of this starting point by arguing that "[t]he theology of liberation insists that the fullness of historical salvation understood as liberation, which includes all salvation, cannot be obtained except from a preferential option for the poor."[63] He specifies this option as an epistemic option, at least to a degree: "Liberation theology attempts to situate itself, really and intentionally, *in the situation and perspective* of the majority populations in order to understand, interpret, and transform reality so as to live out the fullness of the gospel, as much personally as in community."[64] Entering into the perspectives of the majority population—because of his biblical and Christian commitments and his philosophical commitments—opens up a theological perspective. The "option" in liberation theology's "option for the poor" is in this case a call to opt for "the situation and perspective." Without confronting reality, and particularly the reality of coloniality, and then allowing this reality to shape theological reflection, the theologian loses the capacity to speak from an encounter with God. While Ellacuría develops this position by drawing on European thinkers, notably Zubiri, he arrives at a claim about the fundamental importance of ways of knowing and acting within the experience of coloniality, or within the irruption of the poor into history, for theological reflection.

THEOLOGY AS INTELLECTUS AMORIS
AND THE WAY OF THE ADDRESSEE

Ellacuría's way of concretizing the option for the poor becomes clearest in his christology, which Sobrino further developed after Ellacuría was murdered. In Ellacuría's essay most directly concerned with christology, he asks who or what continues Jesus' saving activity in history, or how salvation is realized in history and how humans actively participate in salvation history.[65] His response, in short, is the reality that he calls the "crucified people." Ellacuría develops the idea of the crucified people, the core concept within his christology, as a sign of the times that gives access to the theologal dimension of reality:

> [A]mong so many signs, which are always given, some of which call
> our attention and others which are barely perceptible, there is in each
> time one sign that is primary, from whose light we must discern and
> interpret all others. That sign is always the historically crucified people,
> of whose always distinct historical form of crucifixion is united in its
> permanency. This crucified people is the historical continuation of the
> servant of Yahweh, whose human figure the sin of the world continues
> to take away, and whom the powers of the world strip of everything,
> even his life, especially his life.[66]

Ellacuría understands God to make her or himself present in the crucified people, thus taking on a "theologal concept of poverty," or a recognition that God self-reveals in and through the poor.[67] Focusing on Jesus' incarnation, life, death, and resurrection, Ellacuría posits a real historical continuity, on the soteriological level, between Jesus and the poor of El Salvador.[68] Sobrino maintains that the crucified people "are the actual presence of the crucified Christ in history," such that "in this crucified people Christ acquires a body in history and that the crucified people embody Christ in history as crucified."[69] In coming to an understanding of Jesus Christ through the poor as a theologal sign of the times, or through the crucified people, Ellacuría and Sobrino work from the irruption of the poor into history and allow this irruption to shape the meaning of Jesus and salvation.

Sobrino begins with the "social-theologal setting" of christology, which he concretizes as the world of the poor.[70] The world of the poor "offers thought an epistemological advantage: a light that illuminates its subject matter."[71] He pushes this even further: "The poor and the victims bring theology something more important than contents; they bring light by which we can see the contents properly."[72] Here Sobrino makes a stronger claim than Boff's claim that the poor or their social situation are the material object on which theology reflects; Sobrino claims that the world of the poor, as the historical continuation of Christ, is the perspective from which theological reflection takes place, and is thus the formal object of theology. The conviction to stand under the leadership of the world of the poor is necessary for the Christian (liberation) theologian. As such, the formal and material object of theology cannot be distinguished. The crucified people is not limited to a raw material to be worked on by theological concepts; because it is a theologal sign of the times—that is, a locus that reveals divinity and indicates the possibility for an encounter and relationship with divinity—the crucified people shapes a theological perspective on the formal level.

In order to distinguish the approach of liberation theology, Sobrino describes two approaches Eurocentered theologians generally use to describe the reign of God. Theologians who think from the "notional way" draw on notions or concepts of the reign of God in order to deduce what it meant for Jesus. They do this by looking at the understanding of the reign of God in the Hebrew Bible in order to discern the tradition in which Jesus stood when proclaiming the reign of God, and then, from these ideas about the reign of God, determine how Jesus concretized these notions.[73] Theologians who emphasize "the way of the practice of Jesus" start with Jesus' concrete practices—for example, his miracles, casting out of devils, table fellowship, parables, celebration—in order to understand what he meant when referring to the reign of God.[74] Although both of these ways of understanding the reign of God, and ultimately Jesus, can be productive, neither takes the world of the poor and their irruption into history as a theological source.

In his christology, Sobrino turns to the social-theologal setting of the world of the poor as the primary source to understand the reign of God, which as the final reality for Jesus says something about who Jesus is. Latin American liberation theologians, Sobrino argues, make use of both the approaches that dominate European theology, but also add a third approach, based on the social-theologal setting of the world of the poor, which he calls "the way of the addressee." If the reign of God exists as "good news," Sobrino argues, then "its recipients will help fundamentally in clarifying its content, since good news is something essentially relational, not all good news being so in equal measure for everyone."[75] In this turn to the poor as the addressees of the reign, Sobrino affirms the option for the poor as an epistemological option. This is apparent in his reference to the light that emerges from the world of the poor:

> To accept that there is a light in the world of the poor, and a light that cannot be found in other places, is in the last resort a choice—although one can argue for this in advance on the basis of the transcendental relationship between God and the poor—which acts as a "pre-understanding" of christology. What I want to emphasize, however, is that the so-called option for the poor is more than a pastoral option; it is an all-embracing option to grasp the whole view, but to see it consciously from one position.[76]

Sobrino is clear that this method of thinking from the world of the poor, as a social-theologal setting for christology, but also Christian theology as a whole, is a distinctive move that liberation theology makes.[77] As such, Sobrino, working out of Ellacuría's fundamental intuitions, develops an approach specific to christology that deepens Gutiérrez's claims about the distinctiveness of liberation theology, and he does so by starting with the social-theologal setting of the poor as informing theological reflection.

Because the poor are understood as a theologal reality and as informing theological reflection, the theological task becomes more than critical reflection. Theology becomes an understanding of love, and through this process of understanding, historical transformation. Insofar as the world of the poor "is a mediation of the truth and absoluteness of God," Sobrino underlines a "partiality of divine revelation."[78] This catalyzes an active decision of where to stand as a theologian. This decision is rooted in Christian revelation, but also in a desire to enter into "reality as it is."[79] Taking a stance within the world of the poor elicits, Sobrino argues, a compassion that surfaces on the anthropological level, prior to theology or religion.[80] The task of all theology, including liberation theology, is to move from this posture of compassion to a historical praxis of ending suffering. As such, "liberation theology makes the theological determination of its fundamental object as the Reign of God; and it understands this object as something to be realized now."[81] With this in mind, Sobrino defines liberation theology as *intellectus amoris*.[82] He consistently grounds this anthropological claim christologically:

> Jesus asserts that what is ultimate and absolutely necessary is that persons follow him. Historically, he makes clear that what is most important is not to say "Lord, Lord," but to do the will of the father. Eschatologically, he makes clear that salvation—the final realization

of God's designs and the purpose of revelation—is realized when love
of those in need actually takes place, no matter the explicit awareness
that accompanies such love. . . . It is clear that it is more important for
Christianity that the Christian reality take place than that it be correctly understood, and that what is most fundamental for Christians is
that love happen in this world.[83]

The theological task is to work from the reality of love, which becomes "a
mystagogic reality that gives access to the mystery of God."[84] Understanding this love, allowing it to become more actual in the world, and knowing
and understanding God and salvation, are all intertwined.

Ellacuría and Sobrino provide a fundamental theological basis for undertaking a theological reflection from the irruption of the poor in a way in
which the world of the poor or the crucified people become the criterion
for a Christian theological project. The crucified people, as a particular
reality within historical reality, become the formal object of theology done
within a Christian tradition. As a historical body, the crucified people re-
place what Dussel described as the place from which Latin American theology emerged, "originally the Mediterranean and Europe and today, by
extension, the United States."[85] With the crucified people at the center,
and guided by a posture of love in relation to the crucified people, theological reflection as *intellectus amoris* becomes "post-continental." Jesus
as norm for Christian theology is necessary, but also turned outward, such
that the wisdom of Christ is located in historical reality, and particularly
among the crucified people and in specific relationships with and among
the crucified people.[86] The link to Jesus Christ remains, yet as revealing the
theologal dimension of reality, in this case from a Christian perspective.

There is no direct connection between Ellacuría and Sobrino's work
and the ways decolonial thinkers have responded to coloniality, in the
sense that neither Ellacuría and Sobrino, on the one hand, nor decolonial
thinkers, on the other, are in direct conversation with each other. And,
rather than taking on the discourse of the coloniality of power and decolonization, Ellacuría and Sobrino are concerned with the reign of God as a
transcendent reality of faith, but which is always at the same time historicized. In holding the reign of God as an ultimate orientation, however, the
approach Ellacuría and Sobrino use of connecting the practice of love to
a mystagogical reality that opens up an encounter with and understanding
of God presents possibilities for a decolonial theology.

While Boff, Ellacuría, and Sobrino continue to rely on European sources,
it is possible to see how this reliance manifests in different ways that cannot

be equally grouped together and addressed under an umbrella critique of Eurocentrism. Boff's reliance on Eurocentric sources results in an attempt to legitimize liberation theology in reference to the terms of European disciplinary constructs. In doing so he abandons the foundations of liberation theology in the connection of Christian faith to solidarity with the irruption of the poor into history, to the irruption of the poor as driving critical reflection, and to the irruption of the poor as revealing the reign of God. Ellacuría and Sobrino, on the other hand, transcend the Eurocentricity of their sources by articulating an approach to theological reflection that allows experiences of and responses to the ways reality is experienced as coloniality to inform theological reflection on the formal level.

Bringing out elements in the work of Ellacuría and Sobrino that open up the methodological possibility for theological reflection to become a decolonial project is not an attempt to bring decolonial thought back into a Eurocentered orbit. Decolonial thinkers' move to undo the Eurocentricity of epistemology by contesting the tendency among many intellectuals to over-rely on European sources is a necessary project. Yet, it is also important to show that an approach to theology as intellectus amoris articulated and lived out by Ellacuría and Sobrino pushes critical reflection on historical situations in a genuinely "post-continental" direction that, in being liberationist, can also be decolonial. To continue to actualize the potential for theological reflection to become an option for decolonial thinking and doing, however, calls for expanding the sources of theological thought, de-centering the epistemologies that are pedagogic for theological reflection from a Eurocentered and "continental" orientation, and ultimately decolonizing concrete theological images.

PART II

Decolonial Love

CHAPTER 4

Frantz Fanon's Decolonial Love: A New Humanism in Historical Struggle

Indigeneity as a frame of reference allows one to chart presence, loss, and reconstruction of complex ways of relating to space and creating place. This, in the end, provides another option for theological discourse to free itself from a slavish commitment to "dam up" colonial categories as a means of affirming the plight of a victimized group.

—RUFUS BURNETT JR. AND STEVEN BATTIN, "Indigeneity and Theological Discourse," *Newsletter CLT* 7 (February, 2014): 9

Indigeneity, as Rufus Burnett Jr. and Steven Battin use the term, refers to both "the current life-worlds of indigenous peoples" and the life-worlds of "those who by virtue of the modern project of enslavement and ethnic cleansing had to recast their indigeneity through the production of culture."[1] Through their commitment to indigeneity as a theological resource—or, in the language I have been using, as theologically pedagogic—Burnett and Battin work to peel back the ways colonial categories have "dammed up" in ways that have limited the capacity to transcend modernity from sites of wisdom existing in its cracks.

It is not immediately clear that Fanon was committed to indigeneity in the way that Burnett and Battin offer it as a site for transcending modernity and as informative for theological discourse. Fanon fails to see the blues as more than a "black slave lament,"[2] does not perceive the decolonial possibilities in indigenous Kabyle forms of religion, worship, and dance, and limits the significance of the veil worn by Algerian women to its relationship to the Algerian Revolution. Allowing for these discontinuities, there is at the same time a fundamental continuity between Fanon's political and intellective praxis and the turn toward indigeneity as a site from which to transcend modernity for which Burnett and Battin argue. Fanon is deeply committed to a liberation from the "damming up" of colonial categories. His work is geared toward a reality that exists beyond the modern world-system, which he often calls a new humanity and at times calls love. Fanon momentarily settles on different identities as historicizing this ultimate reality—particularly blackness and the postcolonial nation. But—and here is where Fanon's work decisively offers an example of what Burnett and Battin call indigeneity—Fanon in the end always seeks to transcend the confinement of life-worlds emerging from the colonial difference. He consistently moves from static identities to fluidity. Fanon allows the dynamism that emerges from the colonial difference to constantly surface, rupturing abstract colonial categories. His political and intellective praxis works to actualize this rupture and establish the material conditions for exceeding the imaginative limits of Western modernity.

I refer to both Fanon's praxis and the orientation that guides it as decolonial love and suggest, primarily in the third part of the book, that the decolonial love that surfaces in Fanon's work can be theologically pedagogic in the way that Burnett and Battin propose indigeneity to be. Fanon concretizes his orientation of decolonial love into a historical praxis by breaking open the ways ideology is contained and hypostasized within the modern world-system, situating the human person in relation to a reality that transcends the confines of Western modernity, and committing to a praxis of catalyzing "the end of the world," or a praxis of opening up ruptures in history. This historical praxis of love is perceived as violent from the side of Western modernity.

In this chapter I draw out the chronological development of Fanon's struggle to concretize his orientation of decolonial love into a historical and intellective praxis. I begin with Fanon's time in his native Martinique, move to how fighting for France in the second World War and his studies in psychiatry in Lyon moved his praxis in new directions, and then to ways his work in a hospital outside of Algiers and his involvement with the Front de Libération Nationale (FLN) shaped his articulation of decolonial love as he dictated his last book as he was dying of leukemia at the age of thirty-six. The chapter begins by locating Fanon's understanding of a new humanism within a dialectical perspective shaped by his Caribbean context. In this context, black identity takes center stage for Fanon as a medium of the universal. The chapter then shifts to exploring how the movement of Fanon's dialectics was shaped by his involvement in a nationalist movement while working and living in Algeria. In this context, violence more forcefully catalyzes dialectical movement against ways relationships get frozen within colonial categories and structures. Violence is, in Fanon's work, a constitutive part of a decolonial option, though not a unique conduit of a universal and absolute new humanity.

The Coloniality of Power and Being: The Immanence of the Absolute in the Zone of Nonbeing

Fanon is clear about the limited nature of his own orientation within the world. He begins his first book by proclaiming, "I'm not the bearer of absolute truths. No fundamental inspiration has flashed across my mind."[3] At the same time, he finishes that book by boldly stating, "As a man, I undertake to risk annihilation so that two or three truths can cast their essential light on the world."[4] One vein of scholarship on Fanon has, in light of a trend toward postmodern and postcolonial commitments, tended to emphasize the first statement and minimize the last one.[5] It is extremely difficult to read Fanon, however, while obscuring his positive truth claims. Foremost among these in his first book, *Black Skin, White Masks*, are his claims about the human, and his gestures toward the universal reality of love. Fanon situates the human person in relationship to an ultimate reality that he at times names as love or salvation, which exceeds modern/colonial rationalities.

Toward a New Humanism

Fanon introduces his first book, *Black Skin, White Masks*, by affirming the project of striving for what he calls "a New Humanism."[6] This new humanism is an essential part of the "truths" Fanon wants to uncover and is inseparable from his revolutionary project. The reality that I refer to as decolonial love is fundamental to this new humanism. Fanon's longing for universal human love can be read as a longing for decolonial love—that is, for relations of love liberated from the coloniality of power and what he refers to as the metaphysics of race. Fanon's new humanism originates in the particular historical situation he inhabits in Martinique. Fanon describes racial tensions in Martinique in the 1920s and 1930s to be largely shaped by economic realities:

> The racial problem is covered over by economic discrimination and, in a given social class, it is above all productive of anecdotes. Relations are not modified by epidermal accentuations. . . . A Negro worker will be on the side of the mulatto worker against the middle-class Negro. Here

we have proof that questions of race are but a superstructure, a mantle, an obscure ideological emanation concealing an economic reality.[7]

Fanon writes this in 1955, just after the publication of *Black Skin, White Masks*. In the same essay, Fanon goes on to show how changes in Martinique catalyzed awareness of how race functions within the modern Western network of power. Like Quijano, Fanon sees both the capitalist control over work and its products and resources and race to shape the larger colonial situation. And, also like Quijano, Fanon largely under-theorizes the ways that gender constitutes, and is constituted by, modernity/coloniality.

Fanon identifies 1939, the start of World War II, as a time that changed Martinicans'—and Fanon's—consciousness. Aimé Césaire's publication of *Notebook of a Return to the Native Land*, as well as his actual return to Martinique, announced to Martinicans "that it is fine and good to be a Negro."[8] Césaire not only opened up the possibility for Martinicans to see themselves as racialized in the same way as Africans and others in the African diaspora, he also affirmed that "'*the big black hole*' was a source of truth."[9] The impetus for Césaire's ideological affirmation of Negritude received material justification among Martinicans when a French military fleet commanded by Georges Robert stationed in Martinique at the beginning of the war. With the influx of French sailors, Martinicans experienced "authentic racists" firsthand.[10] The encounter with these French sailors forced Martinicans to undergo their "first metaphysical experience"—they developed a racial consciousness.[11] In the process of the war, "Martinique for the first time systematized its political consciousness" such that "the first metaphysical, or if one prefers, ontological experiment, coincided with the first political experiment."[12] Peter Hudis points out the importance of this moment for not only Martinicans at large, but also Fanon specifically. The concern with the connection between a psychological, or "metaphysical" or "ontological" shift, on the one hand, and a social or political mobilization, on the other, will occupy Fanon throughout the rest of his life and work.[13]

At the age of seventeen, Fanon joined the French to fight against Nazism, although he was quickly dismayed at the racial hierarchies within the French Army and the contradictions between the French rhetoric of freedom and the reality of French soldiers and settlers.[14] Fanon went on to study psychiatry in Lyon, beginning in 1947, where he was also introduced to French philosophy and leftist politics. During his time in Lyon, Fanon began working on *Black Skin, White Masks*. In this work, Fanon would draw on his studies in psychiatry and philosophy to interrogate the themes of alienation/disalienation and humanism in light of his lived experience in Martinique and France.

In Fanon's introduction to *Black Skin, White Masks,* he offers an initial response to the problem of the way the human person is circumscribed within colonial modernity. It becomes evident here that a central tenet of Fanon's decolonial love, and one of the "truths" he wants to bring forth, is the rootedness of the human person in a reality other than the confines of colonial modernity. He articulates this with the concept of a new humanism. Fanon sees the effects of how the coloniality of power gets historicized on the level of being to be both a negative experience and a site from which to actualize a new humanism. He names this site "the zone of nonbeing," which he describes as "an extraordinarily sterile and arid region, an incline stripped bare of every essential, from which a genuine new departure can emerge."[15] From the zone of nonbeing, Fanon turns to writing to interrogate the structure and imposition of this zone, and to thereby liberate the subject from the "veritable hell" of the zone of nonbeing:

> If it be true that consciousness is an act of transcending (*activité de transcendance*), we must also realize that this transcendence is haunted with the issue of love and understanding. Man is a "yes" resonating from cosmic harmonies. Uprooted, dispersed, dazed, and condemned to watch as the truths he has elaborated vanish one by one, he must stop projecting his antinomy into the world. Blacks are men who are black; in other words, owing to a series of affective disorders they have settled into a universe from which we have to extricate them. The issue is paramount. We are aiming at nothing less than to liberate the black man from himself. We shall tread very carefully, for there are two camps: white and black. We shall inquire persistently into both metaphysics and we shall see that they are often highly destructive.[16]

This description of the "act of transcending" in relation to the zone of nonbeing outlines the general project that motivates *Black Skin, White Masks*: an analysis and destruction of the zone of nonbeing, from the possibilities that the zone of nonbeing presents.

Fanon introduces here several elements that ground his articulation of a new humanism. First, when he describes consciousness as an active "transcending" movement, Fanon indicates a dynamic and universalizing dimension of the human person, based on a common ability and desire to love. Colonial modernity negates this dimension of the person by wrenching the potential of the universalizing moment away from the colonized subject. This has the consequence that, from the perspective of those committed to the myth and project of Western modernity, salvation cannot come from the zone of nonbeing. Writing *Black Skin, White Masks* contributes to the praxis of transcending into the human reality. It interrogates a universal position deeply immanent within the human person that is clarified precisely in the zone of nonbeing. Second, the zone of nonbeing is structurally imposed, but then also becomes internally imposed. A praxis of decolonial love that eradicates the zone of nonbeing requires a response to both levels of its imposition. Third, Fanon sees decolonization, as a historical praxis guided by decolonial love, to force the conception of the human out of an ontology or "metaphysics" linked to race. He clarifies that the exit from the zone of nonbeing is not (only) a matter of religious sensibility or a shift in consciousness: "And there's no point sidling up crabwise with a mea culpa look, insisting it's a matter of salvation of the soul. Genuine disalienation will have been achieved only when things, *in the most materialist sense*, have resumed their rightful place."[17] What Fanon calls "disalienation" is a project that addresses the material aspects of life in order to break with inauthentic ways of being, or with ways of being that depend on racial constructions as metaphysical categories. Fanon approaches the universal dimension of the human person, addresses the internal and structural manifestations of the zone of nonbeing, and actualizes a materialist restoration through his own version of dialectical movement.

Fanon's Dialectical Perspective

The irrationality of the coloniality of power produces a situation in which the black subject "has no ontological resistance in the eyes of the white man."[18] Fanon wants to posit the universal dimension of humanity and of human love, yet the modern/colonial situation and the processes of racialization within it exclude this universality as a historical reality or, seemingly, possibility. In the way being is constructed within the coloniality of power, Fanon interprets the black subject as defined in relation to whiteness, as a lack of being vis-à-vis the perceived fullness of being in whiteness.

Fanon charts a way to respond to this lack of ontological resistance. He describes his approach as "sociogeny."[19] Fanon sets aside both the limited analyses of a person's developmental history (ontogeny) and of the species' developmental history (phylogeny) when studying racism and the production of ontological lack, or what Maldonado-Torres refers to as the "subontological difference."[20] He opts rather for an analysis of the entanglement between social relations and the interior life (sociogeny).[21] Fanon affirms the need to analyze the relationship between socio-economic and psychological realities, and then to combat the lack of ontological resistance on both levels.[22] This combat is located within the purview of Fanon's new humanism, which he articulates from the zone of nonbeing, from the colonial difference, and within a dialectical understanding of the movement of history. This reveals another "truth" Fanon conveys in *Black Skin, White Masks,* verified in Fanon's historical praxis: in hypostasizing its own definitions of knowledge, the human person, and history, colonial modernity unjustifiably freezes historical movement and closes alternative options to inclusion within the modern world-system. An orientation of decolonial love implies a historical commitment to creating space for alternatives.

In *Black Skin, White Masks,* Fanon explicitly engages Hegel's "master-slave dialectic" set forth in the *Phenomenology of Spirit* (1807). The movement within Hegel's dialectic between the particular and the universal is central to not only Fanon's first book but to all of his subsequent work. In the *Phenomenology of Spirit,* Hegel works through stages of development toward a true self-consciousness. Hegel's assertion, "*Self-consciousness achieves its satisfaction only in another self-consciousness,*" grounds the movement of this process.[23] The subject requires recognition in order to satisfy self-consciousness, but this recognition has to come from another self-consciousness that the subject recognizes as such.[24] There is, therefore, a need for reciprocal recognitions. Self-certainty only becomes adequate when another self recognizes it: "Each is indeed certain of its own self, but not of the other, and therefore its own self-certainty has no truth."[25]

Hegel describes a two-way action in which each subject stakes its own life in a life-and-death struggle. This act demonstrates that the subjectivity of each individual is more than the immediate form in which it exists: "The individual who has not risked his life may well be recognized as a *person,* but he has not attained to the truth of this recognition as an independent self-consciousness."[26] This assumption of a universal ground is a major assumption that Hegel makes, and that Fanon recognizes: "There is at the basis of Hegelian dialectic an absolute reciprocity that must be highlighted."[27] But, Fanon will not follow Hegel in postulating this universal ground. This "world of reciprocal recognitions" is something that remains to be actualized; confronting colonial modernity from its colonial underside doesn't allow Fanon to start from Hegel's theoretical abstractions.[28] Fanon is concerned with the historical form of the dialectic.

Hegel continues to affirm a reciprocal ground as he proceeds in the dialectic. The life and death struggle does not play out to its end because death would end up negating the other who can offer recognition. Thus, a master-slave relationship is produced. But the tension between the two selves that Hegel envisions only appears to be overcome by one becoming master and the other slave.[29] While this arrangement presents itself as an equilibrium, it is ultimately not a satisfying relationship. The reason behind this is, again, recognition of self-consciousness: only an equal, another self-conscious subject, can provide recognition. Therefore, the master still ceases to be recognized because of the slave's lack of a self-consciousness in the eyes of the master.

In Hegel's master-slave dialectic, there is a dialectical inversion: because the master's consciousness is tied to the things he enjoys, which are produced by the slave, the master is alienated from material reality while the slave works on it. Only the slave's consciousness "will withdraw into itself and be transformed into a truly independent consciousness."[30] Each self-consciousness turns out to be the opposite of what it immediately appears to be.

When Hegel considers servitude in itself—that is, not in relation to lordship—he focuses on two complementary links the slave has to the universal: negatively, the experience of "the fear of death, the absolute Lord," and positively, the ability to creatively transform the world through work by virtue of applying concepts he produces to his environment in a material way.[31] This ability to work on and transform the material world leads to a higher degree of independence for the slave. The creative activity of the slave overcomes the initial fear of the master:

> in fashioning the thing, [the bondsman] becomes aware that being-for-self belongs to *him*, that he himself exists essentially and actually in his own right. . . . Through this rediscovery of himself by himself, the bondsman realizes that it is precisely in his work wherein he seemed to have only an alienated existence that he acquires a mind of his own. For this reflection, the two moments of fear and service as such, as also that of formative activity, are necessary, both being at the same time in a universal mode.[32]

Fanon, while acknowledging the importance of the confrontation with death, emphasizes the second of these two links the slave has to the universal, namely, the creative work of the colonized.[33] The "ultimate" work comes through the decolonial combat. Violence, as Fanon will develop in his later work, is an "absolute praxis. The militant therefore is one who works."[34]

In focusing on the creative work of the bondsman, which Fanon historicizes as the colonized, Fanon takes Hegel in a similar direction that Marx took him. Marx emphasizes the creative work of the proletarian, whereas Fanon emphasizes the creative work of the peasant and the nationalist fighter. Whereas Hegel takes the structure of the state as depending on the institutionalization of class relationships in civil society,[35] Marx and Fanon are both critical of this apparatus. They focus on the alienation embedded within such relationships, and the historical praxis of the subjugated that works toward disalienation. Both, in response, turn to philosophy as a means to reveal this relationship and to ground a different basis for relations.

George Ciccariello-Maher has read Fanon as seriously engaging Hegel's understanding of dialectics, but ultimately as presenting a renewed understanding of decolonial dialectics. Fanon offers, Ciccariello-Maher argues, a "decolonized dialectics" from the colonial difference in four moments. Fanon first diagnoses a blockage in dialectical movement: whereas Hegel posited a shared ground of being, Fanon recognizes a lack of ground, a "zone of nonbeing," that prevents dialectical movement. Second, Fanon turns to the violent assertion of being by those relegated to the zone of nonbeing as a moment that ignites dialectical movement. Third, Fanon recognizes that an assertion of being grounded in blackness risks becoming a false universal under the umbrella of liberal equality, and thus risks closing dialectical motion. Finally, Fanon opens dialectics up beyond determinism, closure, and teleology.[36] Though perhaps not the sort of indigeneity Burnett and Battin have in mind, in Fanon's decolonized dialectics, ways of being, thinking, and imagining from the colonial difference irrupts into being, in opposition to and transcending Europe's modernity.

This decolonial dialectical movement appears within an often-cited anecdote Fanon relays in *Black Skin, White Masks*. In the central chapter of *Black Skin, White Masks*, "The Lived Experience of the Black" (*L'expérience vécue du Noir*), Fanon recounts the experience of standing under the gaze of a white child that objectifies him as a racial other, as lacking ontological ground: "Look! A Negro!"[37] While standing under this objectifying gaze, Fanon refuses to be appropriated into French society on the terms of the white gaze. He becomes angry. He recognizes the reality of the zone of nonbeing and a blockage of the possibility of dialectical movement. In returning to this original moment of anger, Fanon incorporates into the struggle toward a universal reality of a new humanism the particular, and visceral, response to being racialized and objectified.

Fanon recognizes that, within the historical networks of what Quijano described as the coloniality of power, he cannot participate in the white world except on its terms: "Whereas I was prepared to forget, to forgive, and to love, my message was flung back at me like a slap in the face. The white world, the only decent one, was preventing me from participating."[38] In investing in the metaphysics of race, the white world blocks the universalizing potential of the human person. It freezes the mystery of an eschatological reality into a metaphysics circumscribed by race. The child's mother objectifies Fanon: "Look how handsome that Negro is." Fanon rejects this objectification with force: "The handsome Negro says 'Fuck you,' madame."[39] At this moment of rejecting an objectifying gaze, Fanon uses the terms of his signification:

> Whereas I had every reason to vent my hatred and loathing, they were rejecting me? Whereas I was the one they should have begged and implored, I was denied the slightest recognition? I made up my mind . . . to assert myself as a BLACK MAN. Since the Other was reluctant to recognize me, there was only one answer: *to make myself known*.[40]

Fanon affirms the violence of asserting himself as a subject. He "makes [him]self known." He uses the categories given to him by the colonial world: "I finally made up my mind to shout my blackness (*mon cri nègre*). Gradually, putting out pseudopodia in all directions, I secreted a race."[41] Even as Fanon goes on to critique a racialist discourse immediately after this, ironically quoting "our bard," Léopold Sédar Senghor, and asking of Senghor's racial essentialism, "Was this our salvation?,"[42] he uses race as a category to bring forth a mode of ontological resistance. Fanon's outburst of anger, his "Fuck you" and self-assertion within a ground rooted in black identity, is a response to a lack of ontological possession.[43] Fanon violently asserts being from the zone of nonbeing, catalyzing dialectical movement.

Starting from the colonial difference—that is, from the zone of nonbeing—Fanon creates the conditions by which a dialectics can move forward. Ciccariello-Maher refers to this stage in Fanon's decolonized dialectics as a "predialectical struggle to enforce symmetry though combat," which entails a "counterontological violence" that pushes toward disalienation.[44] Fanon gives himself over to black identity, despite his strong misgivings, as an absolute identity from which to move toward a new humanism. He accepts the "irrationality" of race, and asserts black identity in the context of a white supremacist world:

> I had rationalized the world, and the world had rejected me in the name of color prejudice. Since there was no way we could agree on the basis of reason, I resorted to irrationality. It was up to the white man to be more irrational than I. For the sake of the cause, I had adopted the

process of regression, but the fact remained that it was an unfamiliar weapon; here I am at home; I am made of the irrational; I wade in the irrational. Irrational up to my neck.[45]

In claiming—even irrationally—black identity, Fanon sets the stage for "jumpstarting" a dialectics that has been blocked by the historical networks of the coloniality of power.[46]

Fanon perceives the need to resist foreclosing a dialectical movement with the appeal to black identity, but also recognizes the danger in binding black identity as a particular moment within a larger universal untethered from blackness. Fanon sees Jean-Paul Sartre to do the latter in his 1948 essay, "Black Orpheus," written as the introduction to an anthology of the work of Negritude poetry. Fanon cites Sartre at length:

At a blow the subjective, existential, ethnic notion of *Negritude* "passes," as Hegel would say, into the objective, positive, exact notion of the *proletariat* . . . And without doubt it is not by hazard that the most ardent apostles of Negritude are at the same time militant Marxists. But nevertheless the notion of race does not intersect with the notion of class: the one is concrete and particular, the other is universal and abstract. . . . In fact, Negritude appears as the weak stage of a dialectical progression. . . . But this negative moment is not sufficient in itself and the Blacks who employ it well know it; they know that it serves to pave the way for the synthesis or the realization of the human society without race. Thus Negritude is dedicated to its own destruction, it is transition and not result, a means and not the ultimate goal.[47]

For Sartre, class can obtain an absolute quality, but Fanon's experience as black cannot. Race, for Sartre, is merely a moment within a larger and realer dialectic of class. Sartre, in effect, lifts up a European historical experience as a universal and absolute experience, thus undermining the movement and openness of dialectics.[48]

Sartre does not see—and here Fanon sides with Hegel—that the absolute reality is fully immanent in each stage of the dialectic. Fanon remains consistent in his claim that each act of consciousness is "an act of transcending," such that rootedness in history opens up a reality that exceeds the idols of colonial modernity:

This struggle, this descent once more, should be seen as a completed aspect. . . . The dialectic that introduces necessity as a support for my freedom expels me from myself. It shatters my impulsive position. Still

regarding consciousness, black consciousness is immanent in itself.
I am not a potentiality of something; I am fully what I am. I do not
have to look for the universal. There's no room for probability inside
me. My black consciousness does not claim to be a loss. It *is*. It merges
with itself.[49]

Fanon maintains, while "wad[ing] through the irrational," the absolute nature of his consciousness, even in racial terms, within a dialectical movement toward a new humanism, as an image of a radically open and undetermined universal. Unlike Sartre, Fanon doesn't forget the movement
of dialectics and, also unlike Sartre, he approaches dialectical motion from
the colonial difference.

Fanon persists in a historical process of both building and holding open
the mystery of the future, undetermined universal, a universal grounded
in his claim that "[i]f it be true that consciousness is an act of transcending
(*activité de transcendance*), we must also realize that this transcendence is
haunted with the issue of love and understanding."[50] This historical process of forcing dialectical movement from the colonial difference—that is,
Fanon's decolonial dialectics—is a mode of concretizing his decolonial love
into a historical praxis. This praxis lives with Fanon's sociogenic project
of interrogating the connection between social-political and psychological realities. The possibility of the actualization of decolonial love always
exists in relation to both realities. Decolonial love thus always "implies
restructuring the world."[51] Fanon's project of disalienation cannot proceed
without overturning the coloniality of power as a historical structure: decolonial love demands a change "in the most materialist sense."[52] Fanon's
decolonial love initiates "[t]he end of the world, of course."[53] This is why
those beholden to Western modernity perceive the project of disalienation
as violent. The modern/colonial world disallows "the birth of a human
world, in other words, a world of reciprocal recognitions."[54]

A modern/colonial world that seeks to stabilize relations into ontological hierarchy demands a constant effort to force dialectical movement.[55] In
concluding *Black Skin, White Masks*, Fanon turns to fighting as a praxis of
holding open a dialectical movement toward the infinite, and undetermined,
horizon of a new humanism, and thus as a praxis of decolonial love:

> It is obvious—and I can't say this enough—that the motivations for
> disalienating a physician from Guadeloupe are essentially different
> from those for the African construction worker in the port of Abidjan.
> For the former, alienation is almost intellectual in nature. It develops

because he takes European culture as a means of detaching himself from his own race. For the latter, it develops because he is victim to a system based on the exploitation of one race by another and the contempt for one branch of humanity by a civilization that considers itself superior. We would not be so naïve as to believe that the appeals for reason or respect for human dignity can change reality. For the Antillean working in the sugarcane plantations in Le Robert, to fight is the only solution. And he will undertake and carry out this struggle not as the result of a Marxist or idealistic analysis but because quite simply he cannot conceive his life otherwise than as a kind of combat against exploitation, poverty, and hunger.[56]

Ciccariello-Maher notes the short distance between an alienated "physician from Guadeloupe" and Fanon as an alienated psychiatrist from Martinique, suggesting that this is a moment of self-critique in Fanon's work.[57] Fanon recognizes here the need to enter into the motivations of those for whom disalienation requires structural transformation. In this process, Fanon doesn't reduce fighting to a step in the process of affirming the subjectivity of the colonized; the absoluteness of decolonial love exists in the historical process of struggle. There is a fullness to fighting itself. Fighting historicizes another "truth" of decolonial love that Fanon struggles to convey: because decolonial love is eschatological in the sense that it perceives ruptures in colonial modernity that open up to a transcendent reality beyond the hypostasized images of colonial modernity, decolonial love as a historical praxis commits to catalyzing and authenticating historical movement.

The National Struggle as a Conduit of Decolonial Love

Whereas in *Black Skin, White Masks* Fanon affirms the turn to fighting in a way that is not explicitly connected to a concrete historical project, this will soon change. Fanon's shift to placing himself within a historical struggle for decolonization can be seen as a turn to indigeneity—that is, as a turn to the epistemic, ontological, and eschatological options of those communities that perceive the modern/colonial world as alienating in a fundamental way and commit themselves to its end. As Fanon's historical situation changes and his political praxis takes new shape, he deepens his theorization of decolonial love within the historical site of nationalist struggle. Within a nationalist struggle, Fanon maintains his commitment to forcing the dialectical movement of history, as well as to a new humanism.

STRUGGLING FOR THE NEW HUMANITY:
FROM BLACK IDENTITY TO NATIONALIST STRUGGLE

Fanon took a position at Blida-Joinville Hospital, outside of Algiers, at the end of 1953, just a year after publishing *Black Skin, White Masks*. Fanon's move to Algeria would profoundly shape the rest of his life. In his new position, Fanon studied indigenous Kabyle practices and culture and made revolutionary changes within the hospital. He introduced the psychiatric method of sociotherapy, which established more reciprocal relationships between doctor and patient. It included activities such as biweekly forums open to all staff and patients, holiday celebrations, programs in music and film, a weekly publication, and workshops.[58] These changes served to help orient patients—which included French soldiers, pieds noirs, and native Algerians—to move toward a horizon beyond constraints imposed by colonialism.[59]

Early in 1955, the FLN contacted Fanon to work with them as a psychiatrist.[60] As the violence in Algeria escalated through 1955, Fanon became involved with the FLN leadership. Within the context of his deepening relationship with the FLN, Fanon attended the First World Congress of Black Writers and Artists in Paris in September 1956. The talk he delivered at the Congress, entitled "Racism and Culture," indicates ways he was pushing his thought in significantly new directions. In this talk, Fanon situated racism within a larger network of oppression: "The object of racism is no longer the individual man but a certain form of existing."[61] Racism, Fanon argued, "is only one element of a vaster whole: that of the systematized oppression of a people."[62] The effect of racism, along with this "vaster whole," is that culture becomes "closed, fixed"; it ceases to be "open to the future," or to an eschatological reality that exceeds the particular framework of colonial modernity.[63] Ultimately, Fanon presented racism as an alienating force, compelling assimilation.[64] But, Fanon at the same time noted that this process of alienation and assimilation typically isn't permanent. There is a process of reversal in which, upon discovering their alienation, the colonized create a "passionate attachment" to their original culture.[65] In this process, "[t]he sense of the past is rediscovered, the worship of ancestors resumed . . . The past, becoming henceforth a constellation of values, becomes identified with the Truth."[66] Fanon thus outlined a process in which alienation from the original culture through a project of assimilation turns into clinging to the original culture, before colonialism, as the truth.

The key move Fanon makes in this talk is to shift from race and culture to nationalist struggle as his point of emphasis:

> The logical end of this will to struggle is the total liberation of the national territory. In order to achieve this liberation, the inferiorized man brings all his resources into play, all his acquisitions, the old and the new, his own and those of the occupant. The struggle is at once total, absolute. But then race prejudice is hardly found to appear. . . . A people that undertakes a struggle for liberation rarely legitimizes race prejudice. Even in the course of acute periods of insurrectional armed struggle one never witnesses the recourse to biological justifications. The struggle of the inferiorized is situated on a markedly more human level. The perspectives are radically new. The opposition is the henceforth classical one of the struggles of conquest and of liberation.[67]

While the disappearance of race prejudice in a national struggle is overstated, it's clear that Fanon maintains his dialectical position articulated in *Black Skin, White Masks*. He still sees the absolute to be fully present in particular realities, but has shifted his understanding of the conduit of the absolute: anti-colonial combat replaces race as the mediation.[68]

Fanon's commitment to the nationalist struggle and nationalist consciousness as a conduit to the absolute reality of a new humanism compels him to leave his position at Blida. Fanon's resignation from Blida offers a glimpse of the way his orientation of decolonial love will be historicized in a much different way in the latter half of the 1950s. Alice Cherki, a colleague of Fanon's and one of his biographers, notes that Fanon's resignation from Blida could have been prompted by any number of factors: to protest the decision of the resident minister of Algiers to punish workers who participated in a general strike, the danger Fanon and his family were in, or because Fanon's ties to the FLN were in fact stronger than people realized.[69] Cherki acknowledges the difficulty in determining the precise reasons for Fanon's resignation, adding that "[i]n all probability, even he did not entirely comprehend the reasons for his action," and turns to Fanon's letter of resignation to gather any clarity that is possible.[70]

Fanon begins the letter by stating the challenges under which he practiced psychiatry in Algeria while at the same time affirming the importance of this work and the enthusiasm with which he has taken it up. He then indicates a need to broaden the task of psychiatry:

> Madness is one of the means man has of losing his freedom. And I can say, on the basis of what I have been able to observe from this point of

> vantage, that the degree of alienation of the inhabitants of this country
> appears to me frightening. If psychiatry is the medical technique that
> aims to enable man no longer to be a stranger in his environment, I
> owe it to myself to affirm that the Arab, permanently an alien in his
> own country, lives in a state of absolute depersonalization.[71]

Alienation is not only a product of mental illness but also a product of the
social-political structure of Algeria under French colonialism. Through
his sociogenic project, Fanon comes to a conclusion in regard to these
social-political structures: "The function of a social structure is to set up
institutions to serve man's needs. A society that drives its members to des-
perate solutions is a non-viable society, a society to be replaced."[72] With
this letter and his resignation, Fanon's focus resolutely shifts to a praxis of
replacing society.

Replacing Colonial Society through Nationalist Struggle: Fanon within the FLN

Fanon moves into an analysis of alienation within a social world shaped by
what Quijano describes as the coloniality of power, and does so with the
intention of replacing that social world. Disalienation on the level of the
subject demands this social-political engagement. Fanon concretized his
position that decolonial struggle is the site in which the absolute and universal reality of a new humanism could be encountered while he was working as a journalist for the FLN. With the FLN, Fanon contributed articles
to the French edition of the FLN's publication, *El Moudjahid*, which was a
venue for response to, and sometimes propaganda for, the Algerian war for
independence.[73] At the end of 1959, Fanon goes even further in his claim
about anti-colonial struggle as a mediation of the absolute reality of the
new humanity when writing in *El Moudjahid*. He refers to the concretization of nationalist movements at the Bandung conference as capturing a
"carnal and spiritual union at one and the same time."[74] Fanon gives this
idea more substantial grounding in a paper entitled "On National Culture"
that he delivered at the Second Congress of Black Writers and Artists in
Rome, in March 1959. In this paper, Fanon makes a bold claim, in many
ways against the major theme of the conference highlighting the unity of
African and African diasporic cultures: rather than an idea of liberation, a
praxis of national liberation grounds a new humanism.

To present this constructive position of a new humanism grounded in
the praxis of decolonial revolution, Fanon articulates three stages in the

work, but also existential situation, of colonized intellectuals. First, colonized intellectuals attempt to assimilate to the colonizer's culture. This involves a consumption of European culture and intellectual traditions. Fanon thoroughly described this stage of assimilation in *Black Skin, White Masks*.

Second, and often within a context of nationalist mobilization, "the colonized intellectual rejects his accomplishments, suddenly feeling them to be alienating."[75] In this stage, colonized intellectuals affirm their culture as a binary other to European culture. Colonized intellectuals immerse themselves in their previously forsaken culture. Three years earlier, Fanon described this in the First Congress of Black Writers and Artists as an inauthentic attempt to cling to the original culture as truth. This step contains an element of alienation: "since the colonized writer is not integrated with his people, since he maintains an outsider's relationship to them, he is content to remember."[76] The intellectual adopts the indigenous culture, but as an object engaged from an outsider's perspective—as a memory.

In this stage, Fanon alludes to the Negritude movement's attempt to locate a past it can reclaim.[77] In this movement, colonized intellectuals appropriate the "racialization of thought" introduced by Europeans.[78] Fanon departs from Negritude, as he did in *Black Skin, White Masks*: "This historical obligation to racialize their claims, to emphasize an African culture rather than a national culture leads the African intellectuals into a dead end."[79] Fanon is clear that a new humanism has to be found outside European ontologies. He searches for an indigeneity, or "recasts [his] indigeneity," to use Burnett and Battin's term, in the wake of the destruction the coloniality of power renders. Fanon indicates this indigeneity in what will be the third stage that he will affirm as a project to be actualized. Fanon refers to the constructive potential of a nationalist struggle that proceeds from the zone of nonbeing:

> Negritude thus came up against its first limitation, namely, those
> phenomena that take into account the historicizing of men. "Negro"
> or "Negro-African" culture broke up because the men who set out to
> embody it realized that every culture is first and foremost national, and
> that the problems for which Richard Wright or Langston Hughes had
> to be on the alert were fundamentally different from those faced by
> Léopold Senghor or Jomo Kenyatta.[80]

The method of the colonized intellectual "los[ing] himself" in an ancient culture "[i]n order to secure his salvation" is by this point a historically limited project for Fanon: it depends on an abstract idea of race, rather than the historical concreteness of struggle, as a mediation of the absolute.[81]

Fanon names the third stage, which is the constructive position he wants to arrive at, "combat literature." In this stage, colonized intellectuals fully immerse themselves in the nationalist project as a conduit of the universal:

> the colonized writer, after having tried to lose himself among the people, with the people, will rouse the people. Instead of letting the people's lethargy prevail, he turns into a galvanizer of the people. Combat literature, revolutionary literature, national literature emerges. During this phase a great many men and women who previously would never have thought of writing, now that they find themselves in exceptional circumstances, in prison, in the resistance or on the eve of their execution, feel the need to proclaim their nation, to portray their people and become the spokesperson of *a new reality in action*.[82]

This is where Fanon is struggling to be, and where he's trying to push others. In locating the nationalist struggle as the site from which to engage a new humanism, and as "a new reality in action," Fanon moves past an abstract "veneer" of "mummified fragments," to "a dense, subterranean life in perpetual renewal."[83] Colonized intellectuals who engage in combat literature, Fanon argues, connect themselves to the armed struggle and the motion and fluidity it catalyzes. Fanon is clear about the reactionary nature of holding onto an abstraction. To locate the absolute in an abstract notion of culture, detached from nationalist struggle, is to put oneself firmly behind the masses as they struggle for a new humanism.[84] A new humanism is located within the nationalist struggle, "the greatest cultural manifestation that exists."[85] The historically particular nationalist struggle is necessary in order to live into the absolute reality of a new humanism. Decolonial love requires a movement from abstract formulations into the movement of history. That which exceeds the imaginative limits of colonial modernity is encountered in history.

Fanon continues to develop his concept of a new humanism in a book published at the end of 1959 appraising the Algerian Revolution in its fifth year, and translated into English as *A Dying Colonialism* (*L'An Cinq, de la Révolution Algérienne*). In this work, Fanon begins with the premise, already developed in "On National Culture," that the national struggle is a conduit for a new humanity:

> We want to show in this first study that on the Algerian soil a new society has come to birth. The men and women of Algeria today resemble neither those of 1930 nor those of 1954, nor yet those of 1957. The old Algeria is dead. All the innocent blood that has flowed onto the national soil has produced a new humanity and no one must fail to recognize this fact.[86]

It is impossible for colonialism to continue precisely because the new humanity has already come into being in the struggle against colonialism. A decolonial dialectics has been forced into motion. There is a historical and thus existential change in Algeria and in the Algerian, such that an absolute reality has already irrupted into history. Historical stasis ends in the Algerian Revolution. This reality cannot change despite what France does to maintain its colonial domination: "An army can at any time reconquer the ground lost, but how can the inferiority complex, the fear and the despair of the past be reimplanted in the consciousness of the people?"[87]

Because the new humanity that finds historical expression in the nationalist struggle is an absolute reality, there is something deeply human about the Algerian Revolution that extends beyond the particular site of the revolution. Fanon uncovers what he calls the "spiritual community founded in suffering":

> French colonialism since 1954 has wanted nothing other than to break the will of the people, to destroy its resistance, to liquidate its hopes. For five years it has avoided no extremist tactic, whether of terror or of torture. In stirring up these men and women, colonialism has regrouped them beneath a single sign. Equally victims of the same tyranny, simultaneously identifying a single enemy, this physically dispersed people is realizing its unity *and founding in suffering a spiritual community* which constitutes the most solid bastion of the Algerian Revolution.[88]

The spiritual community founded in suffering is a basis for both the revolution and for accessing the absolute. It's the place from which an indigeneity can be recast. The site of the zone of nonbeing provides for Fanon a way of imagining the universal from the colonial difference.

It is clear in Fanon's work within the FLN that he believes in a new humanism as a historical task. Fanon's project, as he affirmed in *Black Skin, White Masks*, is fundamentally materialist. Here I read Fanon in a similar way that Peter Hudis does: Fanon's political project to destroy the metaphysics of race "is not achieved by a mere declaration, through a verbal swearing-off of racial privilege and 'whiteness.' It is achieved through an actual social transformation on the part of the oppressed in which the material and ideological powers responsible for our 'Manichaean world' is thoroughly uprooted."[89] Fanon is concerned with changing the material conditions that allow for a new humanism to irrupt in daily life. This project of replacing society and transforming the material conditions toward the actualization of a new humanism is a project for Fanon that involves violence.

A New Humanism and Decolonial Love in Violence

Within a context of colonial modernity, Fanon recognizes violence as an indispensible conduit to a new humanism. He articulates a new humanism within violence. The concretization of an orientation of decolonial love into a historical praxis occurs in forwarding historical motion in ways that are perceived as violent. At the end of 1960, Fanon found out he was dying of leukemia. He went to the Soviet Union for treatment in January 1961 and then returned to Tunisia and dictated *The Wretched of the Earth* in the span of a few months. He begins that book by claiming that "decolonization is always a violent event."[90] Decolonization happens in a situation that is highly rigid—a "Manichaean" and "compartmentalized world," in which the colonized are separated as a distinct "species."[91] And, decolonization, as a violent event, is constitutive of a new humanity: "Decolonization is truly the creation of new men. But such a creation cannot be attributed to a supernatural power: The 'thing' colonized becomes a man through the very process of liberation."[92]

The first chapter of *The Wretched of the Earth* is significantly different from the introduction and conclusion of *Black Skin, White Masks*. Fanon turns away from his focus on the universal and instead describes static realms in confrontation with each other: "Decolonization is the encounter between two congenitally antagonistic forces that in fact owe their singularity to the kind of reification secreted and nurtured by the colonial situation."[93] And, he appears to no longer look for unity: "The 'native' sector is not complementary to the European sector. The two confront each other, but not in the service of a higher unity. Governed by a purely Aristotelian logic, they follow the dictates of mutual exclusion: There is no conciliation possible, one of them is superfluous."[94] But Fanon has not in fact given up on the absolute, even as it's masked in the colonial situation. Fanon holds onto the position developed in *Black Skin, White Masks* that the decolonial dialectical movement that Ciccariello-Maher identifies emerges from the particularity of the colonial difference, rather than abstract concepts: "Challenging the colonial world is not a rational confrontation of viewpoints. It is not a discourse on the universal, but the frantic affirmation of an originality claimed as absolute (*mais l'affirmation échevelée d'une originalité posée comme absolue*)."[95] Fanon's understanding of the universalizing capacity of the human person comes from the "frantic affirmation" of the colonized—that is, their decolonial praxis of pushing themselves into a historical dialectics of being that emerges from the colonial difference. Fanon claims, in other words, decolonial struggle as a recast indigeneity that transcends Europe's modernity in dialectical movement.

Ciccariello-Maher has argued that violence functions in Fanon's thought as the way to force a frozen dialectics into motion. Fanon doesn't presume, like Hegel, automatic movement within dialectics—thus the need to "jumpstart" dialectical movement.[96] Ciccariello-Maher develops his notion of a "decolonial dialectics" largely by relying on Fanon's work:

> This is a dialectical counterdiscourse that, by foregrounding rupture and shunning the lure of unity, makes its home in the center of the dialectic and revels in the spirit of combat, the indeterminacies of political identities slamming against one another, transforming themselves and their worlds unpredictably in the process. This is a dialectical counterdiscourse that, by grasping the momentary hardening of group identities, grants weight to a separatist *moment* in dialectics—at the expense of premature reconciliation—but does so without succumbing to a hermetically essentialist separatism, be it of class, race, nation, or otherwise. Identities are forged in struggle, and there too they are reforged.[97]

A decolonized dialectics appreciates elements of what Ciccariello-Maher identifies as a radical dialectics emerging in Europe, including the eschewal of all teleology, determinisms, and beliefs in linear progression. It adds to radical dialectics an awareness of the provinciality of Eurocentered conceptions of history, an affirmation of loci outside Europe as historical sources, and a process of thinking from the colonial difference.[98]

Fanon embraces the Manichaeism of the colonial world rather than the false universal of formal equality, and understands decolonial struggle from the zone of nonbeing as necessary in order to push dialectical motion into history.[99] Decolonial struggle, which is for Fanon violent struggle, breaks the stasis of Western ideas: "The colonized intellectual accepted the cogency of these ideas and there in the back of his mind stood a sentinel on duty guarding the Greco-Roman pedestal. But during the struggle for liberation, when the colonized intellectual touches base again with his

people, this artificial sentinel is smashed to smithereens. All the Mediterranean values, the triumph of the individual, of enlightenment and Beauty
turn into pale, lifeless trinkets. All those discourses appear a jumble of dead
words."[100] Smashing the artificial sentinel to smithereens comes within
a commitment "to bring to life the history of the nation."[101] Decolonial
struggle reanimates history, but Fanon's commitment to nationalist consciousness does not entail holding up the nation as salvation. Fanon is clear
about the internal tensions of and conflictive oppositions within nationalist consciousness: national consciousness is not a closure of dialectics, or
a clean unity.

Fanon locates the national bourgeoisie as a contradiction within national consciousness and as a threat to stalling dialectical motion. From the
perspective of the peasant, the national bourgeoisie, or the "town dweller,"
"strives to succeed in the context of the colonial system," and it's in this
sense that "we often hear the peasant say that the town dwellers have no
moral standards."[102] Town dwellers are beholden to the form of ideology
that Clodovis Boff described as justifying the unjustifiable, or of presenting
the immoral as moral, out of a commitment to particular social-political
interests. For Fanon, the response to this situation is for the national bourgeoisie, the town dwellers, to follow the leadership of the peasants:

> Discussions with the peasants now become a ritual for them. They
> discover that the rural masses have never ceased to pose the problem of
> their liberation in terms of violence, of taking back the land from the
> foreigners, in terms of *national struggle* and armed revolt. Everything is
> simple. These men discover a coherent people who survive in a kind of
> petrified state, but keep intact their moral values and their attachment
> to the nation. . . . The men from the towns let themselves be guided
> by the people and at the same time give them military and political
> training.[103]

The "ritual" of these discussions discloses another way of being, thinking, and imagining—a set of alternatives beyond modernity/coloniality.
Violence allows historical movement to occur. Violence not only breaks
the "petrified" state of the colonized, it also breaks the species distinction and Manichaeism with which Fanon started: "The people who in the
early days of the struggle had adopted the primitive Manichaeanism of
the colonizer—Black versus White, Arab versus Infidel—realize en route
that some blacks can be whiter than the whites, and that the prospect of a
national flag or independence does not automatically result in certain seg-
ments of the population giving up their privileges and their interests."[104]

In this situation, "[t]he racial and racist dimension is transcended on both sides."[105] Violence becomes the conduit for a decolonial dialectics: it allows all into "the constantly dialectical truth of the nation."[106]

Although Fanon locates violence as the way to "jumpstart" dialectical motion, he appears to also miss other avenues, and in doing so might limit dialectical movement in unintended ways. Like in *Black Skin, White Masks*, when Fanon assures his reader that complete alienation was not possible, in *The Wretched of the Earth*, he assures his reader that the "petrification" of the colonized is never complete: "The muscles of the colonized are always tensed."[107] Whereas this tension should be directed at the colonist, it finds other outlets: turned against others within the nationalist struggle, relieved through religion, or drained through traditional practices.[108] More carefully considering the latter two practices, which Fanon interprets as deradicalizing moments, opens up ways of forcing decolonial movement by recasting indigeneity that Fanon too easily overlooks.

Fanon fairly clearly sees religion to obstruct dialectical movement and inhibit the "aggressiveness" of the colonized:

> The colonized subject . . . manages to lose sight of the colonist through religion. Fatalism relieves the oppressor of all responsibility since the cause of wrong-doing, poverty, and the inevitable can be attributed to God. The individual thus accepts the devastation decreed by God, grovels in front of the colonist, bows to the hand of fate, and mentally readjusts to acquire the serenity of stone.[109]

Speaking in the first person, Fanon refers to a "magical superstructure that permeates the indigenous society" that loosens the "muscular tension" so crucial to a violent decolonial struggle. Religion leads to a repetition of the colonial world:

> In scaring me, the atmosphere of myths and magic operates like an undeniable reality. In terrifying me, it incorporates me into the traditions and history of my land and ethnic group, but at the same time I am reassured and granted a civil status, an identification. The secret sphere in underdeveloped countries is a collective sphere that falls exclusively within the realm of magic. By entangling me in this inextricable web where gestures are repeated with a secular limpidity, my very own world, our very own world, thus perpetuates itself.[110]

Fighting the colonist, in Fanon's interpretation, loses urgency because the colonist ceases to be ultimate as the sacred enters the picture. He thus separates the decolonial struggle from indigenous forms of spirituality.

Here, it seems that Fanon adopts the Eurocentered critique of the fetish that was the flipside of the European market rationalism that emerged in the fifteenth century as trade networks opened in the North Atlantic.[111] Rather than a way to exceed the boundaries and possibilities of secular thought, religious thought for Fanon becomes a mechanism of leaving behind concerns related to social transformation. In Fanon's understanding of religious thought, a decolonial struggle cannot be ultimate if a religious cosmology is ultimate. Fanon misses ways that religious thought and practice can be a way of relating to reality in light of a faith commitment that exceeds modern/colonial constraints in similar ways that Fanon approaches reality in light of an orientation toward decolonial love.

Fanon marks another channel by which he sees the muscular tension of the colonized to be turned away from decolonial struggle:

> Another aspect of the colonized's affectivity can be seen when it is drained of energy by the ecstasy of dance. The colonized's way of relaxing is precisely this muscular orgy during which the most brutal aggressiveness and impulsive violence are channeled, transformed, and spirited away.[112]

Rituals such as dance produce merely a "pantomime" of liberation, limited to a "symbolic" form of decolonization. Like with religion, Fanon sees a sharp separation between such rituals and decolonization: "During the struggle for liberation there is a singular loss of interest in these rituals. . . . After years of unreality, after wallowing in the most extraordinary phantasms, the colonized subject, machine gun at the ready, finally confronts the only force which challenges his very being: colonialism."[113]

In these instances, it seems that Fanon is too quick to close sites where indigeneity has been recast in ways that might catalyze dialectical movement. Fanon's earlier analysis of women's role in the Algerian Revolution, in *A Dying Colonialism*, sheds some light on how Fanon might too quickly pass over other ways of pushing decolonial movement into history.[114] Fanon uses an analysis of the veil to open up how the revolution impacts the social, familial, and bodily realities of the Algerian people. He describes how European aid societies seek to unveil Algerian women as a function within the larger project of what he calls "a total domestication" of the Algerian population,[115] and how colonial violence thereby determines the veil as one of "the centers of resistance around which a people's will to survive becomes organized."[116] While Fanon's analysis of the veil helps him to uncover important dimensions of colonial violence and resistance, it also raises the question of whether understanding the veil primarily in relation to a culture of resistance—that is, in relation to the nationalist struggle that Fanon privileges as the conduit of a new humanity—obscures a significance of the veil beyond Fanon's understanding of the nationalist struggle. If this is the case, the lens Fanon uses to understand historical praxis through armed decolonial struggle might limit his possibility to see in creative recastings of indigeneity the generative role that Algerian women play in decolonization.

By sometimes understanding women's involvement in passive terms against the criterion of the armed revolution, Fanon reduces the nationalist struggle to a particular mode of expression.[117] Fanon at times describes the involvement of women in the revolution as a moment of assimilation into the nationalist struggle. In these instances, he describes men as making the decision "to involve women as active elements in the Algerian Revolution," such that "women's entry into the war had to be harmonized with respect for the revolutionary nature of the war." Understanding the role of women in reference to a masculine norm, Fanon states that "the women had to show as much spirit of sacrifice as the men" and required a "moral elevation."[118] Fanon is clearly critical of assimilation within the larger scope of his work, yet he interprets the assimilation of women to the form the Algerian Revolution has taken as a positive and necessary element in the dialectical movement toward a new humanity. This raises a question of whether Fanon's decolonial dialectics is sufficiently open to recognize a space where Algerian women can express the absolute nature of a new humanity on their own terms in the context of the revolution. Affirming the revolutionary potential of women wearing the veil gives Fanon the possibility to do this, yet he ultimately limits the site of revolutionary commitment to women's relation to the revolution, and particularly to their participation in armed combat.

In Saba Mahmood's theorization of agency vis-à-vis feminist theory, she indicates how an understanding of the veil might be pushed further. Mahmood questions a feminist conception of agency linked to resistance—and Fanon's conception of the veil here would fit in that category—because such a model "sharply limits our ability to understand and interrogate the lives of women whose desire, affect, and will have been shaped by nonliberal traditions."[119] Mahmood understands agency in terms of the ethnographic research she does within the urban women's mosque movement within the Islamic revival in Cairo. Regarding Egyptian women's practices of piety and their practice of Islamic virtues, Mahmood claims that "what is often made to stand in for 'real motivations' are those authorized by the analyst's categories (such as social protest, economic necessity, anomie, utilitarian strategy), while terms like morality, divinity, and virtue are accorded the status of the phantom imaginings of the hegemonized."[120] Fanon risks eliding actual epistemic practices and forms of self-understanding associated with the veil when he centers his own understanding of the Algerian Revolution as the preeminent locus of the historical manifestation of salvation and decolonial love. If those categories "authorized" by the revolution are primary in an interpretation of the veil, the way Mahmood thinks from the colonial difference is lost.[121]

Fanon concludes his last work by imploring the reader to turn away from Europe's "permanent dialogue with itself."[122] He pushes for dialectical motion: "Today we are witnessing a stasis of Europe. Let us flee, comrades, this motionless movement in which the dialectic has gradually become a logic of equilibrium. Let us return to the question of man."[123] Fanon defiantly sets us on the way for this turn, with violence being the primary avenue of turning from Europe and the wider matrix of the coloniality of power. At the same time, however, there remain options within this decolonial turn. The orientation of decolonial love is historicized in the praxes of exposing ideology, situating the human person beyond the confines of the modern/colonial imagination, and catalyzing and authenticating historical movement. Because of the eschatological nature of decolonial love—that is, its ways of rupturing history and exposing ways colonial modernity eclipses the mystery of its depths and thus forecloses participation in its mystery—the options by which decolonial love is concretized into historical praxis must be held open.

Attempting to see beyond Fanon's privileging of a nationalist struggle is not an attempt to counter Fanon's assertions regarding violence and the nationalist struggle; rather, it's an attempt to offer decolonial options alongside Fanon's, motivated by Fanon's orientation of decolonial love. Fanon recasts indigeneity as a project of unsettling modernity through forcing decolonial motion, and in doing so opens up paths to alternative indigeneities. In Fanon's work, decolonial love is not the violence of nationalist anti-colonial struggle itself; it is the historical process of both building and holding open the mystery of an eschatological reality, which Fanon names a new humanism. Surrendering to the wholeness and unity of this eschatological reality requires options.

James Baldwin's work, which comes out of a different context than Fanon's, presents a related orientation of decolonial love that further opens up such options. Unlike Fanon, who thought within a revolutionary movement that included a demand for national sovereignty, Baldwin thought within a US context that he saw to be shaped not only by a white supremacist power structure but also by ways communities on its underside had constructed worlds and creative responses to that power structure. His work thus demonstrates the importance of pushing past the tendency to crystallize Fanon's prescriptions within the Algerian Revolution, and to instead focus on the fundamental theoretical framework and the orientation of decolonial love from which Fanon thought and acted.

CHAPTER 5

James Baldwin's Decolonial Love: Uncovering the Revelation of the Beat

The challenge before America is not so much eschatological as it is reflective.

— CHARLES H. LONG, *Significations: Signs, Symbols, and Images in the Interpretation of Religion* (Aurora, CO: The Davies Group, 1995), 160

James Baldwin's first novel, *Go Tell It on the Mountain* 1952, is a semi-autobiographical narration of the fourteenth birthday of John Grimes. As Baldwin did, John lives in Harlem. And, like Baldwin, John grows up in a household dominated by his religious stepfather. On his fourteenth birthday, John's mother evokes her go-to scriptural text, telling him, "there's a whole lot of things you don't understand. But don't you fret. The Lord'll reveal to you in his own good time everything He wants you to know. You just put your faith in the Lord, Johnny, and He'll surely bring you out."[1] John's reply—"Yes, Mama. I'm going to try to love the Lord"—causes "something startling, beautiful, unspeakingly sad" in his mother's face.[2] This "strange sadness" on his mother's face is similar to the sentiment that Baldwin elsewhere recalls overcame one of his elementary school teachers, Miss Miller, who had frequently given him books, and took him to see plays and films, when Baldwin told her he had been saved. Baldwin recalls his teacher's response as quite direct: "I've lost a lot of respect for you."[3] The sadness of both Baldwin's mother and Miss Miller in response to his confessions of faith indicates a tension that pervades Baldwin's work. On the one hand, Baldwin presents revelation as a passive experience. His mother's colloquialism and the pride in "being saved" indicate this understanding of revelation. In this case, revelation is simply affirmed. It's something given, which can be accepted or not. On the other hand, Baldwin describes revelation as a task. The sadness that John's/Baldwin's claims of religious fidelity conjure in his mother and in Miss Miller, a sadness produced by their desire for Baldwin to actively reveal the world to himself, expresses this understanding of revelation. While the latter takes precedence in Baldwin's work, the former doesn't disappear.

This tension, and the very meaning and significance of revelation as both something obtained passively and worked for through a historical praxis, shapes Baldwin's orientation of decolonial love. For Baldwin, loving in a decolonial way is intimately connected to revelation, and particularly to the active process of discovering revelation and then working out its meaning and significance. In developing an orientation of decolonial love into the historical task of revealing reality, Baldwin moves toward a reality that he presents as salvation. For Baldwin, salvation is a primarily reflective process, whereas for Fanon, salvation is more explicitly a forward-moving, dialectical concept. Fanon and Baldwin both use the concept of revelation as an eschatological concept. Fanon primarily understands eschatology in relation to "the end of the world" and hastening the ruptures that will actualize the end of the world. Baldwin primarily understands eschatology in terms of historical depth—that is, in terms of encountering reality beyond the way it has been signified and beyond a commitment to idols—rather than in temporal terms as delineating the endpoint of a linear progression. When Charles H. Long delineates the challenge in the US context to be reflective rather than eschatological, he sides with the task Baldwin takes up. As I will show, however, both ways of historicizing decolonial love can be seen as complimentary ways of attending to an eschatological orientation.

In *Go Tell It on the Mountain*, Baldwin's fictional character John leaves home after telling his mother he'll "try to love the Lord." He climbs to the top of a hill in Central Park and, looking over New York City, he "felt like a giant who might crumble this city with his anger; he felt like a tyrant who might crush this city beneath his heel; he felt like a long-awaited conqueror at whose feet flowers would be strewn, and before whom multitudes cried, Hosanna!"[4] John waits on top of the hill:

> He remembered the people he had seen in that city, whose eyes held no love for him. And he thought of their feet so swift and brutal, and the dark gray clothes they wore, and how when they passed they did not see

him, or, if they saw him, they smirked. And how their lights, unceasing,
crashed on and off above him, and how he was a stranger there. Then
he remembered his father and his mother, and all the arms stretched
out to hold him back, to save him from this city where, they said, his
soul would find perdition.[5]

The city housed the glories of success that contradicted "the way of the
cross," which had "given [John] a belly filled with wind and had bent
his mother's back."[6] John stands at the top of the hill: "These glories [of
heaven] were unimaginable—but the city was real. He stood for a moment on the melting snow, distracted, and then began to run down the hill,
feeling himself fly as the descent became more rapid, and thinking: 'I can
climb back up. If it's wrong, I can always climb back up.'"[7] Baldwin never
climbs back up.[8] Rather, he struggles to actualize decolonial love—that
is, to live into the task of revelation, and ultimately the task of salvation—
within the city.

In the person of John Grimes, Baldwin loves by plunging into the city,
in all its ambiguity, rather than by saving or conquering the city, or by remaining above it. Baldwin actualizes revelation and, thus, salvation. In this
sense, Baldwin shares in Fanon's orientation of love rooted in an entrance
into the world in response to the call that reality makes. As Fanon leaves
the walls of the psychiatric hospital and the boundaries of the practice of
psychiatry, Baldwin leaves the walls of the church and the boundaries of
Christian ethics and doctrine. Importantly, for Baldwin, this does not mean
an opposition between the religious and the secular, or the church and the
city; rather, his praxis of love within the city blurs the boundaries of what
is religious, or even theological, and what is nonreligious or nontheologi-
cal.[9] Baldwin's praxis of love, also like Fanon's, emerges with anger—which
is his own and his community's—that he turns into discourse that never
frees itself from that original anger. Whereas for Fanon this discourse is
eschatological in the sense that it serves the "end of the world" and the
construction of a new world, for Baldwin the discourse that emerges out of
his decolonial love reveals the ways communities have survived within, and
despite, the United States. In revealing how communities have constructed
worlds and forged different types of relations within and to the United
States as a social entity, Baldwin uncovers the limitations and incompletion
of what Americans imagine the United States to be. He thus moves to the
eschatological depth of history surfacing in the ruptures forged by those
who reveal the limits of the modern world-system.

Baldwin's plunge into reality forces the revelation of reality, and in this praxis Baldwin loves in a decolonial way. His praxis of love lifts up the veils that legitimize the social, political, economic, and ideological orientation of the United States. This is what Baldwin sets as his task as a writer: "It is this power of revelation which is the business of the novelist, this journey towards a more vast reality which must take precedence over all other claims."[10] Baldwin's task of revealing the historical situation is eschatological insofar as it introduces "a more vast reality" and ultimately a new world: a creative underside of the US social-political imaginary. Unlike the eschatological elements in Fanon's decolonial love, Baldwin's task of revelation does not destruct the "American house" he inhabits. Baldwin claims the United States as his home: "If I am part of the American house, and I am, it is because my ancestors paid—*striving to make it my home*—so unimaginable a price: and I have seen some of the effects of that passion everywhere I have been, all over this world."[11] Baldwin's love is both the anger toward the reality he inhabits and the plunge into its ambiguity. This plunge, which is the manifestation of Baldwin's decolonial love, is not to construct an altogether new city, but to be incarnated into its messiness and particularly into its undersides that have been laboriously made, in order to reveal them.

Baldwin presents salvation, a concept he uses both within and outside a confessional discourse, as already present in daily life, within the "American house" that his ancestors have made a home. He thus links salvation to a praxis of revealing reality. In making this connection, Baldwin's work responds to the challenge of *reflection* that Long sets forward in the context of the United States. Reflection uncovers layers of reality concealed in order to legitimize the idea of the United States, and in doing so operates as a praxis. Baldwin's mode of historical reflection confronts those who sustain a distorted image of the United States and the larger modern/colonial network in which it's situated with their failure to monopolize the construction of worlds. This praxis of reflection, which is ultimately a praxis of revelation, indicates a passive view of revelation insofar as revelation is an already present reality. Yet, revelation is also an activity, and is even sometimes perceived as violent. Revelation strips away the legitimating covers of US identity and of Western modernity more broadly. Revelation, in Baldwin's work, sustains the tension of a reality that simply *is*, and an active praxis of love that brings reality forth. Baldwin thus affirms with Long the historical task of reflection in the United States, but also takes up an eschatological challenge—understood in terms of depth rather than chronology—*through* the reflective task of actualizing revelation. Reflection opens up cracks in the modern world-system out of a commitment to the eschatological reality of decolonial love. Baldwin finds, in these cracks, loci from which to participate in decolonial love.

Although Baldwin does not use terms such as revelation and salvation in ways that are tied to religious discourse in the sense of being controlled by doctrines, creedal statements, or dogmatic theology, they do have religious—and here I argue theological—significance.[12] Showing how Baldwin develops decolonial love as an orientation and a praxis, and then developing how this response entails a religious orientation, opens up an orientation of decolonial love that both diversifies the loci from which decolonial love emerges beyond Fanon's conception of decolonial love in armed struggle, and opens up decolonial love as theologically pedagogic.

Decolonial Love: A Praxis of Revelation

Like Fanon's orientation of decolonial love, and like the way Chela Sandoval has theorized decolonial love, Baldwin's orientation of decolonial love is both a means for interpreting the social world and a tool for political action. As a hermeneutic, Baldwin's orientation of decolonial love is a mode of consciousness that overrides normative ethical, ideological, or religious claims. This implies decolonial love's function as a political tool, insofar as it guides political action toward an end of decolonization. For Baldwin, this in part takes the form of entering into networks of relation in the world and writing to reveal them.

As the process of John Grimes's decision to run down the hill and into the city indicates, the church has an ambiguous position in Baldwin's work. His orientation of decolonial love isn't free from this ambiguity. Baldwin describes his entrance into the church as a flight from the world, as a place of refuge from the tensions and ambiguities of the world.[13] While the church as an evasion of the reality of the world is certainly an undercurrent in Baldwin's work, there remains a powerful capacity within the church, although often unrealized, that he wants to maintain. Baldwin describes this potential with respect to the relation between black communities in the United States and Christianity: "The blacks did not so much use Christian symbols as recognize them—recognize them for what they were before the Christians came along—and, thus, reinvested these symbols with their original energy."[14] Here, Christian symbols contain an underlying revelation—revelation that simply *is*—and yet this revelation has to be brought out. Bringing out this revelation is, Baldwin shows, a valuable inheritance handed down within the black church. He defines this revelation as such:

> One is confronted with the agony and the nakedness and the beauty of a power which has no beginning and no end, which contains you, and which you contain, and which will be using you when your bones are dust. One thus confronts a self both limited and boundless and born to die and born to live. The creature is, also, the creation, and responsible, endlessly, for that perpetual act of creation which is both the self and more than the self.[15]

Even as Baldwin critiques the church's tendency to evade reality, he takes revelation, as one of the central inheritances passed down within the church, to be his central task. He understands the church to have the capacity to be a revelatory and creative site that interacts with a reality that goes beyond the self, both spatially and temporally. The "power" Baldwin refers to, what he calls elsewhere the "beat," points to a similar structure of reality that Zubiri and Ellacuría call the theologal. Baldwin perceives this structure to be tangible within his historical context—or at least almost tangible—within black religious communities and artistic expression.

The praxis of decolonial love, which Baldwin finds to be both suppressed and present within the black church, involves the violence of forcibly undoing the "system of reality" held by white Americans.[16] Baldwin sees that "a vast amount of the white anguish is rooted in the white man's . . . profound need to be seen as he is, to be released from the tyranny of his mirror."[17] White Americans have not made the commitment to, in the metaphorical sense, run into the city. More concretely, white Americans have not run into reality. Love is the violent process of forcing this confrontation with reality, of incarnating "America" in the messiness of reality, and exposing its ambiguities:

> Love takes off the masks that we fear we cannot live without and know we cannot live within. I use the word "love" here not merely in the personal sense but as a state of being, or a state of grace—not in the infantile American sense of being made happy but in the tough and universal sense of quest and daring and growth.[18]

Love, as Baldwin understands it, both depends on revelation and is the activity of revelation. Decolonial love takes off the masks necessary to sustain the legend or the history that allows for the legitimization and perpetuation of the culturally dominant idea of the United States and the social-historical reality that it is, and thus the persistence of the coloniality of power. In this praxis, love can be perceived as violent. The love to which Baldwin refers is a "menaced love,"[19] a love that shows that salvation exists within the "hurricane" of existence in the United States. Salvation is something that Baldwin is compelled to unveil and enter into, not always and necessarily something to be created anew. The "creation" for Baldwin involves the act of revelation.

Decolonial Love as a Religious Orientation

Baldwin's decolonial love guides a praxis of revelation that ultimately opens up the possibility of salvation. It is a way of situating oneself in the world—often within traditions—that shapes meaning. As such, Baldwin's decolonial love can be understood as informing an understanding of a religious reality. Three categories come through in Baldwin's work that shape his orientation of decolonial love as a religious reality by which he makes sense of and commits to salvation: revelatory experience, suffering, and love. Together, these categories give meaning to a religious perspective that catalyzes a deepened fidelity to history. Revelation, suffering, and love all take place in history and are oriented toward historical realities.

Revelatory Experience

Baldwin encapsulates revelatory experience—an element of the plunge down the hill in *Go Tell It On the Mountain*—in an early nonfiction essay, written as a letter to his nephew and published in *The Fire Next Time*:

> it was intended that you should perish in the ghetto, perish by never being allowed to go behind the white man's definitions, by never being allowed to spell your proper name. You have, and many of us have, defeated this intention; and, by a terrible law, a terrible paradox, those innocent who believed that your imprisonment made them safe are losing their grasp of reality. But these men are your brothers—your lost, younger brothers. And if the word *integration* means anything, this is what it means: that we, with love, shall force our brothers to see themselves as they are, to cease fleeing from reality and begin to change it.[20]

In this early essay, Baldwin brings forward a number of commitments related to the category of revelation that remain central to his work. First, in going "behind the white man's definitions," Baldwin sees in his nephew a capacity to overcome the failure of the "innocents"—those who have imprisoned his nephew with the intention of keeping their myth intact—to enter into reality. His nephew, in other words, takes up the task of revelation. Second, Baldwin understands integration as forcing the irruption of reality into a constructed myth. Reality in this sense is an object of revelation that remains present, even if unseen. Third, this irruption is a revelatory experience, and those who rely on a myth that necessitates the concealment of his nephew perceive this irruption as violent. In framing revelatory experience as such, Baldwin maintains the connection between salvation and violence that Fanon located within love, yet positions this violence outside a revolutionary struggle, and within the realm of daily life. Revelatory experience, which involves both an active presence and recognition of an already existing reality, opens up the possibility of salvation in forcing a fuller encounter with reality.

Long's work helps to draw out the need for the revelatory praxis for which Baldwin calls, and shows why revelatory experience is a necessary task within a US context. In short, Baldwin's work supports and deepens Long's contention that the *absence* of revelatory experience is crucial to US identity and to ways Americans orient themselves in the world. Long uses the term "signification" to refer to a process of naming the other without regard to the concepts through which an "other" people know themselves. To signify is to arbitrarily designate meaning from a hegemonic position.[21] Long uncovers the obvious manifestations of this within a US context within the European conquest of the Americas beginning in the fifteenth century and in the subsequent Atlantic slave trade. These significations produced European and Euro-American myths connected to political and economic objectives.[22] Relative to colonial modernity, Long argues that these myths assign meaning to particular realities constructed as "silent"—for example, the New World in 1492—and that these myths in turn shape colonial modernity.[23] The "linguistic conquest" of ascribing meaning to realities perceived as silent and lacking the capacity to name themselves created a new form of orientation within the world that shapes modern consciousness.[24] Fanon also describes the normalization of a metaphysical world imposed through the conquest of the Americas and Africa that is also a linguistic conquest. Fanon's description of the metaphysics of blackness and whiteness is, in Long's understanding of the term, a description of an orientation within the world. In attempting to force the obliteration of the metaphysical world established by Europe (that is, the project of "the end of the world"), Fanon's decolonial love disallows the possibility of the continuity of the European myth. Signification, therefore, is not only a discursive reality; it also shapes an orientation and experience within the world.

As such, Long's concept of signification indicates the historical manner in which dominant US imaginaries have avoided revelatory experience.

Long describes black communities within the United States as having been signified within the matrix of the modern world-system, yet also, and Baldwin emphasizes this as well, as always having existed as more than this signification:

> one must also take account of those peoples who had to undergo the "creativity" of the Western world—those peoples and cultures who became during this period the "pawns" of Western cultural creativity. They were present not as voices speaking but as the silence which is necessary to all speech. They existed as the pauses between words— those pauses which are necessary if speech is to be possible—and in their silence they spoke. As opposed to the existential and historical presumptions of human beings making their world, those who lived as the *material prima* (raw material, I think, is the economic way of expressing this) *kept the ontological dimension open through their silence.* This silence was as necessary as it was forced.[25]

In encountering the New World, Europeans first perceived it as silent, and then, out of this (mis-)perception, signified the silence. The recognition of the incompleteness of Western creativity—and here I mean the inherent incompleteness, not an incompleteness needing to be brought to completion—and its inability to signify the silence of its other indicates the ontology that exists outside Western creativity. The "pauses between the words," as Fanon, Baldwin, and Long show, occupy a position that the Western imagination cannot recognize, as this recognition would be self-destructive. This is why, as Fanon points out, the modern/colonial situation demands that the colonized "lack ontological resistance."[26] This lack legitimizes the continuation of the project of Western modernity. Both Fanon and Baldwin shape praxes of forcing the ontology of the "pauses" into being. In other words, their orientations of decolonial love bring forth the silence that always remains more than what it is signified as. This is revelatory experience.

Baldwin particularly focuses on how culturally dominant discourses signify black communities and mythologize their position within the United States. He develops an understanding of revelation out of this context. Baldwin responds to signification by affirming that the praxis of revelation, and subsequently the experience of revelation, is made concrete when subjects go behind these significations. This is an intellective process of confronting reality, and is Baldwin's own task. The writer is called to recognize the ways the signified are already going behind significations, and, in this recognition, contribute to the task of moving behind significations. Baldwin describes this praxis of the writer as uncovering truth, or as connecting to a meaning that already exists.[27]

In view of the task of revelation, which is the fruit of the incarnation into the world that shapes Baldwin's orientation of decolonial love, Baldwin responds to signification and the social-political reality it imposes. This response opposes the dominant view in which the black subject stands in need of what Baldwin often calls "the alabaster Christ," or salvation that results in "becoming white." Baldwin thus rejects a Christian theological position that imposes a shameful past on African Americans, which can only be erased by the alabaster Christ and ultimately through assimilation:

> As he [the black subject] accepted the alabaster Christ and the bloody
> cross—in the bearing of which he would find his redemption, as,
> indeed, to our outraged astonishment he sometimes did—he must,
> henceforth, accept that image we then gave him of himself: having
> no other and standing, moreover, in danger of death should he fail to
> accept the dazzling light thus brought into such darkness.[28]

Baldwin's vision of salvation entails revealing that the black subject already stands on legitimate ground, thus obviating the need of the dazzling light of the alabaster Christ. When the task of the writer is understood as revelation, the writer participates in the process of salvation by uncovering ways of being human from meaning-making loci other than the significations and images of Western modernity.

Baldwin sees the church as inhabiting an ambiguous position. It sometimes upholds the task of revelation and at other times fraudulently presents the dazzling light of the alabaster Christ in a distorted "theology." In a dialogue with Nikki Giovanni, Giovanni tells Baldwin that she "really dig[s] the church," to which Baldwin responds that he does too. Giovanni continues: "I can't dig theology, but the music and the energies of the church." Baldwin again affirms Giovanni's position. Giovanni illustrates what she means by this: "I went up to an A.M.E. Zion church and a lady was singing 'Yes, Jesus Loves Me' and people started shouting. People were shouting. And it hit me as I was sitting there—my God, as a so-called black militant I have nothing stronger to offer than Jesus." Baldwin's response is no longer simply affirmative. He ambiguously responds, "Baby what we did with Jesus was not supposed to happen."[29] Baldwin perceives a positive potential to the church, and even Jesus, yet one that has been distorted.

In exploring a possible way the church can initiate revelatory experience and thus work toward and actualize salvation, Baldwin recalls the religious language of the black church but without shedding the ambiguities he perceives in it. He describes being "counselled, from time to time, to do our first works over"—that is, "to reexamine everything. Go back to where you started, or as far back as you can, examine all of it, travel your road again and tell the truth about it. Sing or shout or testify or keep it to yourself: but *know whence you came*."[30] This practice of moving back through history is what people in the United States who become white cannot do without calling into question the legitimacy of the project of Western modernity. At Ellis Island, "one becomes a white American," and leaves her or his identity behind: "One is mysteriously shipwrecked forever, in the Great New World."[31] This process of becoming white—"The price the white American paid for his ticket"—remains to be interrogated. The task of revelation still calls. The "first works," so to speak, are left behind, and the relationship becoming white has to becoming black remains concealed: "I know very well that my ancestors had no desire to come to this place: but neither did the ancestors of people who became white and who require of my captivity a song. They require of me a song less to celebrate my captivity than to justify their own."[32] Just as he counsels his nephew to continue to go behind the definitions of white America, Baldwin will not provide this song for those who became white, as it justifies these processes of becoming. His task is, on the contrary, revelation: to force, or at the very least catalyze, the process of doing one's first works over. This revelatory experience actualizes salvation. It entails destroying the "American" identity built on what Fanon identified as the "lack of ontological resistance" in the "zone of nonbeing." This sets the stage for Baldwin to argue that revelatory experience within the United States cannot but go through lived experiences of inhabiting the undersides of US identity and the US imaginary.

Revelation from Contexts of Suffering

When Baldwin connects communities' experiences of suffering to salvation, he does so without positing a direct correlation between suffering and salvation.[33] Rather than positing a direct link between suffering and salvation, Baldwin focuses on responses to suffering as opening up salvation. From a theological perspective, Victor Anderson has lifted up the creative productions that emerge from suffering and, like Baldwin, connects these creativities to salvation. Anderson develops a constructive theological position that values suffering, but as an epistemic rather than soteriological locus. Anderson argues that in the experience of suffering, creative capacities come forth: "These virtues are not sequential effects of suffering. Rather, they are copresent or emergent potentialities in the creative exchange of human beings themselves with suffering and evil."[34] He sees a creative potential that suffering can occasion, but that is not derivative of suffering. Suffering does not cause salvation, but can occasion it.[35] In his task of actualizing a process of revelation in his work, Baldwin, like Anderson, recognizes that suffering can provide a common basis out of which a response that transcends suffering can be formulated. In other words, suffering does not cause redemption, yet responses to suffering can be revelatory and thus salvific.[36]

One of the primary ways Baldwin uncovers a response to suffering that is revelatory and salvific is through music. In his short story "Sonny's Blues," the narrator recognizes the capacity of music to connect disparate experiences and create an order when listening to his brother:

> All I know about music is that not many people ever really hear it. And even then, on the rare occasions when something opens within, and the music enters, what we mainly hear, or hear corroborated, are personal, private, vanishing evocations. But the man who creates the music is hearing something else, is dealing with the roar rising from the void and imposing order on it as it hits the air. What is evoked in him, then, is of another order, more terrible because it has no words, and triumphant, too, for that same reason. And his triumph, when he triumphs, is ours.[37]

Through its capacity to witness to suffering, music indicates something about reality and the experience of reality that transcends an individual situation. Baldwin shows that music can be a type of revelation, which is always both connected to a specific historical situation and transcends it.

Suffering provides for Baldwin a context for an alternative way to make sense of the world, which is a creative process rooted in expressing and passing down revelation. In music, Baldwin discovers a different way of signifying reality, including different sources for this constructive process, and not just a different signification. Suffering occasions creativity, as Anderson phrases it, that allows for a re-positioning within what Baldwin calls the "American house." This different way of signifying implies a reflective task that is also eschatological. Whereas for Fanon a decolonial vision entails "the end of the world," for Baldwin, a decolonial vision enters into worlds created on the undersides of the modern world-system. Through sites such as church, music, and literature, Baldwin locates these creative processes and different ways of signifying. These sites offer decolonial imaginaries that go behind dominant forms of signification and offer alternative possibilities for revelation.

Baldwin reflects on the alternative form of signification—again by turning to music—in a more explicit way in a 1979 essay, "Of the Sorrow Songs: The Cross of Redemption." In this essay, he puts forth jazz, an expression that makes sense of the world out of an experience of suffering, as a possibility for articulating salvation within a US context.[38] If experiences of suffering are allowed to come forth as a locus from which to understand reality, Baldwin argues that jazz can offer Americans the possibility to come to terms with, or "conquer," their history. For this reason, music presents a locus of salvation.

"Of the Sorrow Songs" is technically written as a review of James Lincoln Collier's *The Making of Jazz*. Though Baldwin only uses this book as a starting point in the essay, Collier's work is significant for Baldwin because he sees Collier's attempt to define jazz as an attempt to define Baldwin's own history and his own life.[39] Baldwin feels obligated to respond to Collier because of the fear that his nephew "or, for that matter, my Swiss godson or my Italian godson," will believe it.[40] Baldwin tries to undo the possibility that Collier's definition of reality conceals the revelation laboriously passed down in the black church and in black music, and plays into the processes of becoming both white and black in the modern/colonial world. Baldwin wants to reclaim jazz, from Collier, as a medium that allows for a presentation of the human condition that is salvific.

Baldwin is clear that jazz arose, in part, as a response to Europe's naming of history. As a way of seeing the world, jazz emerges out of necessity. Jazz speaks the language that cannot be spoken from a Eurocentered perspective. It emerges as a task of revelation, from the underside: "not only to redeem a history unwritten and despised, but to checkmate the European notion of the world."[41] It's a language, an expression, which presents another way of thinking, another way of conceptualizing reality. Jazz affords musicians a possibility to name the world from an epistemic site the European does not inhabit.

Jazz, as Baldwin articulates it, "came into existence as an exceedingly laconic description of black circumstances, and as a way, by describing these circumstances, of overcoming them."[42] As laconic, jazz resists being decoded. It creates a world on the boundaries of Western modernity. It functions as what Mignolo refers to as border thinking. In the cracks of Western modernity Baldwin uncovers jazz as, to use Dussel's term, a transmodern expression. Jazz establishes a distance between European languages and the experiences such languages express. As musical expression jazz is related, in a fundamental sense, to life—to a life that refuses to be signified as something it's not.[43] In a way that "History" cannot, jazz responds to the life that exists beyond what is captured by the European notion of the world. And, at the same time, jazz participates in the creation of this life. Jazz—and Baldwin moves easily between jazz and "black American music" more broadly—makes of the "captivity" of black existence in the United States "a song."[44]

Significations are most illuminating in the way they reflect back on the world that produces them. Baldwin speaks of "History," but a similar point can be made of "Theology": as an invention, theology describes the inventor/theologian more than it does its subject. Jazz might do the same, but it also creates a world in different a way than these disciplines presenting themselves as objective have created a world. The laconic, coded expression of jazz begins elsewhere, and in doing so offers a transmodern expression of reality. It "make[s] a world" that is not beholden to the confines of colonial modernity.[45]

Baldwin does not pretend that jazz, or black music more broadly, doesn't begin with the hardness of his lived experience of being "officially, and lethally, despised."[46] But jazz also comes out of the hardness of despising others, and out of the hardness of resurrecting, out of the hardness of loving. Jazz "begins on the auction block."[47] It begins in that site that reveals Europe for what it is. But, at the same time, jazz includes "the 'beat,' which is the key to music, and the key to life."[48] The beat "recognizes, changes, and conquers time."[49] The beat makes a world that is not imprisoned by significations. The beat offers a world not imprisoned by Eurocentered disciplines, and releases time from its significations. The beat allows for history to become "a garment we can wear, and share, and not a cloak in which to hide." It allows time to become "a friend."[50] The beat creates a world—a laconic, coded world that resists decoding by Eurocentric categories. Baldwin holds this creative act, which is at the same time an act of uncovering, as the possibility for salvation. Jazz is salvific because it actualizes revelation.

Baldwin brings out the beat in music as a decolonial world within a center of Western modernity. He uses the beat as a metaphor for the footholds of decolonial love within a modern/colonial world. To touch the beat requires coming to terms with the history in which we are situated. The beat is the foundation of historical experience. It allows for the salvation of history and salvation in history, and is the reality to which the praxis of revelation seeks access. The beat allows for salvation, and provides its foundation, insofar as it is the locus for "making the world" in a way that respects the inheritance of revelation. In this respect, the beat is something actively produced, yet at the same time something that conquers and dominates the human subject. Baldwin's turn to the beat is certainly iconoclastic as he attempts to destroy the false signification rendered on his community and its creativity, in part by the alabaster Christ. But with recourse to the beat, Baldwin also positively affirms the content of salvation. He ties salvation to living into a foundational element of life in the modern/colonial world that hierarchies within the coloniality of power conceal. In putting forth the beat as a principle of salvation, Baldwin articulates salvation as a conquering of history that principally comes from the praxis of those signified as lacking ontological resistance.

REVELATION AND LOVE

For Baldwin, salvation happens in the irruption into history of an eschatological reality that lies underneath the way history has been signified. The creative capacity of the ways decolonial love his historicized—that plunging into reality that opens up the salvation present in the beat— motivates the iconoclastic destruction of the dominant orientation of the US imaginary. Love as a historical praxis violently forces an irruption into history. Passing down revelation through modalities such as the church, music, and literature, Baldwin particularly shows how communities have created worlds and alternative ways of signifying reality that challenge the culturally dominant ultimate orientation within the United States. These creative, iconoclastic acts express an orientation of love onto which Baldwin latches.

Baldwin concretizes this love in his address to the World Council of Churches in 1968, an address in which he presents himself as "one of those people who have always been outside [the church], even though one tried to work in it."[51] The experience of the cross has the effect, Baldwin claims, to "make us, the blacks, very early distrust our own experience and refuse, in effect, to articulate that experience to the Christians who were our oppressors."[52] Baldwin describes this as a great loss for himself but "also a great loss for you, as white people."[53] The "alabaster Christ" of Christianity prohibits the black subject from living, thinking, and creating from a ground outside the dazzling light of the alabaster Christ. The resilience of the alabaster Christ closes creative possibilities that move beyond assimilation. The alabaster Christ negates the possibility of the blues, which Baldwin describes as "not a racial creation" but "an historical creation produced by the confrontation precisely between the pagan, the black pagan from Africa, and the alabaster cross."[54] By rejecting the possibility to sing the blues, a possibility that arises out of "a certain kind of spontaneity, a certain kind of joy, a certain kind of freedom, which a man can only have when he is in touch with himself, his surroundings, his women and his children,"[55] the church wedded to the alabaster Christ loses its capacity to reveal. The alabaster Christ, therefore, in closing transmodern loci, closes the encounter with salvation. Baldwin, motivated by an orientation of decolonial love, brings forth a praxis of revelation that emerges in creative ways from the underside of modernity that can open the encounter with salvation.

Baldwin maintains that black subjects play a crucial role in the revelation of the US social situation and of the identity of individuals who make up the United States. In this capacity to reveal, and thus also to save, the black subject is wrapped up with the concept of God:

> To be with God is really to be involved with some enormous, overwhelming desire, and joy, and power which you cannot control, which controls you. I conceive of my own life as a journey toward something I do not understand, which in the going toward, makes me better: I conceive of God, in fact, as a means of liberation and not a means to control others. Love does not begin and end the way we seem to think it does. Love is a battle, love is a war; love is a growing up. No one in the world—in the entire world—knows more—knows Americans better or, odd as it may sound, loves them more than the American Negro. This is because he has had to watch you, outwit you, deal with you, and bear you, and sometimes even bleed and die with you, ever since we got here, that is, since both of us, black and white, got here—and this is a wedding.[56]

In continuing to live in a US context, Baldwin describes the black subject as both a loving and revelatory subject, and thus a principle of salvation. "To be with God" opens up an encounter with revelation and ultimately salvation, and it requires breaking the process of signification that Long describes. "To be with God" requires divesting the power to signify. Love is significant in "being with God" because love is the praxis of entering into reality and revealing it. Love shatters the significations of colonial modernity. This love is not passive: it confronts Americans with ideologies we use to cover up reality and to prevent revelation and salvation. Baldwin's decolonial love, which indicates the potential of the salvific process of signifying reality differently, is violent insofar as it breaks down protective veils. His decolonial love opens up space for a historical encounter with the mystery of an eschatological reality, and thus salvation, but does so by destroying the idols that sustain socially dominant US illusions of stasis. As a "growing up," love requires a revelation that the American who is committed to sustaining the coloniality of power cannot afford. It requires "smash[ing] that mirror before which he has been frozen for so long."[57] This revelatory capacity of love is what makes love "war," what makes it violent. Baldwin's orientation of decolonial love ultimately spells the end of "America," as it exists as a legend and a myth. This destruction allows for the encounter with the beat—that is, for salvation. In the violence of love, the presence of salvation is concretized in history.

Baldwin's orientation of decolonial love manifests as a praxis of revelation that is often perceived as violent. While the following two chapters indicate how this praxis can be understood as theologically pedagogic with respect to the image of salvation in a more systematic way, Baldwin already presents decolonial love as a religious orientation. In *Go Tell It on the Mountain*, Baldwin rejects a pull back to the church when religion is understood in a way that prohibits an incarnation in reality. Baldwin instead turns to the traditions of handing down and creating revelation in the church, music, and literature as sites where decolonial love is actualized, and as possible locations for decolonial futures. When different ways of making sense of the world and situating oneself in the world are uncovered in the midst of experiences of suffering, subjects outside the physical and narrative centers of Western modernity can effect salvation within, and also beyond, their respective communities. This irruption of revelation, and thus salvation, is the materialization of an orientation of decolonial love. Decolonial love violently shatters the false sense of reality to which Americans are able to cling as long as dominant forms of signification remain unchallenged.

In seeing decolonial love, revelation, and salvation to exist in everyday lives, the making of worlds, and cultural expressions, Baldwin's work can push past some of the limits in Fanon's transmodern turn. The orientation of decolonial love evident in Baldwin's work is not limited to movements directly concerned with instituting a new political system; decolonial love and salvation are also encountered—and perhaps primarily encountered—in the mundane quality of life. In the struggle to understand what is fundamental to reality and to our experience of reality, Fanon and Baldwin both open up important loci for beginning to think about, and ultimately encounter, divinity. They already make important connections between how these loci generate orientations of decolonial love, and thus perspectives on how the human person might encounter and respond to divinity.

PART III

Theological Reflection as a Decolonial Option

CHAPTER 6

The Theological Pedagogy of Frantz Fanon and James Baldwin

Liberation does not entail moving to the "great beyond," but instead
implies a posture of radical attention and steadfastness in reality. This
radical attention and steadfastness particularly involves relationship
with those who struggle under the burdens of injustice and poverty.

MALIK J. M. WALKER, "Just Sit: Liberation as Abiding in an Urban
Future," *Newsletter CLT* 11 (June 2015): 5–6

The ways Fanon and Baldwin live out orientations of decolonial love
through a radical attention and steadfastness in reality offers an intellective praxis, an epistemic framework, and content that can be "theologically
pedagogic," to use a term from Marcella Althaus-Reid.[1] Decolonial love, as
an orientation by which to make sense of one's place in the world and face
up to reality, offers a way of understanding an encounter with a divine reality. As such, decolonial love provides a basis from which to expose idolatry
and construct theological knowledge and images. Specifically, decolonial
love can offer a way to understand revelation and history as grounds for a
theological image of salvation.

As a theological pedagogy, decolonial love can, on a basic level, inform
a way of thinking theologically. Orientations of decolonial love can ground
forms of theological reflection outside conversion to the epistemic norms
produced within the coloniality of power. When theology emerges from
decolonial love as an instance of encounter with divinity and an epistemically generative site, theology becomes a form of border thinking, or a way
of thinking that emerges from the limits of the modern world-system. In
this chapter, I read Fanon and Baldwin as demonstrating that orientations

of decolonial love are epistemic loci from which communities have thought theologically on their own epistemic terms. Understanding the historicizations of orientations of decolonial love as theologically pedagogic sites that exceed modern rationalities establishes the possibility to situate a decolonized theological image of salvation within understandings of revelation and history shaped by decolonial love. I take up the latter task in the second part of this chapter by arguing that Fanon and Baldwin face up to reality in a way that allows history to become a locus of revelation and of encounter with an eschatological reality. This encounter provides the context of salvation.

Theological Ways of Thinking: The Theological Pedagogy of Frantz Fanon and James Baldwin

Liberation theologians broadly understand theology as critical reflection on historical praxis or a historical situation in light of faith, in the service of social transformation.[2] Phillip J. Linden Jr. specifies the form of that critical reflection as one that, rather than accommodating to the modern world-system we inhabit, "seeks to incorporate the Divine Mystery beyond the material and the power that the material can have over creation."[3] From this fundamental understanding of theological reflection, Vincent Lloyd draws out two specific tasks of Christian theological reflection: on the one hand, to "rightly and rigorously" say "what God is not" in a way that exposes idols, and on the other, to hold up "wisdom of the oppressed," or of those who inhabit sites in which the demystification of idols is most clear.[4] The orientations of decolonial love in the work of Fanon and Baldwin can work within the broad understanding of theology as a critical reflection on history in light of the divine reality encountered in—but exceeding—the material world, and can inform both of the more specific tasks Lloyd identifies. Reading the orientations of decolonial love in the work of Fanon and Baldwin to be theologically pedagogic advances a form of critical reflection that catalyzes and authenticates social transformation.

The Critical Task: Exposing Idols

Fanon's decolonial love rests on the conviction that dialectical movement proceeds from the colonial difference. Revolutionary movement from the zone of nonbeing irrupts within a situation in which the colonizer has "turned the colonized into a kind of quintessence of evil," in which "[t]he 'native' is declared impervious to ethics, representing not only the absence of values but also the negation of values."[5] Fanon sees clearly the ways Christian thought has incorporated the epistemic racism within colonial relations of power into its own framework and has come to be one of the primary forms of signifying "the native" as evil. Christian thought functions, Fanon argues, on the same level as the chemical DDT: as DDT "destroys parasites, carriers of disease," Christianity "roots out heresy, natural impulses, and evil."[6] Through a process of signification, the historical development of Christian thought within colonial modernity serves the elimination of the colonized. This is both a literal and physical elimination, in the form of modern/colonial genocides, and an elimination that takes the form of assimilation: "The Church in the colonies is a white man's Church, a foreigners' Church. It does not call the colonized to the ways of God, but to the ways of the white man, to the ways of the master, the ways of the oppressor."[7] Fanon recognizes ways Christian thought functions as an idol in the modern/colonial world. In Lloyd's terms, the Christian thought that Fanon identifies has become secular thought, wherein religion is excluded or managed "by the powers that be" such that "there is nothing beyond the ways of the world."[8] Rather than forming a posture that exposes idols, Fanon argues that Christian commitments function to solidify idols—that is, Christian thought serves the modern world-system by proposing a particular form of historical stasis as ultimate.

Fanon is thus deeply suspicious of positive theological claims, especially when made with some sort of loyalty to the Christian tradition and from epistemic contexts where the existence and violence of idols is easily concealed. Fanon's decolonial love smashes to "smithereens" the "sentinel on duty guarding the Greco-Roman pedestal" and turns "[a]ll the Mediterranean values, the triumph of the individual, of enlightenment and Beauty" into "pale, lifeless trinkets."[9] The violence involved in this act of smashing idols—and not just on the discursive level, but the revolutionary movement required to change structures that legitimize such idols—propels historical movement. This is the decolonial dialectical movement from the zone of nonbeing. The violence within decolonial love destroys the solidification of concepts into Eurocentered idols, whether Christian or secular.

Fanon's critical work clears space. Exposing idols makes room for something else, beyond that which has been idolized within the modern world-system and the coloniality of power. The dialectical movement Fanon aims to catalyze opens up options; Fanon's decolonial dialectics are not contained within a linear progression laid out by Eurocentered modernity. Fanon's intellective task of exposing idols, in other words, implies a hope

or a faith that neither he nor many contemporary secular decolonial thinkers explicitly acknowledge: an eschatological faith in a reality that exceeds
the modern world-system and its rationalities. Reading Fanon and Baldwin as intellectuals committed to an eschatological reality and as having
thought theologically, and reading them alongside theologians, can help to
clarify the decolonial turn as not only a critical posture but also one that
opens up options for encountering and recognizing an eschatological, un-
namable reality.

Baldwin takes up the negative theological task Lloyd identifies, although
in different ways than Fanon. Within the scope of an orientation of decolonial love, Baldwin critiques idolatrous commitments central to US identity and posits an unnameable alternative. When Lloyd reads Baldwin in
relation to the two-fold task of theology he sets forth, he focuses on Baldwin's identification of blackness as a "tremendous spiritual condition."[10]
Blackness names a lived situation in which the danger of idols is readily
apparent, and thus a lived situation that facilitates the critique of idolatry. Blackness functions in Baldwin's work, Lloyd argues, to name a site
in which faith operates as a negative theology rather than a structure of
adhering to a positive understanding of a transcendent reality. In Lloyd's
reading, Baldwin does not reject a transcendent object, but he does reject
the ultimate authority of the transcendent object to demand full adher-
ence. Baldwin exposes what is perceived as absolute authority "as less than
absolute," but in doing so, Lloyd argues, he has a difficult time accepting
traditions and norms.[11]

Lloyd sees Baldwin's "lasting import" to be his "negative political theology," or his successful way of addressing the first task of theological reflection of critiquing idolatry.[12] He appreciates the rigor of Baldwin's critique,
but he also indicates Baldwin's limitations with respect to the second task
of providing a constructive alternative that holds up the wisdom of the
oppressed. Lloyd sees the constructive element of Baldwin's work that
coalesces in the reality that Baldwin calls love to lack sufficient political
concreteness: Baldwin, Lloyd argues, "ultimately idolizes a vague, postracial concept of love."[13] In Lloyd's reading, a racial consciousness shapes
Baldwin's critical lens, but Baldwin then lets go of this racial consciousness
when he moves to a constructive project. Lloyd wants to hold up blackness—understood paradoxically as both "ontological symbol" and "visible
reality"—as a generative theological site with tradition and norms in a way
that he sees Baldwin to abandon.[14] The alternative Baldwin holds up as
love is, for Lloyd, politically impotent. This presents a potential problem
in reading Baldwin's work as theologically pedagogic. Does Baldwin work

to clear a space for a transcendent reality only to fill it with a vague concept of love?

Lloyd and I read Baldwin similarly as prioritizing the task of revelation. Baldwin's task of examining reality requires, as Lloyd points out, shedding simplistic significations and recognizing "the sacred opacity of each human and so reverencing each human (this is, for Baldwin, salvation)."[15] The task of revelation is that which opens up the possibility for salvation. Lloyd and I differ, however, in assessing Baldwin's turn to love. Baldwin offers, in Lloyd's reading, a love without norms, a love without judgment and condemnation, and thus a "[p]olitically troubling" love without justice.[16] In other words, it is clear for Lloyd that love is connected to revelatory experience in Baldwin's work, but it is not clear what it reveals.

Understanding Baldwin's notion of love as decolonial love through Ignacio Ellacuría's theological perspective brings out its political dimension, although in a different way than how Lloyd wants love to be political. Baldwin's constructive account of love implies a political project of deepening one's presence in reality, rather than adhering to norms. Baldwin holds reality to be, in itself, sacred. The "beat" bears witness to an eschatological reality encountered in history that exceeds the constraints of the modern world-system. Jazz, and African American music in general, does not make a normative claim about reality; it rather opens up the possibility to encounter reality. This encounter with reality is, for Baldwin, a historical instance of salvation. Baldwin's normative claim, therefore, rests in the need to encounter reality—that is, to take on "a posture of radical attention and steadfastness in reality," as Malik J. M. Walker puts it. Distorting reality, which includes signifying other people, closes the possibility for reality to give of itself in revelatory ways and thus for salvation history. Distorting and concealing reality excludes the capacity to encounter reality, and particularly what Xavier Zubiri and Ellacuría named as its theologal structure. The distortion of reality occludes the possibility of encountering the divine reality through material reality. Justice is present in Baldwin's work as a response to the intellective task of facing up to reality, and occurs in taking responsibility for reality, to draw on Ellacuría's terms.

Lloyd convincingly argues that Baldwin does not offer love primarily in connection to a call to adhere to norms, yet this does not mean that justice or norms are absent. The struggle to encounter reality is primary for Baldwin. The primary normative function of decolonial love, as both Baldwin and Fanon develop it, is shedding significations and ideologies that sustain a historical stasis that for them specifically has its point of origin in European colonialism. When reading the work of Fanon and Baldwin as theologically pedagogic, the imperative to encounter reality includes, as its most fundamental aspect, an encounter with the eschatological reality of the divine mystery that prompts decolonial movement. Within a context of colonial modernity, this primary norm plays out historically as decolonization, or as unsettling the manifestations of the coloniality of power in being, knowledge, and eschatology. Justice thus emerges in salvation, in a freedom to be in reality and to encounter its deep structure, beyond the modern/colonial stasis. This dynamic is political: it involves forcing historical movement against social and political structures, and imaginaries that seek historical stasis.

THE CONSTRUCTIVE TASK: ARTICULATING ALTERNATIVES FROM AN ENCOUNTER WITH THE DIVINE MYSTERY

As Fanon and Baldwin take up a political and intellective task of encountering and facing up to reality, they both focus on race as a crucial element in the modern world-system. Like in Quijano's analysis, Fanon and Baldwin situate race within a broader historical context and structure than is immediately apparent from the perspective of Western modernity. This move to locate race within a wider purview is part of Fanon's decolonial dialectics and Baldwin's intellective task of revelation.

One way Baldwin articulates the function of race within the modern world-system he confronts is with reference to the blues. Whereas Fanon is more explicitly dialectical than Baldwin, the blues function for Baldwin as a historical articulation that provides an alternative to modern/colonial forms of stasis. In his 1964 essay, "The Uses of the Blues" Baldwin claims that his title "does not refer to music; I don't know anything about music. It does refer to the experience of life, or the state of being, out of which the blues come."[17] The blues function for Baldwin as a way of facing up to reality. When he turns to "the American Negro's experience of life" in the same essay, Baldwin makes a similar move: "I want to be clear that when I talk about Negroes in this context I am not talking about race; I don't know what race means."[18] In claiming to not know "anything about music" or "what race means," Baldwin frees his project from modern/colonial significations, even as he recognizes the ways in which they become real. Like with the blues, Baldwin uses "Negroes" as a way to articulate private life and the experience of being powerless and without a solution, rather than a reified position within the modern world-system.[19] This lived experience of a particular relationship within and to colonial modernity is often too easily elided in "liberal jargon," and talk of progress. Such discourse is used, Baldwin argues, to "avoid the facts of this life":

> in order to face the facts of a life like Billie [Holliday]'s or, for that matter, a life like mine, one has got to—the American white has got to—accept the fact that what he thinks he is, he is not. He has to give up, *he has to surrender his image of himself,* and apparently this is the last thing white Americans are prepared to do.[20]

The blues, for Baldwin, are about this process of surrender. They evoke a praxis of surrender that counters "America," which Baldwin compares to a "forty-year-old virgin . . . who has spent his or her life in a kind of cotton batting."[21] The entity of "America" has failed "to accept the reality of pain, of anguish, of ambiguity, of death," which "has turned us into a very peculiar and sometimes monstrous people."[22] "The blues" articulates experiences of the limits of Western modernity and confronts the "disaster" of the American situation.[23]

Baldwin continues to use the blues as a way of encountering and making sense of reality in a 1968 speech to the World Council of Churches in Sweden. In this speech, Baldwin positions Christian and blues perspectives in opposition to each other:

> One of the things that happened, it seems to me, with the rise of the Christian Church, was precisely the denial of a certain kind of spontaneity, a certain kind of joy, a certain kind of freedom, which a man can only have when he is in touch with himself, his surroundings, his women and his children. It seems to me that this shows very crucially in the nature, the structure of our politics and in the personalities of our children, who would like to learn, if I may put it this way, how to sing the blues, *because the blues are not a racial creation, the blues are an historical creation produced by the confrontation precisely between the pagan, the black pagan from Africa, and the alabaster cross.* I am suggesting that the nature of the lies the Christian Church has always helplessly told about me are only a reflection of the lies the Christian Church has always helplessly told itself, to itself, about itself.[24]

Baldwin situates the blues within the modern/colonial encounter between Europe, Africa, and the Americas. He latches onto the "spontaneity," "joy," and "freedom" that are crucial to the blues but obscured by Christian significations. Baldwin stakes his project with this blues perspective. While this differs from staking his project with the category of race or within

Christian identity, Baldwin does not make the "postracial" turn that Lloyd suggests that Baldwin makes; rather, Baldwin sees race within the broader contours of the coloniality of power and contests this entire matrix by thinking within a perspective oriented toward a transcendent—even theologal, to again draw on Zubiri and Ellacuría's term—reality encountered by deepening roots in history. Baldwin is centrally concerned about surrendering one's image of oneself, and forcing an imposed stasis into historical motion. The turn to the beat and to love are his central images for this praxis of facing up to reality. The beat, like love, includes and is even grounded in the "auction block," but at the same time articulates an encounter with the divine depth of history.

Although not in reference to Baldwin or Fanon, Linden develops a theological perspective that authenticates a struggle to encounter and bear witness to the divine depth of history. The task of encountering reality compels Linden to develop a "theological-historical view" in which he uses Fernand Braudel's *longue durée* approach to history. This long historical view establishes an "integrity" for "understanding what the black experience means" in the North Atlantic world.[25] Linden sees Braudel's challenge to historians to engage the long time span, or longue durée, as a challenge to theologians to engage the "real" historical situation.[26] When historians focus on the history of the longue durée rather than *l'histoire événementielle*, or the history of events, Braudel holds, they can perceive a coherence of historical movement and historical upheavals. The longue durée entails an attention to the "semistillness" of history around which events gravitate.[27] When Linden brings this perspective into theological reflection, he challenges theologians to search for and respond to "the root causes of an apparent historical deviation experienced in the creation of the modern nation-state."[28] A longue durée view establishes a basis of integrity for theological reflection that stands in opposition to becoming enchanted by concepts and tools within the parameters of understanding of those who are successful within colonial modernity, which theologians can use in seeking a stake in the modern world-system.[29]

Using the language of salvation, Fanon describes the sort of inclusionary praxis that elides conflict. Linden sees this inclusionary praxis to come out of a failure to analyze long historical processes, and he thus strongly rejects it as a viable response to the modern project. Like Linden, Fanon presses his readers to not be enchanted by opportunities for inclusion without conflict. Fanon's particular focus is the nationalist bourgeoisie. Historical analyses and interventions based on an ideology of inclusion into the modern world-system buy into what Fanon refers to as "the atheist's form of salvation." The decolonial struggle in Algeria that Fanon prioritizes as a site of the eschatological reality of decolonial love brings all Algerians together because "in reality *everyone* will be discovered by the French legionnaires and consequently massacred or else *everyone* will be saved. In such a context, the 'every man for himself' concept, the atheist's form of salvation, is prohibited."[30] As a movement that ruptures the long history of colonial modernity, the revolution stands in contrast to the atheist's form of salvation as a genre of salvation rooted in self-interest. Fanon adamantly rejects this atheism: it is "prohibited" within the decolonial struggle that is already a site of the new humanity. An individual quest for salvation as inclusion, for both Fanon and Linden, is merely collusion with the modern world-system. It is a form of salvation that conflates events occurring within the modern/colonial world-system with the eschaton. The "atheist's form of salvation" perceives salvation in and by colonial modernity.

As a way of asserting a constructive theological project that offers alternatives, Linden insists on situating theological reflection within an encounter with the theologal structure of reality:

> The theologian of today must be one who seeks to incorporate the Divine Mystery beyond the material and the power that the material can have over creation. . . . Such a discourse goes beyond being right. For the theologian, knowing the teachings of the Church (orthodoxy) is vital to the life and tradition of the Church. However, for the theologian, orthopraxy or doing right (martyrdom), namely witnessing with one's life to the presence of the Divine, is of greater value in the midst of the capitalist materialization of the Mystery than being right.[31]

The theologian has the task of exposing idols—for Linden, specifically the power of capitalist materialities—in the service of making space for the encounter with the divine mystery. An encounter with the divine mystery, and the bearing witness to the divine mystery as martyrdom, is both the point of access from which theological reflection can take place and the historical presence of salvation. The latter provides the opportunity for the former. Recognizing that which exceeds the modern world-system requires an analysis that that can see its long history, and a posture toward reality that refuses to be caught up in the enchanting possibilities offered in particular events within the modern/colonial matrix.

As in all theology, there is a tension between having a foretaste of the mystery of the eschaton and the eschaton itself. While the temporal sense of the eschaton as the endpoint of a linear progression is abundantly present in scripture—the obvious exceptions are the wisdom books of Ecclesiastes,

Proverbs, and Job—Linden, Fanon, and Baldwin all suggest an interpretation of both the foretaste of the eschaton and the eschaton itself, which is fundamentally mystery, primarily as the fullness of time (*kairós*) that occurs in spatial realities rather than as the consecutive unfolding of time (*chrónos*). Eschatological significance is present in immediate historical situations.[32] Decolonial love makes present an encounter with the mystery of the eschaton, yet never eclipses, controls, or fully grasps the eschatological reality. Salvation, then, is the encounter with the divine mystery, and a participation in the depth of the divine mystery in the struggle to face up to reality. Clearing away the mystification by idols, or the "atheist's form of salvation" makes salvation possible.

Fanon and Baldwin can inform theologians' struggle to critically reflect on a historical situation out of an encounter with the mystery of an eschatological reality in history—that is, out of an ultimate concern with salvation. Fanon and Baldwin operate out of a posture that incorporates what theologians refer to as the divine mystery, historicized by Fanon and Baldwin in praxes of decolonial love, into their apprehension of and engagement with the world. Exposing idols opens up the martyrial praxis of "witnessing with one's life to the presence of the Divine," to which Linden refers.

When read purely as humanists, Fanon and Baldwin become less politically potent. The claims Fanon and Baldwin make about eschatological dimensions of reality and how to live individual and communal life in relationship to that ultimate mystery—which coalesce around decolonial love—ground their political stance. The task of revealing reality that Fanon and Baldwin uphold is a way of apprehending reality—and in doing so, encountering its theologal depth—in historical contexts deeply shaped by the modern/colonial world-system.

Reading Fanon and Baldwin as humanists who can provide raw material on which the theologian can work is akin to using Clodovis Boff's theological method that depends on three distinct moments within theological work: first a moment of social analysis that, second, theology as a separate discipline and way of thinking works on, which then, third, leads to praxis. Reading the work of Fanon and Baldwin in this way weakens it politically—decolonial love can be reduced to a moment within, but not of, theological reflection. Reading the work of Fanon and Baldwin as theologically pedagogic, in contrast, recognizes their orientations of decolonial love to shape theological claims. When read as theologically pedagogic, decolonial love can shape a theological image of salvation that grounds both a witness to a divine reality and political life.

Revelation and History: A Foundation for Salvation

Salvation—as it is presented in the work of Fanon and Baldwin, and also, as I will bring out in the subsequent chapter, in the work of self-identified theologians—requires breaking forms of historical stasis that conceal reality. Both Fanon and Baldwin take up an intellective praxis of breaking forms of historical stasis that are falsely perceived as ultimate in order to clear space for decolonial love. Though they prioritize historical motion, Fanon and Baldwin recognize and attend to what Braudel refers to as the "semistillness" of the longue durée within their intellective praxis. Though each thinker settles, at times, on particular identifications of a positive subjectivity, they both work to constantly move past these particular iterations to engagements with the semistillness of the longue durée to make sense of historical reality.

One image Braudel uses to illustrate the longue durée in relation to the history of events is watching fireflies in the night: "their pale lights glowed, went out, shone again, all without piercing the night with any true illumination. So it is with events; beyond their glow, darkness prevails."[33] The history of events is important to both Fanon and Baldwin, yet they are careful to situate the history of events within the larger historical reality to which Braudel refers as the night in his metaphor. Decolonial love manifests for both as a political praxis of forcing one's way into reality, which is expressed in events. Baldwin imploring his nephew to go behind definitions, and Fanon leaving Blida and working for the Front de Libération Nationale (FLN) are both examples of this political praxis. But at the same time, decolonial love names a structure of reality, or a foundation within reality to which all of reality is pulled.

This deep structure of reality that guides political commitments is crucial to a theological approach that emerges from Christian commitments. As Ellacuría and Sobrino have argued, Christian theology begins from historical sites of marginalization and oppression, and from these sites strives to take on the perspective of those whom Sobrino calls "the victims." Communities on the undersides of dominant structures determine the perspective for engaging the world and uncovering revelation within Christian theological reflection. For Ellacuría the possibility of Christian theology rests on the capacity to "face up to the reality" of the world of the poor (enfrentarse con la realidad de los pobres) and the perspectives that emerge in this world. Ellacuría articulates this process in three steps: "grasping what is at stake in reality" (hacerse cargo de la realidad), "assuming responsibility for reality and paying the price for it" (cargar con la realidad), and "taking charge of reality" (encargarse de la realidad).[34] Within this process, theological reflection attends to the reality of suffering and the hope of liberation, both of which are concealed and distorted within modern/colonial rationalities.

In the first dimension of the encounter with reality, the noetic dimension of "grasping what is at stake in reality" (hacerse cargo de la realidad), Ellacuría focuses on the moment of option within reality. Theology has to always come from and be directed toward reality itself, rather than be focused on an idea of reality.[35] Without an orientation toward the theologal dimension of the poor, or to ways in which the world of the poor opens up into a theological pedagogy, theologians are left with what Sobrino calls an "enbourgeoisied" theology—that is, a theology that seeks a stake in the modern world-system. Such a theology chooses "its own sphere of reality, swimming around in it like a fish in water, while ignoring the deeper reality: the reality of the poor and the victims."[36] An enbourgeoisied theology foregoes revelation as a historical task; it attaches itself to a fossilized, objectivist understanding of revelation.[37] It takes the stasis of the modern world-system as its point of departure. For Fanon and Baldwin, the option to take up the intellective praxis of grasping the reality of decolonial love in the limits of the long history of colonial modernity constitutes this first dimension of facing up to reality.

In the ethical dimension of apprehending reality, "assuming responsibility for and paying the price for reality" (cargar con la realidad), the option of place is crucial. Social forces and social interests create intellectual production, such that opting for a particular place has direct implications for articulating the encounter with reality.[38] Because doing theology among the poor is the place where Ellacuría affirms that God is most present from a Christian perspective, assuming responsibility for reality is, on a physical and sensory level, connected to the option for the poor.[39] The struggle Fanon and Baldwin take up to stand in solidarity with those who inhabit the colonial undersides of Western modernity and their option to orient themselves in reality based on this commitment—an orientation of decolonial love demonstrated concretely in Baldwin's run down the hill in Central Park and Fanon's letter of resignation from Blida—expresses this ethical dimension of facing up to reality.

In the praxis-oriented dimension of apprehending reality, "taking charge of reality" (encargarse de la realidad), Ellacuría focuses on human knowing as a praxis, but only insofar as knowledge is verified and concretized through historical praxis.[40] The goal of Christian theology, therefore, is not apologetical, but is instead aimed at collaboration with God's sav-

ing transformation of reality through the call to solidarity with the crucified people, the historical continuation of God's self-offer in Jesus Christ.
Fanon and Baldwin connect the intellective praxis of discovering the reality
of decolonial love within reality with the political praxis of making decolonial love present. Concrete political commitments—for Fanon, writing
combat literature and his work within the FLN, and for Baldwin, writing
to reveal, particularly vis-à-vis historical movements such as the civil rights
and Black Power movements—historicize the vaster reality of decolonial
love in concrete events that contest the modern world-system.

Understanding decolonial love as theologically pedagogic prioritizes an
understanding of revelation connected to eschatology but understood as a
metaphysically dense rather than chronologically determined event. Sobrino refers to a metaphysical notion of eschatology in his understanding
of Jesus' resurrection, which New Testament authors present "as the action
of God by which the eschatological irrupts into history and in which the
true reality of Jesus begins to be made plain."[41] When Sobrino describes
the resurrection "irrupting into history," he uses the term "eschatological"
in two senses. In one sense, the eschatological refers to the end-times in
a temporal sense.[42] In a second sense, which for Sobrino is the primary
sense, the eschatological refers to a metaphysical reality. The eschatological denotes "a manifestation of what the ultimate really is."[43] In this sense,
the eschatological refers to a density within a given historical situation.

Fanon and Baldwin attend to and think from realities that indicate the
density of the historical present. Fanon interprets the Algerians' struggle
for liberation as opening up an encounter with the mystery of the eschaton
because, in their struggle, Algerians forge themselves as a new people as
they live into and shape the reality of decolonial love. The Algerian Revolution sheds the mystification of idols that signify a pseudo-eschatology
within the coloniality of power. For Fanon, a decolonial struggle is a privileged site of a preliminary encounter with an eschatological reality because
it incarnates decolonial love. Decolonial struggle historicizes a way of being human, a way of thinking, and a posture toward reality that collectively
makes up an orientation that allows Algerians to live into an ultimate reality that colonial domination has suppressed.

This sense of the eschatological is equally apparent in the connection between decolonial love and revelation in Baldwin's work. Baldwin's
orientation of decolonial love focuses on the praxis of catalyzing an irruption of reality into a history signified on the terms of colonial modernity. The propagation of the alabaster Christ as a religious image in
the United States has suppressed the reality of the beat and the ability to

encounter and witness to the beat. Communities that have prohibited the elision of the beat—or communities that have held out for the possibility of revelation—have actively struggled against idolatry, and have thus actively opened up the possibility of an an initial encounter with the mystery of an eschatological reality in history. Neither Fanon nor Baldwin, therefore, develop an eschatology that is primarily oriented toward a temporal endpoint, but rather an eschatology that deepens roots in history, drawing out historical encounters with the divine mystery.

Reading Sobrino's christology through orientations of decolonial love can open up a way of encountering an eschatological reality rooted in the historical process of decolonization. Sobrino makes two claims with regard to perceiving the irruption of the eschatological into history that indicate his understanding of the encounter with God in history. On the one hand, an eschatological reality comes from God as grace. Like the resurrection appearances in the New Testament, eschatological realities are initiated "from outside, from God."[44] This language, which points to a faith claim, indicates a deductive element within theological reflection. On the other hand, to grasp what is contained in the presence of the eschatological in history, it is necessary to take on the hope of the victims. This praxis allows those who follow Jesus to "rebuild—with different, though ultimately similar, mediations—the process followed by Israel's faith in a God of resurrection."[45] Thus, a deductive element of faith in a liberating and transcendent God who "gives" revelation goes hand-in-hand with an inductive element of entering into the hope of the victims.[46]

The inductive movement within the process of theological reflection is necessary because theology for Sobrino is ultimately not concerned with gaining knowledge "*about* the resurrection and *about* the disciples' experiences but real experiences *of* the resurrection (and of God)."[47] Theology is not only critical reflection from ultimate principles; it is also—and more fundamentally—the building up of these principles and historical transformation. This is Lloyd's constructive task of holding up the wisdom of the oppressed. For Sobrino, access to God is a physical access, related to the experience of religation, or the experience of being tied back to the theologal reality that, from a Christian perspective, he refers to as God. An encounter with God and God's self-revelation, therefore, is connected to the physical pull of reality, to deepening one's roots in reality. Sobrino specifies this within Christian faith commitments as manifesting in the option for the poor.[48] In other words, Sobrino brings forth an anthropological dimension of faith, rooted in the physical pull toward the theologal dimension of reality, and describes the access to this reality from a Christian and confessional perspective by centralizing the hope of the victims. It is at this point that Christian and decolonial projects can work constructively together. Both work to encounter an eschatological reality through a historically particular avenue in order to open up critical and constructive avenues.

Within the theological understanding of reality Ellacuría and Sobrino provide, revelation develops through the experience of religation. From a Christian perspective, the gravitational pull toward the divine depth of reality comes from the world of the poor as a theologal reality. The struggle to encounter reality is thus centered on an encounter with God that is congruent with entering into the hopes irrupting from the colonial undersides of Western modernity. Decolonial love is one example of the way this theologal reality is manifest historically. Decolonial love provides a way for theologians to attend to the dynamic sense of revelation as God's gradual self-disclosure in history.

Though the way Fanon and Baldwin present and make a wager for decolonial love does not need Christian faith, or does not depend on the christological event, it is also not opposed to Christian faith. Decolonial love unfolds outside the control of Fanon, Baldwin, or any other individual or community. Yet, at the same time, Fanon and Baldwin wager that it comes from a specific place, from those not invested in the modern worldsystem. Here their wager can live with Christian faith. In reading the work of Fanon and Baldwin as theologically pedagogic, I do not intend to subordinate Fanon and Baldwin to Christian claims, or interpret their politics within a Christian framework; rather, I refer to reading them as making a claim about salvation. Salvation, as the next chapter argues, depends on living into decolonial love as revelation. Salvation occurs in the struggle to unveil, encounter, and participate in a sacred reality that exceeds the modern world-system, which is the core of the intellective work of both Fanon and Baldwin. What is perceived as violent in the work of Fanon and Baldwin is a struggle to introduce salvation into a historical context that rejects it in its commitment to the modern/colonial stasis—that is, into a society that already believes, in an idolatrous way, that it has been saved by colonial modernity.

The process of theological thinking that Fanon and Baldwin take up, and that Ellacuría articulates in a more systematic way, involves exposing idols in the task of apprehending reality. Exposing idols entails unveiling the limitations of a perceived salvation in and by colonial modernity in order to open space for a more authentic encounter with reality. Read as theologically pedagogic, the orientations of decolonial love that Fanon and

Baldwin actualize help them to both refuse to idolize particular concepts as spaces or events in which an eschatological reality settles and to stand in relation to a divine mystery. Their bearing witness to this sacred reality shapes them as intellectuals. Read as theological thinkers, Fanon and Baldwin can decolonize salvation and inform a project of re-imagining salvation within colonial modernity.

CHAPTER 7

Decolonizing Salvation

The future of this world depends on everybody in this
room and that future depends on to what extent and
by what means we liberate ourselves from a vocabulary
which now cannot bear the weight of reality.

—"JAMES BALDWIN's National Press Club Speech 1986,"
YouTube, December 22, 2014, https://www.youtube.com/
watch?v=CTjY4rZFY5c&t=1657s

In December 1986, Baldwin concluded his address to the National Press
Club in Washington, DC, from which the epigraph comes, by stating that
"whereas the slave must know the master . . . and the master cannot fool
the slave, the slave can fool the master, *because the master wants to be fooled.*"
Baldwin tried to convince the audience of the danger of this process of
being fooled—that is, of those committed to the advancement of the mod-
ern/colonial project continuing to be fooled, or rather fooling themselves,
in the creation of others who "live quite beyond the confines of the American imagination." He described this as a paralysis infecting an interdepen-
dent world. The future, Baldwin averred, depends on liberation from this
ideological distortion.

The doctrine of salvation is often part of that "vocabulary which cannot
bear the weight of reality," and from which we must be liberated. Decolonizing the image of salvation contributes toward a liberation from vocabulary that allows for the perpetuation of the coloniality of power and a constant process of being "fooled," as well as a liberation for an openness to an
eschatological reality and a bearing witness to the divine mystery.

This chapter proceeds by first mapping three soteriologies oriented toward liberation, from Ignacio Ellacuría, Ivone Gebara, and Marcella Althaus-Reid. It then reads these theologies of salvation through orientations of decolonial love, and vice versa, in view of presenting decolonial love as a historical locus of the encounter with a divine reality and thus as informing the theological image of salvation. It then turns to how the conflict and perceived violence embedded within decolonial love relate to salvation. Decolonial love as a locus of salvation, it argues, includes a posture of violence toward Western modernity and the matrix that supports and legitimizes it. This violence entails letting go of an identity within Western modernity, on the one hand, and an encounter with the divine mystery, on the other.

Salvation in Theologies Oriented Toward Liberation

Ellacuría, Gebara, and Althaus-Reid all claim a new way of doing theology. The new approaches to theology they propose each shape how they reimagine theological concepts. Each theologian's way of doing theology leads to his or her constructive account of salvation. Considering the attitude or posture toward reality from which Ellacuría, Gebara, and Althaus-Reid each imagine salvation and the concrete images of salvation in their work offers points of reference in the movement toward a decolonized image of salvation.

Ignacio Ellacuría: Salvation within the Historical-Theologal Structure of Reality

The way Ellacuría perceives the structure of history allows for a connection between, on the one hand, the praxis of unveiling reality and entering into its deepest dimensions and, on the other, salvation. Ellacuría uses a Christian hermeneutic to ground the imperative to encounter reality. While the orientations of decolonial love in the work of Fanon and Baldwin share this imperative, they demand a posture of attention within reality in ways that do not depend—as it does for Ellacuría—on the christological event.

Ellacuría posits a unity in history between the political and theological, or between liberation and salvation, that precedes the distinction between these terms in theoretical explanations of historical reality. He draws on both the story of the Exodus and the Gospels to demonstrate "that there are not two histories, a history of God and a human history, a sacred and profane history. Rather, there is a single historical reality in which both

God and human beings intervene."[1] Though divine and human actions differ and are important to distinguish, they occur in the same history. In the Exodus narrative, salvation happens through both God's divine action and Moses' human action within the context of the historical struggle of the Israelites. Likewise, in the Gospels, salvation happens both through Jesus as human and through Jesus as divine. In each account, human and divine action happen within a single history.

Ellacuría identifies a problem in the way that the theoretical subdiscipline of soteriology has ended up obscuring the real issue of salvation by separating theoretical discourse on God from real historical experience. There has been a "conceptual separation" within the long tradition of theological ways of thinking, such that concepts within soteriologies have increasingly stood in for reality. This is opposed to the biblical tradition, wherein there is a unity between historical experiences and the understanding of God (recall Prevot's distinction that Ellacuría's work is shaped by biblical faith more than metaphysics). "Truth" has shifted from reality to theological concepts, and this shift has served social and political interests.[2] By unearthing this shift, Ellacuría raises the question of how to understand history vis-à-vis the discipline of theology. Theological discourse, he argues, has obscured the real theologal structure of history. Scripture affirms a primordial experience of historical-theologal existence that theologians have forgotten and obscured. Ellacuría draws theologians back to this experience and interpretive tradition of historical unity as the point of departure, and pushes us to let go of dualistic concepts referring to reality that have been distorted over time. As José Sols Lucia puts it, there has been an error in taking a plurality of concepts used to describe reality articulated within secular reflections as "automatic translations" of reality as such.[3]

Ellacuría's attempt to return to the real theologal structure of history, or the experience of history conceptually before the plurality of concepts that emerge with secular modernity, within a biblically informed Christian perspective, shapes his understanding of the metaphysical density of "historical reality." He provides a theological rationale for the historical-theologal structure of reality in his account of creation:

> Creation can be seen as the grafting (*plasmación*) *ad extra* of the trinitarian life itself, a freely desired grafting. It would not be an idealistic exemplary causality, but an act of communication and self-giving by the divine life itself. This grafting and self-communication has degrees and limits, whereby each thing, within its own limits is a limited way

of being God. This limited way is precisely the nature of each thing. God's communication, the grafting *ad extra* of the divine life, has gone through a long process toward the grafting of that divine life in the human nature of Jesus and ultimately the "return" of all creation to its original source.[4]

A commitment to God who has opened outward, from Godself, profoundly shapes Ellacuría's understanding of reality as structured theologally. This Christian hermeneutic forms his understanding of both humanity and history: "The *theologal* dimension of the created world, which should not be confused with the *theological* dimension, would reside in that presence of the trinitarian life, which is intrinsic to all things, but which in human beings can be apprehended as reality and as the principle of personality."[5] It is because of who God is, in other words, that we have the capacity to stand within and apprehend history as a theologal reality.

Through this lens shaped by a Christian understanding of God as trinitarian, Ellacuría opens a way of understanding the absolute dimension of all of creation: "All created things are a limited way of being God, and the human being in particular is a small God because the human being is a relative absolute, an acquired absolute."[6] In postulating both history and the human person as relative absolutes open to divine presence, Ellacuría's work finds a point of connection with Fanon's claim that challenging the colonial world requires "the frantic affirmation of an originality claimed as absolute."[7] Ellacuría and Fanon are not, of course, saying the same thing here. Fanon operates out of an image of the absolute as a new humanity, while Ellacuría is committed to the Christian God as an image of the absolute. But Ellacuría's unpacking of a theologal-historical structure through Christian terms recognizes a similar dimension of reality to which Fanon appeals. Both thinkers' appeals to the absolute allow for the absolute to be both historical and transcendent in a way that informs where they understand the locus of salvation to be, particularly within a modern/colonial context.

Ellacuría couches his understanding of salvation within the way he concepetualizes historical reality and its theologal structure. He connects revelation with salvation, and sees the history of revelation to be, at its core, a history of salvation.[8] The mode of God's self-revelation, as laid out in scripture, is a history of salvation. God has chosen history as the locus of salvation and has structured history theologally:

> History can engender salvation . . . if God so wills it and to the degree
> that God wills it. This does not happen extrinsically to history, because

history itself, with its own structure, brings forth salvation from the womb without changing its structural elements and maintaining all its appearance as historical reality. This of course presupposes that history has been chosen by God as the midwife of salvation and that in that election, it has been radically elevated to the mission for which it is chosen.[9]

As such, history itself is not sufficient as the subject of salvation: history as salvation history depends on God and on the appearance of salvation as historicized salvation.[10] Because of the action of God, history takes on an "extraordinary metaphysical density" that manifests in a theologal structure.[11] In line with his understanding of the theologal structure of history, Ellacuría commits to history as transcendentally open to God in a way that allows all of creation, and especially humanity, "to participate in God's own Trinitarian life."[12]

Ellacuría sees Christ to be that which allows for the presence of an absolute reality, transcendence, and ultimately salvation within history. He affirms that "God has spoken definitively through the Son," such that "all revelation and tradition must be placed within this context."[13] Further, the openness of history depends on the incarnation. It is only "because God has first become present within it" that history has a transcendent nature.[14] This leads Ellacuría to posit Jesus as a unique locus of salvation:

> Salvation by definition is the ever-increasing presence of God in human life and in human history. God is the principle of holiness and happiness, principle of fullness and progress, Alpha and Omega of human beings and of history. The truth of this God is the incarnate *Logos*, and the way to God's life *is Jesus alone*, who died and was resurrected for our sins and our salvation.[15]

To move toward a decolonial theology, which offers decolonial options rather than a mission, it is helpful to read Ellacuría's soteriology through the orientations of decolonial love that Fanon and Baldwin lay out. Salvation depends on the christological event for Ellacuría because the theologal structure of reality depends on the christological event. Reading Fanon and Baldwin as theological thinkers implies, however, more humble theological claims: an orientation of decolonial love sees the "darkness" of history that Braudel articulates, and commits to a posture with respect to this darkness but does not name a necessary cause of its structure, as Ellacuría does with the Christ event. The condition for the possibility of the mystery is not, in the work of Fanon and Baldwin, Jesus Christ or any other confessional claim.

As I argued in the third chapter, Ellacuría's theological-philosophical framework provides the possibility of a decolonial response. In a similar way, Ellacuría's soteriology provides the possibility for a decolonized image of salvation. He opens up the loci from which salvation can emerge, yet at the same time limits the cause of the possibility of a human encounter with an eschatological reality to faith in Jesus Christ. From an ecofeminist perspective, Gebara pushes Ellacuría's position further by collapsing persisting dualisms within his theological epistemology.

IVONE GEBARA: SALVATION IN RELATEDNESS

Like Ellacuría, Gebara engages in theological reflection in order to respond to a particular reality, but in doing so, she draws on different sources for theological reflection than Ellacuría did. Gebara's soteriological framework is similar to Ellacuría's understanding of historical reality in the ways she perceives the divine depth of reality, but also departs from his notion of reality as historical reality in decentralizing the christological event. In this process, Gebara's soteriological framework opens up the possibility to articulate decolonial love as a historical site in which we encounter the eschatological mystery, and thus, from which we experience salvation.

Though Gebara acknowledges she is profoundly shaped by Latin American liberation theology,[16] she takes issue with the claim among some liberation theologians that they have developed a "new" way of doing theology. Gebara's basic critique of liberation theology concerns its understanding of history, which she takes to be in line with how Eurocentered theologies have understood history.[17] Gebara reads Gutiérrez as maintaining an epistemological structure in which "[t]he judgment on history is still of a transcendent nature, and is defined by the fact that Christian revelation precedes it."[18] While I have argued that the way Ellacuría conceptualizes reality within a historical-theologal structure offers an opportunity to get out of the dualism between history and transcendence, Gebara breaks with what she calls the traditional, patriarchal epistemology of theology by drawing on a different philosophical foundation. The nature of Gebara's rejection of Eurocentered theological frameworks, which is not indebted to a biblical faith in the ways that Ellacuría's approach is, can further open up cracks in theological epistemologies in ways that allow for decolonized images of salvation.

Gebara's alternative, ecofeminist epistemology rests on her concept of relatedness. While Gebara relies on relatedness throughout her theological work, she is clear that the way the concept of relatedness shapes her theological anthropology grounds all other theological concepts, including her way of imagining salvation.[19] Whereas Ellacuría starts with scripture as a justification for his philosophical-theological understanding of history, Gebara builds an understanding of the human person out of the experience of relatedness, which then grounds her understanding of history.

There are a couple of tensions in Gebara's understanding of the human person in terms of relatedness that provide the basis for her understanding of salvation. First, there is a tension between universality and particularity. Gebara critiques the tendency within Western theology to exaggerate what might initially be helpful concepts, such as human autonomy or freedom, or an essence that connects all humans, such that they cease to be helpful. Western perspectives, in other words, have some value but become limited when they exaggerate, absolutize, and, in a sense, universalize, their concepts and insights.[20] When Gebara develops an understanding of the human person in an ecofeminist perspective, she hangs on to a universalist perspective. Relatedness simply *is*. It is the "primary reality" and "foundational reality of all that is or can exist," and is "the constitutive relationship of communion we have with all beings."[21] Relatedness exists beyond our consciousness of it.[22] It is our "earthly condition," or that reality that shapes us as part of the larger cosmos.[23] We can discern that relatedness does indeed exist because it is revealed within the natural order, within our experience of reality.[24] In this way that Gebara uses relatedness, it makes a universal claim about how reality is—or even the "nature" of reality or the cosmos.

At the same time, and in contrast to the way the Western theological tradition has absolutized and exaggerated concepts, Gebara develops "a more open-ended attitude toward our established concepts. This means accepting the fact that none of these concepts is more than a perspective, a tentative point of view adopted in order to deal with everyday life and with the broader sweep of history."[25] This way that Gebara develops relatedness suggests a perspective born in a particular context—which is, of course, not to say that such a perspective does not have implications outside that context: "We can begin only from the limited point that is ourselves. So it is our own situation that prompts us to build a discourse that begins with our world and with ourselves."[26] In this sense, relatedness grows out of our very limited capacities to know other human beings and our environments.[27]

This tension between universality and particularity within the concept of relatedness opens up a second tension—between relatedness as a descriptive and normative category.[28] When using relatedness as a descriptive term in close connection with the universalist perspective above (i.e., relatedness as a primary, foundational, constitutive reality), Gebara is explicit that relatedness "*is not* a synonym for moral goodness; rather, it points to the vital power of the interconnection among all things, independent of any anthropological ethical judgment we might make about them."[29] In this sense, relatedness describes how reality is; it does not make a claim about how things should be. As a descriptive category, relatedness becomes a metaphysical category, or a concept that helps us grasp how the reality that we encounter actually is.

At the same time, Gebara also uses relatedness to make ethical claims. Reality itself (that is, relatedness) implies an ethics. The reality and experience of relatedness implies an ethics in a different way than a religious creed implies an ethics because the former is not a rule that's created, but is simply the way things are, or the way we experience reality to be.[30] This experience of relatedness contains an "ethical dimension" that "implies respect for all kinds of living beings [and] can be apprehended by human beings in the very act of welcoming the extraordinary relatedness that animates all living things."[31] It makes a claim about how reality ought to be and how humans ought to act within reality. In this sense, relatedness is an epistemological claim as well, or a claim about the best way to understand reality.

Relatedness, as it exists as constitutive of reality and as an ethical claim, grounds Gebara's understanding of salvation. The concept of relatedness drives Gebara's understanding of Jesus Christ, the cross, and the resurrection. Whereas Ellacuría begins with christology and then makes sense of reality in light of who Christ is (that is, proceeding from christology to articulating the historical-theologal structure of reality), Gebara works in the other direction, making sense of Christ through the experience of reality as relatedness.[32] Relatedness allows Gebara to "open up our understanding of 'salvation' to a broader process," and to one that focuses on the material and quotidian nature of salvation.[33] Jesus is important for Gebara, but she sees him within the more fundamental concept of relatedness. She ultimately holds to "a more biocentric understanding of salvation" in which the earth "is both the subject and object of salvation."[34]

Gebara shares Ellacuría's understanding of the theologal structure of reality but doesn't posit Jesus as the unique historicization of this eschatological reality or as the event that allows humans to encounter the eschatological dimension of history. Rather, Gebara affirms that the incarnation "is more than Jesus of Nazareth."[35] Jesus is, for Gebara, a "metaphor of the divine presence" or a "symbol," rather than a metaphysical reality.[36] There is no "salvific uniqueness" of Jesus; he is rather a symbol of the divine presence in all of creation.[37] Salvation resides in the relatedness that is constitutive of all reality. Thus, both Ellacuría and Gebara imagine a transcendental openness of history but differ on the cause of this historical structure that allows for salvation. Ellacuría grounds this christologically, such that Christ shapes the meaning of history and of persons, whereas Gebara sees Christ as an example of a historical structure that precedes Christ.

MARCELLA ALTHAUS-REID: SALVATION IN QUEER HOLINESS

Like Ellacuría and Gebara, Althaus-Reid offers a way of doing theology that she understands to question the hermeneutical and epistemological foundations of theological ways of thinking within European modernity. She refers to this alternative way of doing theology as "Indecent" or "Queer." Her Indecent theology seeks to explicitly crack open modern/colonial confines to which theological discourse is often relegated, and discover the foundations of the experience of salvation in material realities. In doing so, Althaus-Reid offers an approach to theology in which realities such as decolonial love that exceed the imaginative limits of colonial modernity are more explicitly theologically pedagogic than they are in the soteriologies of Ellacuría or Gebara.

Althaus-Reid critiques ways that systematic theology has been deeply shaped by the introduction of "a systemic sexuality" in the European conquest of the Americas. She argues that Latin American liberation theologians, as "decent theologians," have in large part bought into this systematic theology shaped by a Euorcentered systemic sexuality as a guiding epistemological structure.[38] Althaus-Reid pejoratively refers to Enrique Dussel,[39] Gustavo Gutiérrez,[40] Jon Sobrino and Ignacio Ellacuría,[41] and Ivone Gebara,[42] as decent theologians, and could certainly have placed Clodovis Boff in this category as well. Decent theologians obscure real human praxis and relationships through the discourse of theology.[43] Liberation theology, like all theologies, is a sexual theology but relies on "sexual categories and heterosexual binary systems" brought to the Americas in the Conquista such as "the virginal conception by Mary or the theocratic filiation of Jesus."[44] Althaus-Reid argues that introducing social analysis centered on class never allowed liberation theology to break with these sexual categories concretized in the Conquista—that is, class analysis never dealt with the epistemological ramifications of the construction of gender within the modern/colonial moment. The result of this failure on the part of liberation theologians is that they have only been able to articulate idealist

theologies that easily accept the systemic sexuality formalized in the Conquista and the ways this shapes discourse on the sacred.[45] Liberation theologians have used idealist and Eurocentric ideologies shaped by systemic
sexuality to signify the subject of their theology: the poor.[46] In this process,
Althaus-Reid sees liberation theology to become an apologetic theology
that attempts to reconcile Latin American realities with European sexual
logics and theological frameworks.[47]

When Althaus-Reid turns to the theological image of salvation, she uses
a materialist starting point to critique the ways it has been constructed
within liberation theologies. She uses the image of "Queer redemptions"
to draw attention to alternative geographical sites and routes to God's
grace. Queer redemptions emerge from revelatory loving relationships
that "are not necessarily translatable into imperial theological language."[48]
In the movement to revelatory relationships outside the scope of what she
calls "Colonial Theology," Althaus-Reid moves into the realm of what
she calls "demonology," which starts with "rebellious spirits" outside the
constructed sacred order.[49] Concrete forms of relationships that cannot
be represented within modern/colonial knowledge frameworks are, in
Althaus-Reid's theology, instances of God's self-offer in history, or God's
grace. These relationships, rather than the more vague signifier of "the
world of the poor," are the historical sites of encounter with a divine mystery. They are the sites of the historical experience of salvation, and thus,
the sites that generate theological reflection.

Althaus-Reid understands salvation as a process of disrupting the repetition of an imperial past and imperial knowledge. While she acknowledges
that salvation can function as the alabaster Christ does in Baldwin's work,
it can also symbolize the embrace of a rebellious demonology.[50] As a reality
that moves past ways colonial theology is limited in its capacity to bear the
weight of reality, Althaus-Reid envisions salvation emerging from queer
relationships, or from rebellious ways of loving that subvert norms within
colonial theology. She locates this claim christologically, in the "kenosis of
sexuality" that Jesus' incarnation represents and in the disruption of a pattern of eternal repetition that the incarnation actualized.[51]

There is a "holiness" that emerges within sites of the demonic, within
rebellious spirits, that disrupts, rather than retains, colonial theology and
its laws. Althaus-Reid turns to "Queer holiness" as an option for a historical project of resistance to the imposition of redemption as retention.[52]
Queer holiness is an unrepresentable reality that stands outside the colonial processes of duplication to which Christian theology is indebted.
Queer holiness resides in the places where capitalist spirituality cracks. It

plays a dissenting role, emerging from sites outside of conversion to culturally dominant conceptions of salvation. It embraces those spaces where the god of colonial theology is perceived to be absent.[53] Queer holiness elects options that are "alternatives to salvation."[54] In turning to queer holiness as a form of relation emerging in the imaginative limits of colonial modernity, Althaus-Reid opens up the possibility of a theological posture that takes decolonial love as theologically pedagogic in more explicit ways than Ellacuría or Gebara.

Decolonial Love as a Locus of Salvation

Ellacuría, Gebara, and Althaus-Reid all recognize problems in the ways the doctrine of salvation has been presented and the ways that it functions in a modern/colonial world. At the same time, however, they don't give up on the praxis of struggling to encounter an eschatological dimension of reality. They each imagine and articulate anew an image of salvation linked to history and revelation as a way to respond to the modern world-system. Bringing the ways Ellacuría, Gebara, and Althaus-Reid articulate the theological image of salvation into conversation with the decolonial love of Fanon and Baldwin as theologically pedagogic can offer a decolonized image of salvation that more explicitly confronts the coloniality of power.

DECOLONIAL LOVE AS A SITE OF THE HISTORICAL-THEOLOGAL STRUCTURE OF REALITY

For Ellacuría, Jesus' life, the cross, and God's action of resurrection ground the capacity to encounter the theologal structure of historical reality. This christological basis becomes more concrete in Sobrino's christology developed after Ellacuría's death. Sobrino's starting point for understanding salvation in the reality of Jesus of Nazareth as liberator of the oppressed prompts the centrality of conflict in Sobrino's christology.[55] During his life, Jesus stands in a special relationship to the ultimate realities of the kingdom of God and to God as Father. Jesus' relationship to the kingdom produces conflict insofar as Jesus proclaims and initiates the kingdom within a historical context opposed to the kingdom. As such, Jesus' practice in relation to the kingdom is a struggle against specific historical forces.[56] Without this struggle that emerges from Jesus taking a stand with the poor and against their oppressors, and without recognizing how the "Kingdom stands in *combative relation* to the anti-Kingdom," Jesus' love is rendered abstract.[57] Jesus' relationship to the ultimate reality of God produces conflict because such an orientation allows Jesus to grasp "the theologal-idolatric structure of reality," and thereby oppose, at an ultimate and fundamental level, the reality of the anti-kingdom.[58] At stake in Jesus' controversies is "a vision of the reality of God."[59] Thus, Sobrino argues that the christocentric nature of Christian salvation must be understood as conflictive if Jesus' two fundamental relations, to the kingdom of God and to God, are taken seriously.

Following Ellacuría's way of doing theology, the setting from which theologians work plays a crucial role in Sobrino's process of discerning the content of Jesus' love, which manifests as conflict laden. A Christian faith commitment implies engaging in the work of theology from "a particular historical situation in which God and Christ are believed to be continuing to make themselves present; this is therefore a theologal setting rather than a theological setting."[60] This "social-theologal setting" is "the world of the poor," which takes on the status of a formal object of theology, or as a site that provides the basic perspective for theological reflection.[61] As such, Sobrino's christological starting point catalyzes a movement to the world of the poor as the locus of encounter with Christ and thus as an epistemically generative site.[62] As a formal object of theology, the "world of the poor," or "the victims" clarify the conflictual aspect of Christianity.

Taking on the task of theological reflection from the world of the poor motivates a focus on Jesus' cross, which allows for a further specification of the theologal dimension of reality, as well as a further elaboration of how the Christian understanding of revelation manifests through conflict. Jesus was killed because, within a climate of persecution, he put forth an exclusive alternative in opposition to the status quo, namely, the kingdom of God.[63] Christian faith has subsequently found meaning in the death of Jesus because the tradition has linked the cross to salvation. Sobrino locates this meaning by referring back to Jesus' life, and seeing the cross as a consequence of his life but also as a reality that reveals something new about God. The cross shows the credibility of God's love to the victims.[64] The theologal reality of the cross allows Sobrino, following Ellacuría, to affirm contemporary sites of crucifixion as "social-theologal realities." In making this claim, Sobrino argues that "[t]he mere existence of the crucified people is what can—and in the last resort the only thing that can—unmask the lie by which the world's reality is concealed."[65] The reality of crucifixion, in other words, is a conflictual reality that both exposes the idolatry of the modern world-system and reveals the ultimate character of reality.

For Sobrino, Jesus' resurrection is the irruption of an eschatological reality into history, which refers Christians back to Jesus' life and the cross, and offers new insight into the theologal dimension of reality. The resurrection provides hope for the crucified. The hope of those who are crucified in the contemporary context is the key hermeneutical lens through which Sobrino understands the resurrection: "slot[ting] ourselves into" the hope of the victims allows theologians to "rebuild—with different, though ultimately similar, mediations—the process followed by Israel's faith in a God of resurrection."[66] From this perspective, Sobrino focuses on how the resurrection indicates again the conflictual aspect of Christianity. God's action of resurrection is against humans' action of crucifixion, and the dialectic between God and idols is essential to God's revelation.[67] As such, Christianity "is a religion of struggle and conflict, given the theologal structure of history, shot through as it is with the God of life and the idols of death."[68] The theologal structure of history is clarified within the specific religion of Christianity through conflict. Conflict—and taking a particular side in conflict—is the locus of both divine revelation and the divine gift of salvation.

Reading the work of Fanon and Baldwin through the historical-theologal structure that Ellacuría and Sobrino develop, decolonial love becomes a site that clarifies the theologal structure of history by illuminating idols and concretizing a historical commitment. The way Sobrino sees the historical Jesus to clarify this structure through conflict grounds the continuity of such a move in the Christian tradition, in both the understanding of history and, as I will demonstrate below, in the understanding of an encounter with the divine in sites of historical conflict.

At the same time, taking decolonial love as a starting point opens up a perspective beyond the Jesus-centric focus of Ellacuría and Sobrino. Whereas the way of doing theology that Ellacuría and Sobrino propose would suggest that decolonial love is a site of salvation because of the historical and metaphysical reality of Jesus, understanding salvation from the decolonial love of Fanon and Baldwin does not depend on Jesus. In the work of Fanon and Baldwin, decolonial love is a historical site of salvation in itself. The movement of history that decolonial love propels is the locus of salvation in a way that is neither opposed to nor dependent on Jesus as the Christ.

DECOLONIAL LOVE AS A SITE OF RELATEDNESS

In Gebara's work, relatedness as a metaphysical category, as "something that is primary, that constitutes our being," leads to relatedness as an epistemological category, as "a complete acceptance of our corporal historic reality."[69] This tension provides a framework for understanding the way decolonial love functions in the work of Fanon and Baldwin, and indicates how decolonial love can be theologically pedagogic without depending on a christological move. Decolonial love can be understood as both a metaphysical and epistemological, or normative, category and as residing within this tension in a similar way as Gebara's understanding of relatedness. Recognizing decolonial love to function in this way brings up a further question about where God is within the context of salvation. Reading decolonial love through the way that Gebara develops relatedness can begin to respond to this question.

Gebara closely identifies relatedness and God—to the point that she calls God relatedness.[70] As relatedness, God is both physical and metaphysical, both continuity and difference, and both the material nature of reality and the opening and possibility of reality.[71] Ultimately, God cannot be "a pure essence existing in itself," but rather "God is *relationship*."[72] God is "concomitant with," rather than existing before, creation.[73] In rejecting a personal god, Gebara opts for the language of "a divine milieu" over the typical way of speaking of God within liberation theology as "the God of life."[74] This way of understanding God is particularly amenable to the theological pedagogy of the orientations of decolonial love that Fanon and Baldwin offer. It also allows for a significant response to the modern world-system that Quijano describes with the concept of the coloniality of power.

In grounding her theological thought on an understanding of the human person re-imagined within relatedness, Gebara indicates a way to understand decolonial love as establishing an understanding of the human person that grounds subsequent reflection. Fanon calls attention to a site from which the human person emerges. The new humanity is expressed within the way the nationalist struggle historicizes an ultimate reality, or within the "spiritual community founded in suffering" that emerges in the Algerian Revolution.[75] Baldwin implores his nephew to "go behind the white man's definitions."[76] For both thinkers, the human person emerges in conflict with the modern world-system. The desire of decolonial love opposes inclusion into that system. Fanon's nationalist struggle and Baldwin's projects of going behind definitions, smashing mirrors,[77] and taking off masks,[78] open up a foundation of the human person beyond categories of Western modernity.

Fanon and Baldwin offer decolonial love as a description of reality and of the human person underneath the significations within Western modernity. Relationships within "spiritual communities" and without the distortions of masks, mirrors, and definitions, are loci where the depths of reality can be encountered. This is the universal and descriptive aspect of decolonial love. At the same time, an encounter with reality involves a praxis: the praxis of nationalist struggle, and the praxis of tearing off masks, smashing mirrors, and going behind definitions implies normative claims. Decolonial love thus both describes the historical structure in which the human is situated and makes a claim about human action as a process of encountering that structure. The structure of reality is already given as salvific, though the coloniality of power—as one way to describe historical oppression—distorts this structure and creates the need for a specific praxis of encountering reality.

Gebara's use of relatedness likewise offers a way for decolonial love to challenge manifestations of the coloniality of power on the level of knowledge. With relatedness, Gebara steps beyond absolute claims about Jesus' metaphysical status with regard to human salvation without throwing out Jesus as a symbol and metaphor of salvation. Salvation is not caused by or dependent on the metaphysical quality of Jesus; rather, it is grounded in the material experience of reality, which Gebara describes as relatedness. Likewise, while decolonial love describes reality, is constitutive of reality, and ultimately is salvation, salvation is not dependent on the historically specific ways Fanon and Baldwin express orientations that I interpret as decolonial love; rather, decolonial love expresses a fundamental experience of reality, one that moves past dominant epistemic categories within the coloniality of power, and it is this experience of reality that grounds salvation. Decolonial love as a theologically pedagogic category can disentangle theological concepts from what Aimé Césaire referred to as the "gobbledygook" in which the modern Western intellectual tradition, including Christian theology, often works.[79]

When decolonial love unsettles the way the coloniality of power manifests on levels of being and knowledge, it opens up the possibility for a decolonized eschatology. Theology, Gebara argues, "is particularly the domain of the symbolic production of meaning and a special place for reproducing the dominant social and cultural structure."[80] Theology, and specifically soteriology, is a colonial task insofar as it aids the stabilization of Western modernity and its basis of the coloniality of power through processes of inclusion. Gebara's concept of relatedness, however, allows for a decolonized image of salvation: an image that opens up to an alternative way of imagining and encountering reality outside the interests of colonial modernity. Decolonial love offers the hope of the "end of the world,"[81] and ultimately a commitment to a different sort of eschatology, wherein, as Fanon asserts, "things, in the most materialist sense, have resumed their rightful place."[82] Within this hope, the orientation of decolonial love includes options for historical praxis, or for ways of historicizing this orientation.

Decolonial Love as a Site of Queer Holiness

Whereas Ellacuría employs a substantivist ontology in which he sees the world of the poor as the site of divine revelation, Gebara leans toward a social-relational ontology, perceiving relationships as revelatory of the divine. Althaus-Reid takes this latter perspective even further, and in doing so contributes to a basis for a decolonized image of salvation. Althaus-Reid specifically perceives loving relationships as revelatory. Ways of loving can exceed the limitations modern/colonial structures have put on the divine mystery, and in exceeding these limitations can both reveal and be loci of salvation.

Althaus-Reid consistently asserts that human relationships are theologically pedagogic.[83] She agrees with liberation theologians such as Ellacuría that what we know of God is from how God self-reveals in history, but she sees liberation theologies to have missed "that such revelation of God in history is also a revelation made *through the history of human relationships, and intimate relations*": God's revelation is in "the native's orgy" and "the perceived tainted vulgarity of the Other's intimate loving exchanges."[84] This is different than seeing the being and existence of marginalized peoples (for example, the crucified people or the world of the poor) as the historical continuation of Jesus Christ, as is the case in Ellacuría's theology.

In Althaus-Reid's proposal of divine revelation in intimate relationships, indecent loving relationships—and this includes human liberative action, which is always done in a relationship to a people—are theologically pedagogic. Revelation occurs in queer holiness and exceeds the institutional delineation of God:

> what we have here in essence is how Queer holiness finds God, as a
> stranger at the gates of Hegemonic Theology, amongst loving expres-
> sions of relationships at the margins of the defined decent and proper
> in Christianity. Indecent love becomes pedagogic because it teaches the
> difference between the church as a heterosexual colony (or neo-colony)
> and the church as the Queer *Kingdom* where the love which exceeds
> institutions (as God exceeds Godself in Christ and in the Trinity)
> knows more and knows better about alternative projects for justice
> and peace.[85]

Queer holiness and indecent love are the spaces where the Christianity/ idolatry binary constructed on the terms of the modern world-system is thrown out. Indecent love—and within the historical context of the colo- niality of power, decolonial love—is a way of loving that rejects standard paths toward salvation within Christian imaginaries entangled with the historical matrix of the coloniality of power.

Rather than reordering relationships to fit into a concept of divine rev- elation, Althaus-Reid allows queer holiness and indecent love to be theo- logically pedagogic. She frames the need to engage queer holiness and indecent love in Marxian terms: without a theologically pedagogic role of queer holiness and indecent love, theological work becomes alienated from "the workers." The textualization and disciplinization of queerness as a liberative force that becomes "valuable in a theological market" loses the original force queerness has in history.[86] Althaus-Reid turns to material and epistemological sites that have been rendered indecent by the church, and resists interpreting these sites "from our central, doctrinal thoughts adapted to the margins."[87] She avoids the standard tendency among theo- logians to abstract material experiences of suffering and appropriate suf- fering as "the intellectual property of the owner of the intellectual system of production, the theologian."[88] Against this tendency, Althaus-Reid ar- gues that immediate claims about lived experience are already theological claims:

> The real suffering of the oppressed . . . becomes an item of merchan- dise which, following Marx's analysis, becomes an abstraction separated from the system which nurtures and locates it. . . . The wealth of the theological Western bourgeoisie is then represented in the Systematic Theology which has forgotten in its abstractness the living suffering and praxis of the oppressed which precedes it, that is, the real "theo- logians" who are the people who reflect and act from their sufferings under the theo/ideological structures of oppression.[89]

When professional theologians (to continue the link with Marxism, the "owners of the means of production") sever the connection between the oppressed, "the workers," and the sacred, they deny the theologically peda- gogic role of historical responses to oppression. In an effort to "own" theo- logical reflection, theologians sever theological discourse from the the- ologal dimension of reality that is encountered and brought out in history. When the discipline of theology is construed within a market logic, the op- pressed lose their right to produce discourse. In other words, theological discourse gets alienated from those struggling against the modern/colonial world-system. Communities on the undersides of Western modernity can provide a voice, but not a thought system that supports theological claims.[90] Boff's separation of theological epistemology into three distinct mediations serves this process of alienation.

This process of alienation is a core element of the apparatus of colonial modernity. It is a pernicious effect of the operation of the coloniality of power on the epistemic level that maintains the lack of ontological resistance to which Fanon refers. Althaus-Reid addresses the lived experience of alienation by broadening the understanding of revelation to that which "reveals (unveils, undresses) God in our historical circumstances, and assumes a materialist twist in our understanding," rather than holding to "the almost mediumistic art of pulling down a Platonic idea of an abstract absolute idea of God."[91] To think theologically from queer holiness and indecent love, rather than primarily from theological concepts concretized within Eurocentered intellectual traditions, assumes this "materialist twist."

Reading decolonial love as occupying the central place of queer holiness within Althaus-Reid's soteriology allows for an understanding of decolonial love as a site of salvation that affirms historical motion. Jesus occupies a central place for Althaus-Reid but in a different way than how the Christ event indicates an irruption of an eschatological reality into history for Ellacuría and Sobrino, or how Christ functions as an example of relatedness for Gebara. Grounded in a relational ontology, Althaus-Reid affirms a dialogical christology that is open and in process. Her christology operates from an anchor in material reality but never definitively stabilizes an understanding of liberation or Christ. For Althaus-Reid, Christ is "made" in the dialogue between a subjugated people and the Jesus they interpret in scripture, similar to the dialogue between Jesus and the Syrophoenician woman in the New Testament.[92] Jesus, as a "messiah in process," entails "becoming Christ in a process of popular conscientization where the roles are reversed, and it is the poor people and the suffering women who teach him, with their questions, their rejections and their proposals, what it means to be God in the midst of the poor."[93] This is the theological pedagogy to which Althaus-Reid refers. The gospels for Althaus-Reid are a "part of an incomplete process of conscientization," and communities construct Christ as a communitarian rather than an individual messiah in the opening of praxes that break historical stasis.[94] This model of a "flowing christology" that grounds salvation in community leads Kristien Justaert to argue that for Althaus-Reid, "Jesus Christ is no longer a male subject, but a dynamic collective of individuals who are not considered to be subjects (e.g. poor women). The 'collective Jesus' evolves continually (in space and in time) in a process of becoming-Messiah. Wherever this process takes place, Jesus Christ is alive among us."[95] The collective Jesus as a process of "becoming-Messiah" is, therefore, a fluid and communal construction, rather than a singular event or metaphysical principle. This relational process, grounded in a flowing christology, is for Althaus-Reid the always-historicized encounter with salvation.

Violence, Salvation, and Decolonial Love

Both Fanon and Baldwin take up a praxis of creating the possibilities to encounter the mystery of an eschatological reality in history. Decolonial love is a historical sign that expresses something decisive about the divine, opening up the possibility of encounter with the divine mystery, and thus salvation. Fanon frames this encounter as the new world and new humanity that are forged within the context of the Algerian Revolution. Baldwin describes it as the revelation of the fundamental character of reality and of relationships within history that are concealed in the historical quest to legitimize "America." Both thinkers also recognize the violence of this encounter. Exposing idols in order to open up the possibility to participate in the depth of a divine mystery requires shattering the significations of reality that the modern/colonial matrix has concretized—in the "Greco-Roman pedestal," the "zone of nonbeing," the "alabaster Christ," the "masks," the "mirrors." Precisely for this reason, both thinkers work to encounter the mystery of an eschatological reality in history in a praxis of decolonial love that is often perceived as violent.

If decolonial love historicizes the theologal character of reality, decolonial love also opens an encounter with God in history, or actualizes a historical praxis that Sobrino describes as "overcoming the distance between God and humans."[96] Connecting decolonial love and salvation brings us to the question of how to understand normativity—for example, in terms of ethics, Christian doctrine, liberation, or love—within an encounter with, and the subsequent articulation of, salvation. The question of what becomes normative is particularly germane in the connection of violence and love, which both Fanon and Baldwin affirm in different ways. Jorge A. Aquino has illuminated the complexity of the acceptability of violence within Christian theology vis-à-vis the question of norms in arguing that the role of love in revolutionary action is "ambivalent." Aquino describes historical claims of love to constantly fluctuate between authentic love and violence.[97] He considers violence to be outside the realm of love, and argues for the need to confront the ambivalences within love that allow for violence. He thus challenges theologians to deal with how tactics represented as within the realm of love in fact allow for different sorts of violence.

Because of the closeness of their orientations of decolonial love to conflict and even violence, Fanon and Baldwin show the strength and perceptivity of Aquino's argument regarding the ambivalence of love and also push the understanding of this ambivalence further. Aquino notes a set of elisions in Chela Sandoval's work on decolonial love. Her work obscures the ambivalence between love and violence in authorizing tactics among the oppressed that are uncomfortably close to tactics of capitalist hegemony. It fails to deal with the question of the formation of those Sandoval refers to as "U.S. third world feminists" within elite intellectual circles. And, Sandoval doesn't fully consider the similarities between the methodologies of differential consciousness that she affirms and the methodologies of late capitalism.[98] The crux of Aquino's argument is that "liberation theologians have more squarely set up shop in the midst of the poor" than those who practice the differential consciousness Sandoval draws out, which has had the result that liberation theologians have "more systematically explored the ambivalences and elisions that haunt Sandoval's work."[99] Aquino's goal is not to solve these elisions he uncovers in Sandoval's work but to be clear about the closeness of love and violence. He aims to avoid the tendency of academic elites to claim for ourselves the "authorship" of the oppressed and tries to distinguish tactics of late capitalism and love.

Fanon and Baldwin theorize love with careful attention to the ambivalences between love and violence, and in doing so they push Aquino's understanding of the ambivalence of love and violence further. Unlike Aquino, neither Fanon nor Baldwin set up love and violence as polarities. Aquino defines love and violence in a way that in large part produces ambivalences within a paradigm of mutual exclusivity:

> Revolutionary violence typically arises from materialist articulations of self- or class-interest seeking to disrupt or displace the institutions or actors who uphold an oppressive regime, often through violent means. On the other extreme lie strategies rooted in the value of self-abnegation, or *agape*, which carry on acts of nonviolent (self-) sacrifice in the name of a large collective good or utopian ideal, but without commitment to violence.[100]

By locating revolutionary violence and *agape* as "extremes," and love as "without commitment to violence," Aquino suggests a paradigm that strongly differs from what Fanon and Baldwin present in their orientations of decolonial love. Unlike Aquino, who sees revolutionary change that does not exclude violence, on the one hand, and Christian *agape*, on the other, to be opposed,[101] neither Fanon nor Baldwin argue for any fundamental contradiction between processes of revolutionary social change—even if they are violent—and love. Whereas Aquino sees "love as an axis of revolutionary praxis [to be] compromised by the question of how to overcome systems of political economy established through violent means,"[102] Fanon and Baldwin do not suggest any compromise in love by the actions of those not seeking inclusion into the modern world-system that are perceived as violent. And, to make a stronger claim, both Fanon and Baldwin show that love is in fact compromised if nonviolence is understood as intrinsic to love, or if violence and love are seen as mutually exclusive.[103]

Understanding the orientations of decolonial love that Fanon and Baldwin offer as theologically pedagogic can lead to a difficult claim: when violence functions within orientations of decolonial love, violence itself has the capacity to make present the theologal. This is a vexing claim—one that does not fit within the fences of a paradigm that holds to an essential relationship between nonviolence and a Christian understanding of divinity or between nonviolence and salvation. It is, however, a necessary claim when taking orientations of decolonial love to be theologically pedagogic.

To use Fanonian terms to articulate a theological project, revolutionary love often calls on a degree of violence to smash to smithereens the material possibilities of God-talk that strategically conceals and distorts reality.[104] Taking seriously Ellacuría's connection of the material and formal objects of theology, such that historical reality provides a foundation for the theological task that is exemplified in Sobrino's "way of the addressee" means that theological reflection cannot avoid or seek to contain this type of violent force that manifests on the material level. In the violence of a historical irruption against the coloniality of power, theologians can perceive divinity incarnate in history. The encounter with the sacred happens in both the violence that opens space for the divine and in the encounter with the divine. Both elements are part of the same process of love.

The violence in Fanon's work is directed toward Western modernity as a general phenomenon, which he experiences in material and immediate ways as a colonial subject. But this violence could also be applied particularly to theology as an academic discipline and as a way of framing reality that distorts and conceals reality, and in doing so, legitimizes the coloniality of power. For Fanon, the new world and new humanity can only be adequately imagined when moving beyond perspectives of Western modernity.[105] Fanon finds, in the revolutionary decolonial struggle, a process of both losing an identity that depends on modern/colonial rationalities and, simultaneously, a process of reclaiming humanity and of opening space for the eschatological dimension of reality that signification within the modern world-system conceals. When this struggle toward opening the possibility of an encounter with the eschatological dimension of reality manifests as violence, Fanon embraces dialectical movement.

Like Fanon, Baldwin does not separate love from violence. When the abstract concepts of love and violence are concretized historically, their relationship becomes much more complicated. Baldwin's conception of love is consistent with Fanon's on a fundamental level. Unsettling significations central to US identity is perceived as violent because shifting this edifice "so profoundly attacks one's own reality," such that "heaven and earth are shaken to their foundations."[106] Baldwin provides an iconoclastic response in his advice to his nephew: "we, *with love*, *shall force* our brothers to see themselves as they are, to cease fleeing from reality and begin to change it."[107] In this understanding of love, which remains consistent with his articulation of the manifestation of decolonial love as running down the hill into the city, Baldwin advocates a praxis that is often felt as violent. Decolonial love forces the irruption of reality into a construction of reality built to sustain the coloniality of power. By forcing a confrontation with reality, and in doing so denying the forms of identity attached to the structures of "America," Baldwin opens up the possibility to encounter the theologal. This process of salvation is a violent process insofar as it obliterates the foundations of dominant logics Americans have constructed in order justify prevailing structures.

In the work of Fanon and Baldwin, a praxis of deepening one's roots in reality is both violent and loving. The demand to confront reality and build something new, in Fanon's case, and the demand to recognize worlds that have already been made, in Baldwin's case, take away the possibility for Western modernity to signify its other. This is sensed as violent when a dominant society—France or the metropolis for Fanon, and the United States and its foundation as a white settler colony for Baldwin —depends on this signification for its self-legitimization. Breaking this construction shatters the structures in which those seeking inclusion in the modern world-system claim their identity.

Love, as both Fanon and Baldwin show, cannot reside above the historical situation. To love is not to distance oneself from reality, moving to a plane that transcends from reality and resides above the conflicts and violence within reality. To love is to be in reality more fully, and more passionately. Fanon did this by moving from behind the confines of psychiatry and the boundaries of European intellectual trajectories into the messiness and violence of the Algerian Revolution. Baldwin did this by working to shatter the tactics Americans use to prevent an encounter with reality. Both used writing as a tool within their political praxis. This movement into reality, for Fanon and Baldwin, is both decolonial love and salvation, and violence is a constitutive part of this movement.

Perceiving a historical movement of liberation or decolonization as a historical site of salvation and therefore as theologically pedagogic opens up a way of articulating the reality of salvation within a theological perspective that is also decolonial. This means that the loci of decolonial struggles and the epistemologies and orientations that take shape in these historical sites inform the theological meaning of salvation because they already are salvation historicized. This differs from interpreting a decolonial struggle theologically, in the sense of looking to see the elements within a decolonial struggle that might be shaped by understandings of divinity. It also differs from first rendering a decolonial movement Christian, and then drawing out the Christian elements of a decolonial struggle as theologically pedagogic. Understanding historical struggles as theologically pedagogic requires recognizing the decolonial love that orients these struggles as generating encounters with salvation and thus as informing the meaning of salvation.

Sharpening Decolonial Options in the Present Moment

This book frames a theoretical problem and potential response directed toward, and with a concern for, communities that identify as Christian and reflect on historical situations in light of a Christian faith commitment. It asks whether the theology of Christian communities is useful, relevant, and can operate in an authentic way in the present context of global coloniality. Taking seriously the traditions that make up liberation theology, which claim that Christian theology must be responsible to those who experience social, political, and economic structures as structures of domination, and ultimately must work against oppression, it suggests an option for a positive response.

When Frantz Fanon and James Baldwin were writing, they wrote within particular struggles. Fanon's writing was a part of his political praxis within a nationalist struggle that "authorized" this struggle, clarified its objectives, and convinced readers to push the struggle forward. Baldwin wrote to reveal realities underneath social myths, clarify ways in which the interior lives of individuals and communities are deeply political, and search for a unity that bound the everyday struggle of existence. Both sought to push decolonial movement forward, breaking the historical stasis of the modern world-system.

Those within the decolonial traditions in which Fanon and Baldwin stand and within the traditions of theologians of liberation have articulated the need to interrogate social-historical realities as a praxis that can respond to brutalities such as those imposed by US social, political, and economic structures. This intellective work demands an analysis of the historical contours of this nation that was invented within colonial modernity: from the establishment of a white settler colony within the constrained social imagination of the coloniality of power, to the various evolutions and intensifications of this modern/colonial legacy. Within such a context, decolonial options need to be sharpened. The US context forces a decolonial option within theology.[1] Turning to an encounter with the divine, as Christians understand divinity to be incarnate and revealed in Jesus, is not the only option to respond to the coloniality of power. But, the struggle for salvation, as a struggle to unveil, encounter, and participate in the eschatological depths of reality, is needed to both clarify the historical situations with which we are confronted and to ground a political praxis of transforming culturally dominant illusions of stasis. Decolonizing salvation, and in doing so re-imagining the locus, experience, and orientation that guides theological reflection, is one part of responding to the coloniality of power. Theological reflection is one tool within the project of clearing space for an encounter with reality.

When Ignacio Ellacuría and Jon Sobrino were writing in the 1970s and 1980s, they were doing so in the midst of living through the Salvadoran Civil War. Within this context, they entered into the political fray as theologians. Their approach to theological reflection was rooted within a political context grounded in conflict, and their theological writing intervened in this historical situation. In the context of critiquing forces within the Salvadoran Civil War and holding up an alternative option, Ellacuría and Sobrino operated in a fairly clear way as organic intellectuals. Likewise, Fanon and Baldwin articulated orientations of decolonial love—and, in my reading, thought theologically—within specific political contexts. Combat literature is for Fanon a praxis of writing within nationalist struggle, as revelation is for Baldwin a praxis of writing within a US context that continues to signify reality in an attempt to turn away from it. In these contexts, Fanon and Baldwin took sides. What does it mean to do liberation theology in the present context of global coloniality when the material conditions are different, even if still conflictual and embedded within the long history of the coloniality of power? What does reading the orientation of decolonial love that Fanon and Baldwin offer as theologically pedagogic mean for those who work as "professional" theologians?

Decolonial love is an eschatological reality that is also a historical reality. Fanon and Baldwin teach theologians how to struggle to participate in an eschatological reality and be held accountable to such a reality. This is their theological pedagogy. They hold together a rejection of the modern/colonial world-system that leads them away from a politics of inclusion with a faith in the eschatological reality of decolonial love that overpowers them and leads them to praxes perceived as violent. They surrender to the mystery of decolonial love rather than aspire to a stake in the modern world-system. Their participation in the eschatological reality of decolonial love—which is a way of being radically present in history, touching the depths of its theologal structure—shapes how they live faithfully in history. Fanon and Baldwin offer an orientation to theologians. They offer a posture toward reality wherein intellective work, or the struggle to apprehend reality, implies a commitment to opposing Western modernity and its ways of delineating being, knowledge, and eschatology. Fanon and Baldwin push theologians to live into an alternative eschatological commitment and to do intellectual work from this commitment.

While liberation theologians such as Gustavo Gutiérrez, Clodovis Boff, Ignacio Ellacuría, Ivone Gebara, and Marcella Althaus-Reid all claim a novel contribution on the level of methodology, a theology of God precedes and informs their projects in a fundamental way. They struggle to live faithfully in history in relation to God. The subversive and challenging aspects of these liberation theologians is who or what they claim God to be and how God is connected to revelation and history and, ultimately, to salvation.[2] Doing theology within a decolonial commitment does not necessarily entail changing the tasks of liberation theology. Doing theology within a decolonial project also does not necessarily entail moving on from the primary topics and commitments of liberation theology. It does, however, require investing in new forms of analysis and continuing to struggle to ground theological language more strongly in historical realities while doing so in light of the imagination of and commitment to the sacred. I refer to decolonial love as an eschatological reality, rather than simply love as an abstract category, because within a Christian perspective the divine is not abstract. Divinity is incarnate and revealed in those condemned by the status quo, in those who reveal the limits of social arrangements. The decoloniality of the present struggle shapes the liberation that is folded into salvation. Decolonial love, as a reality that emerges in the cracks of the modern/colonial world-system, is one option from which theologians can construct and articulate the sacred. Surrender to a divine reality, and the struggle to create the social and political conditions in which this encounter and surrender can be actualized, shapes a decolonial theology.

The form of analysis that decolonial thinkers provide, and the image and theorization of decolonial love that Fanon and Baldwin actualize can help theologians to decipher the present "signs of the times." Decolonial love provides an orientation to theologians as we struggle to apprehend reality. Decolonial love offers to theologians a foothold within the modern/colonial context from which to commit to the sacred and to face up to reality from a historical encounter with the divine mystery.

ACKNOWLEDGMENTS

Fr. Phillip J. Linden Jr. first introduced me to theology as a way of respond-ing to the world. He impressed upon me the need to take up theological reflection as a response to suffering peoples and out of a commitment to a particular struggle for liberation. He pushed me to understand libera-tion in terms of an encounter with a divine mystery, and why such an en-counter entails a liberation from European modernity and the imaginative constraints of the political economy that this half-millennium process has introduced. I continue to strive to do theology out of the perspective that Linden passed on to me and so many other students at Xavier University of Louisiana, and hope that this book gives some glimpse of that struggle.

As an intellectual, philosopher, and friend, Andre C. Willis has con-tinued to have a major impact on my struggle to figure out exactly what it is that I want to do through theological reflection and the study of reli-gion. Without his guidance and mentorship, I would be lost in the strange world of academia. Andre's readiness to listen to me work through my positions, his generous feedback on various drafts of this manuscript, his help in clarifying my arguments, his encouragement, and his friendship were instrumental in completing this book.

I am extremely grateful for the support of Jacques Haers and Kristien Justaert, who guided me in writing the initial draft of this manuscript. They were my most immediate discussion partners as I began writing what would become this book. Our frequent discussions and the tremendous amount of time we put into continuing the tradition of the Centre for Liberation Theologies at the Catholic University of Leuven (KU Leuven), as a locus for critically reflecting on and advancing theologies of libera-tion, formed the academic context that provided the space for me to work through the central ideas of this book. Kristien read countless drafts of this work, and has always been willing to engage the ideas I presented. Jacques repeatedly pushed me to bring my own voice forward, and helped to give me the confidence to do so. This book is significantly shaped by their constructive and critical feedback, and would not have been possible without their support. I could not have asked for better academic mentors. Funding through KU Leuven, the Centre for Liberation Theologies, and the Anthropos Research Group provided me with the time and resources to write this manuscript.

Having frequent conversations with a group of Fr. Linden's students—particularly Malik J. M. Walker, Steven Battin, and Rufus Burnett Jr.—has pushed me to continue to come back to the theological perspective we first learned at Xavier as a generative starting point. Malik has been a constant discussion partner since I was an undergraduate, and his critiques and encouragement helped me make it through my graduate work and writing this book. This book would not have been possible without his friendship. Steve and Rufus introduced me to decolonial thought while I was in graduate school, which helped me find a new way of using theological reflection to respond to the present context.

This book has also been shaped by the feedback of many friends and colleagues who read the manuscript. Mayra Rivera, M. Shawn Copeland, and Yves De Maeseneer provided constructive criticisms that were foundational as I moved into this project. Vincent Lloyd provided substantial feedback on the entire manuscript, and pushed me in new directions as I reworked it. It would be difficult to overstate his generosity. Georges De Schrijver, Bob Lassalle-Klein, Ivan Petrella, Emilie Townes, Steven Battin, and Jessica Coblentz gave me feedback on different chapters of the manuscript at various points that helped me to clarify my presentation of ideas. Richard Morrison at Fordham University Press and the blind reviewers solicited by the Press were also immensely helpful in the last stages of manuscript revisions. I'm extremely grateful to Richard for first encouraging me in this project. And, conversations with students at Saint Mary's College of California around potential intersections between de/coloniality and theologies of liberation forced me to continue to consider new questions, and articulate my positions with greater clarity.

My family—my parents, Laura Drexler and David Dreis, and sisters, Anna and Leah Drexler-Dreis—passed on to me the values and commitments that were the seeds for this work. The conversations I've had with my uncle, Tom Drexler, shaped my decision to study theology and the choices I have made in my studies. My family's support while I was writing this in Belgium and then California has meant much more to me than I could express.

I am most profoundly indebted to LaToya Drake. She was my immediate discussion partner before this project and throughout the duration of it, and steadily challenged me to respond to the concreteness of reality and, above all, engage with honesty the topics I was dealing with. Always up for long conversations about the ideas in the book, LaToya continues to challenge me to pursue academic inquiry not as an abstract process of fulfilling requirements, but as a response to something real that has to be as intellectually precise as possible. Her feedback on drafts, and her support, enthusiasm, humor, and love inspired me to keep going with this project.

Chapter 3 is a substantially revised version of a previously published article, "Latin American Liberation Theology as a Decolonial Project? Considering the Theological Approaches of Clodovis Boff and Ignacio Ellacuría," *Louvian Studies* 39 (201516): 218–39. This article is used by permission of Peeters Publishers.

Chapter 5 is a substantially revised version of a previously published article, "James Baldwin's Decolonial Love as Religious Orientation," *Journal of Africana Religions* 3, no. 3 (2015): 251–78. *Journal of Africana Religions* is edited by Edward E. Curtis IV and Sylvester Johnson. This article is used by permission of The Pennsylvania State University Press.

INTRODUCTION: WHAT IS DECOLONIAL LOVE?

1. See Sylvester A. Johnson, *African American Religions, 1500–2000: Colonialism, Democracy, and Freedom* (New York: Cambridge University Press, 2015).

2. Ibid., 121.

3. Throughout this book, I have not capitalized "black" or "white" as racial descriptors. I follow Cedric Johnson's reasoning in making this choice: "Such racial markers are not transhistorical, nor are they rooted in some biological essence. Instead, my usage [i.e., of not capitalizing 'black' and 'white'] reflects the view that racial identity is the product of historically unique power configurations and material conditions." (Cedric Johnson, *Revolutionaries to Race Leaders: Black Power and the Making of African American Politics* [Minneapolis: University of Minnesota Press, 2007], xvii).

4. Walter D. Mignolo, *Local Histories/Global Designs: Coloniality, Subaltern Knowledges, and Border Thinking* (Princeton, NJ: Princeton University Press, 2000), ix.

5. Ibid.

6. Gustavo Gutiérrez, *A Theology of Liberation: History, Politics, and Salvation* rev. ed., trans. Sister Caridad Inda and John Eagleson (Maryknoll, NY: Orbis Books, 1999), 96–97.

7. See ibid., 87.

8. See ibid., 88.

9. See ibid., 89.

10. Ibid., 97.

11. Ibid., 94.

12. See ibid., 86.

13. Gustavo Gutiérrez, *We Drink from Our Own Wells: The Spiritual Journey of a People*, trans. Matthew J. O'Connell (Maryknoll, NY: Orbis Books, 1984), 93.

14. Gutiérrez, *A Theology of Liberation: History*, 11.

15. On the option for the poor, see for example, Gustavo Gutiérrez, "Option for the Poor," in *Mysterium Liberationis: Fundamental Concepts of*

Liberation Theology, ed. Ignacio Ellacuría and Jon Sobrino, trans. Robert R. Barr (Maryknoll, NY: Orbis Books, 2004), 235–50; José M. Vigil, "The Option for the Poor is an Option for Justice-and not Preferential," *Voices from the Third World* 27, no. 1 (June 2004): 7–21; and Ada María Isasi-Díaz, "Mujerista Discourse: A Platform for Latinas' Subjugated Knowledge," in *Decolonizing Epistemologies: Latina/o Theology and Philosophy*, ed. Ada María Isasi-Díaz and Eduardo Mendieta (New York: Fordham University Press, 2012), 44–67.

16. Mayra Rivera has uncovered a version of this tendency in Enrique Dussel's work, which she describes as at times appropriating the locus of the alterity of those he names as victims as his own discourse in order to gain authority. See Mayra Rivera, *The Touch of Transcendence: A Postcolonial Theology of God* (Louisville, KY: Westminster John Knox Press, 2007), 75–76. Nelson Maldonado-Torres also recognizes this in Dussel's work, arguing that "[f]or Dussel, the Other becomes first a concrete subject, then a certain people with a history, and finally *myself*, that is, the poor of Latin America and the philosophy of the periphery." (Nelson Maldonado-Torres, *Against War: Views from the Underside of Modernity* [Durham, NC: Duke University Press, 2008], 183). In naming himself as the Other, the Other becomes for Dussel a ground of knowledge that legitimizes his own work.

17. See Jon Sobrino, *The Principle of Mercy: Taking the Crucified People from the Cross* (Maryknoll, NY: Orbis Books, 1994), 41.

18. See Maldonado-Torres, *Against War*, 122–59; and Chela Sandoval, *Methodology of the Oppressed* (Minneapolis: University of Minnesota Press, 2000).

19. Other interpreters of Fanon have centralized dialectics in his thought, including George Ciccariello-Maher, *Decolonizing Dialectics* (Durham, NC: Duke University Press, 2017); Peter Hudis, *Frantz Fanon: Philosopher of the Barricades* (London: Pluto Press, 2015); and Ato Sekyi-Otu, *Fanon's Dialectic of Experience* (Cambridge, MA: Harvard University Press, 1996).

20. Frantz Fanon, *Black Skin, White Masks*, trans. Richard Philcox (New York: Grove Press, 2008), 191; translation modified.

21. See James Baldwin, *James Baldwin: Collected Essays*, ed. Toni Morrison (New York: The Library of America, 1998), 23.

22. James Mossman, "Race, Hate, Sex, and Colour: A Conversation with James Baldwin and Colin MacInnes," in *Conversations with James Baldwin*, ed. Fred L. Standley and Louis H. Pratt (Jackson, MS: University Press of Mississippi, 1989), 48.

23. See Josiah Ulysses Young III, *James Baldwin's Understanding of God: Overwhelming Desire and Joy* (New York: Palgrave Macmillan, 2014), 9.

24. Frantz Fanon, *The Wretched of the Earth*, trans. Richard Philcox (New York: Grove Press, 2004), 11.

25. Baldwin, *Collected Essays*, 404.

26. Fanon, *Black Skin*, xi.

27. Carol Wayne White reads Baldwin as a "religious humanist," as ultimately affirming our "sacred humanity." See Carol Wayne White, *Black Lives and Sacred Humanity* (New York: Fordham University Press, 2016), vii–viii.

28. In this respect, I read Baldwin in a similar way as Vincent Lloyd. See Lloyd, *Religion of the Field Negro* (New York: Fordham University Press, 2017), 47–48.

29. James Baldwin, *The Fire Next Time* (New York: Vintage International, 1993), 95. Ed Pavlić describes Baldwin's allergy to stasis: "For Baldwin, the enemy was clear: the energies of separation; the forces that enclosed the self with itself; the mirrors that refused to reflect, shift, challenge, distort; the deforming logics of American history and the West that based itself on property and insisted on considering itself 'white.' Races, social classes, metaphors such as masculinity, were designed to confine, to stop the wheel and thwart the living disturbances of actual human encounters; they were social—at bottom, commercial—concoctions designed to prevent recognition of strangers, make Yes-men or No-women out of the mirrors of reflection and refraction." (Ed Pavlić, *Who Can Afford to Improvise? James Baldwin and Black Music, the Lyric and the Listeners* [New York: Fordham University Press, 2016], 104).

30. Walter D. Mignolo, *The Darker Side of Western Modernity: Global Futures, Decolonial Options* (Durham, NC: Duke University Press, 2011), xii.

31. See Mignolo, *The Darker Side of Western Modernity*, xxvii–xxviii.

32. See, for example, Walter D. Mignolo, "Delinking: The Rhetoric of Modernity, the Logic of Coloniality and the Grammar of De-Coloniality," *Cultural Studies* 21, no. 2–3 (2007): 463; and Mignolo, "Epistemic Disobedience and the Decolonial Option: A Manifesto," *TRANSMODERNITY: Journal of Peripheral Cultural Production of the Luso-Hispanic World* 1, no. 2 (2012): 45–46.

33. Marcella Althaus-Reid writes, for example, about the "pedagogic role" that Queer Holiness should "play in church and in society" (Althaus-Reid, *The Queer God* [London: Routledge, 2003], 169), or how "Indecent love becomes pedagogic because it teaches the difference between the church as a heterosexual colony (or neo-colony) and the church as the Queer *Kingdom* where the love which exceeds institutions (as God exceeds Godself in Christ and in the Trinity) knows more and knows better about alternative projects for justice and peace." (Ibid., 171).

34. Gustavo Gutiérrez, "The Irruption of the Poor in Latin America and the Christian Communities of the Common People," in *The Challenge of Basic Christian Communities*, ed. Sergio Torres and John Eagleson (Maryknoll, NY: Orbis, 1981), 108.

35. Gustavo Gutiérrez, *On Job: God-Talk and the Suffering of the Innocent*, trans. Matthew J. O'Connell (Maryknoll, NY: Orbis Books, 2009), 91–92.

I. COLONIAL MODERNITY AS A HISTORICAL CONTEXT

1. See Richard Wright, *The Color Curtain* (Jackson, MS: University of Mississippi Press, 1995).

2. See Aimé Césaire, *Discourse on Colonialism*, trans. Joan Pinkham (New York: Monthly Review Press, 2000).

3. See José Carlos Mariátegui, *Seven Interpretive Essays on the Peruvian Reality*, trans. Marjory Urquidi (Austin, TX: University of Texas Press, 1971).

4. For more on Quijano's formative role within the wider emerging field of decolonial theory, see Walter D. Mignolo, "Modernity and Decoloniality," *Oxford Bibliographies*, last modified 28 October 2011. Regarding the term "modern world-system," Wallerstein makes the following clarification: "Note the hyphen in world-system and its two subcategories, world-economies and world-empires. Putting in the hyphen was intended to underline that we are not talking about systems, economies, empires *of the* (whole) world, but about systems, economies, and empires *that are* a world (but quite possibly, and indeed usually, not encompassing the entire globe). . . . It says that in 'world-systems' we are dealing with a spatial/temporal zone which cuts across many political and cultural units, one that represents an integrated zone of activity and institutions which obey certain systemic rules." Immanuel Wallerstein, *World-Systems Analysis: An Introduction* (Durham, NC: Duke University Press, 2004), 17.

5. See Aníbal Quijano, "Coloniality and Modernity/Rationality," *Cultural Studies* 21, nos. 2–3 (March/May 2007): 169.

6. Ibid., 170.

7. See Aníbal Quijano, "Coloniality of Power, Eurocentrism, and Latin America," *Nepantla: Views from South* 1, no. 3 (2000): 544–45; and Aníbal Quijano, "Colonialidad del poder y clasificación social," *Journal of World-Systems Research* 6, no. 2 (Summer/Fall 2000): 345.

8. Quijano explains these modes of legitimization throughout the corpus of his work. See especially, Quijano, "Coloniality of Power, Eurocentrism, and Latin America," 533–80.

9. Quijano, "Colonialidad del poder y clasificación social," 350.

10. Ibid. Emphasis in original.

11. David Harvey reads Marx's position to be much closer to the constructive position Quijano sets forward than the critical way that Quijano reads Marx. See David Harvey, *A Companion to Marx's* Capital (London: Verso, 2010), 190–97.

12. See Quijano, "Colonialidad del poder y clasificación social," 372.

13. Karl Marx, *Capital: A Critique of Political Economy, Volume I*, trans. Ben Fowkes (London: Penguin Books, 1990), 175, n35; see Harvey, *A Companion to Marx's* Capital, 198.

14. Quijano, "Colonialidad del poder y clasificación social," 366.

15. See ibid.
16. See ibid., 371.
17. See ibid., 371–72.
18. Ibid., 376.
19. Quijano, "Coloniality and Modernity/Rationality," 171.
20. Cedric J. Robinson's work on racial capitalism points out that this racial classification of labor had a precedent in a medieval European economic system that had already been invested in racial categories. See Cedric J. Robinson, *Black Marxism: The Making of the Black Radical Tradition* (Chapel Hill, NC: University of North Carolina Press, 2000), 9–28.
21. See Aníbal Quijano, "'Raza,' etnia' y nación' en Mariátegui: Cuestiones abiertas," in *Cuestiones y horizontes: de la dependencia histórico-estructural a la colonidalidad/descolonialidad del poder* (Buenos Aires, CLASCO, 2014), 757.
22. See Quijano, "Colonialidad del poder y clasificación social," 377–78.
23. María Lugones, "Heterosexualism and the Colonial/Modern Gender System," *Hypatia* 22, no. 1 (Winter 2007): 193. Quijano is fairly clear in his understanding of sex, like age, as a "biological attribute"; see Quijano, "Colonialidad del poder y clasificación social," 373.
24. Lugones, "Heterosexualism and the Colonial/Modern Gender System," 195.
25. Ibid., 196. In making claims about the role (or the lack of the role) of gender within non-European societies before colonial contact, Lugones relies on Paula Gunn Allen's *The Sacred Hoop: Recovering the Feminine in American Indian Traditions* (Boston: Beacon Press, 1986); and Oyéronké Oyewùmí, *The Invention of Women: Making an African Sense of Western Gender Discourses* (Minneapolis: University of Minnesota Press, 1997).
26. Ibid., 187–89.
27. See ibid., 186.
28. Ibid., 202.
29. See ibid.
30. Sylvia Wynter, "Unsettling the Coloniality of Being/Power/Truth/Freedom: Towards the Human, After Man, Its Overrepresentation—An Argument," *CR: The New Centennial Review* 3, no. 3 (Fall 2003): 286.
31. Enrique Dussel, *The Underside of Modernity: Apel, Ricoeur, Rorty, Taylor, and the Philosophy of Liberation*, trans. and ed. Eduardo Mendieta (New Jersey: Humanities Press, 1996), 217.
32. Enrique Dussel, "Europe, Modernity, and Eurocentrism," *Nepantla: Views from South* 1, no. 3 (2000): 472.
33. See Sylvia Wynter, "1492: A New World View," in *Race, Discourse, and the Origin of the Americas: A New World View*, ed. Vera Lawrence Hyatt and Rex Nettleford (Washington, DC: Smithsonian Institution Press, 1995), 14.

34. See ibid., 26.

35. Willie James Jennings, *The Christian Imagination: Theology and the Origins of Race* (New Haven, CT: Yale University Press, 2010), 84.

36. See Wynter, "1492: A New World View," 28.

37. See ibid., 43. Wynter sees race as central: other categories of otherness—based on gender, sexuality, etc.,—are generated from the "ultimate mode of otherness based on 'race,'" Wynter, "1492: A New World View," 42.

38. See Nelson Maldonado-Torres, "Race, Religion, and Ethics in the Modern/Colonial World," *Journal of Religious Ethics* 42, no. 4 (2014): 699.

39. See Nelson Maldonado-Torres, "AAR Centennial Roundtable: Religion, Conquest, and Race in the Foundations of the Modern/Colonial World," *Journal of the American Academy of Religion* 82, no. 3 (September 2014): 646–51.

40. See Maldonado-Torres, "Race, Religion, and Ethics," 699.

41. See Maldonado-Torres, "Race, Religion, and Ethics," 700; Maldonado-Torres, *Against War*; and Nelson Maldonado-Torres, "On the Coloniality of Being," *Cultural Studies* 21, no. 2–3 (March/May, 2007): 240–70.

42. Maldonado-Torres, "Race, Religion, and Ethics," 703.

43. See Wynter, "Unsettling the Coloniality of Being," 260; and Sylvia Wynter and David Scott, "The Re-Enchantment of Humanism: An Interview with Sylvia Wynter," *Small Axe: A Caribbean Journal of Criticism* 4, no. 2 (September 2000): 159–60.

44. See Wynter and Scott, "The Re-Enchantment of Humanism," 177.

45. Ibid., 183.

46. Quijano, "Coloniality and Modernity/Rationality," 169.

47. Ibid.

48. Quijano, "Coloniality of Power, Eurocentrism, and Latin America," 549.

49. Quijano, "Colonialidad del poder y clasificación social," 343.

50. Ramón Grosfoguel, "The Epistemic Decolonial Turn," *Cultural Studies* 21, no. 2 (2007): 213.

51. Quijano, "Coloniality of Power, Eurocentrism, and Latin America," 549.

52. Linda Martín Alcoff, "Mignolo's Epistemology of Coloniality," *CR: The New Centennial Review* 7, no. 3 (Winter, 2007): 82.

53. Charles W. Mills, *The Racial Contract* (Ithaca, NY: Cornell University Press, 1997), 18.

54. See Jennings, *The Christian Imagination*, 33–34.

55. Frantz Fanon, *Black Skin, White Masks*, trans. Richard Philcox (New York: Grove Press, 2008), xiv.

56. See James Baldwin, *James Baldwin: Collected Essays*, ed. Toni Morrison (New York: The Library of America, 1998), 19.

57. Ibid., 20.

58. Ibid., 23.

59. Gustavo Gutiérrez, *A Theology of Liberation: History, Politics, and Salvation* rev. ed., trans. Sister Caridad Inda and John Eagleson (Maryknoll, NY: Orbis Books, 1999), 11.

60. Jon Sobrino argues that, in contrast to European theology, Latin American liberation theology has an intentional component of historical transformation toward liberation. See Jon Sobrino, *The True Church and the Poor*, trans. Matthew J. O'Connell (London: SCM Press, 1985), 7–38.

2. THE ENTANGLEMENT OF CHRISTIAN THEOLOGY AND THE COLONIALITY OF POWER: THE POSSIBILITIES OF A RESPONSE

1. Frantz Fanon, *The Wretched of the Earth*, trans. Richard Philcox (New York: Grove Press, 2004), 149, translation modified.

2. See, for example, the essays in *Race and Epistemologies of Ignorance*, ed. Shannon Sullivan and Nancy Tuana (Albany, NY: SUNY Press, 2007); and Toni Morrison, "Unspeakable Things Unspoken: The Afro-American Presence in American Literature," in *The Black Feminist Reader*, ed. Joy James and T. Denean Sharpley-Whiting (Malden, MA: Blackwell Publishers, 2000), 24–56.

3. Scholars who think within a decolonial vein often cite Charles Taylor as an example of someone who falls victim to this problem in his analysis of Western modernity, in his development of the modern self and secularism as processes internal to Europe. Joseph A. Massad, for example, develops an alternative understanding of the development of Western liberal secularism than Taylor's *A Secular Age* (Cambridge, MA: Harvard University Press, 2007), which Massad argues presents secularism "as a development internal to Europe and its Christian populations." Massad, *Islam in Liberalism* (Chicago: University of Chicago Press, 2015), 13. Enrique Dussel cites Charles Taylor's *The Sources of the Self: The Making of the Modern Identity* (Cambridge, MA: Harvard University Press, 1992) as an example of how modern thinkers have generally posited the development of modern identity as a phenomenon internal to Europe. Dussel shows that Taylor's use of exclusively European thinkers is not without consequences. Taylor's "manner of interpreting modern identity is Eurocentric, that is to say, provincial, regional, and does not take into account modernity's global significance and, thus, the inclusion of Europe's periphery as a 'source,' also constitutive of the modern 'self' as such." Dussel, *The Underside of Modernity: Apel, Ricoeur, Rorty, Taylor, and the Philosophy of Liberation*, trans. Eduardo Mendieta (Atlantic Highlands, NJ: Humanities Press, 1996), 131. Theologians thinking in decolonial terms most often cite the group of theologians who self identify as "radical orthodox" as an example of this Eurocentric critique of modernity. See, for example,

the critiques of radical orthodoxy in the essays in *Interpreting the Postmodern: Responses to "Radical Orthodoxy,"* ed. Rosemary Radford Ruether and Marion Grau (New York: T&T Clark, 2006).

4. Enrique Dussel, "World-System and 'Trans'-Modernity," *Nepantla: Views from South* 3, no. 2 (2002): 233–34.

5. Miranda Fricker, *Epistemic Injustice: Power and the Ethics of Knowing* (Oxford: Oxford University Press, 2007), 17.

6. Ibid., 44.

7. Linda Martín Alcoff describes this as one argument for why epistemologies of ignorance exist. See Alcoff, "Epistemologies of Ignorance: Three Types," in *Race and Epistemologies of Ignorance*, ed. Shannon Sullivan and Nancy Tuana (Albany, NY: SUNY Press, 2007), 40–41.

8. See Fricker, *Epistemic Injustice*, 6.

9. Ibid., 153.

10. See ibid., 161.

11. See Nelson Maldonado-Torres, "The Topology of Being and the Geopolitics of Knowledge," *City* 8, no. 1 (April 2004): 34; and Nelson Maldonado-Torres, "Frantz Fanon and C. L. R. James on Intellectualism and Enlightened Rationality," *Caribbean Studies* 33, No. 2 (2005): 151–52.

12. See Eduardo Mendieta, "Ethics of (not) Knowing: Take Care of Ethics and Knowledge will Come of its own Accord," in *Decolonizing Epistemology: Latina/o Philosophy and Theology*, ed. Ada María Isasi-Díaz and Eduardo Mendieta (New York: Fordham University Press, 2011), 260.

13. Aníbal Quijano, "Colonialidad del poder y clasificación social," *Journal of World-Systems Research* 6, no. 2 (Summer/Fall 2000): 380.

14. Sylvia Wynter and David Scott, 'The Re-Enchantment of Humanism: An Interview with Sylvia Wynter," *Small Axe: A Caribbean Journal of Criticism* 4, no. 2 (September 2000): 120.

15. Ibid., 165.

16. See ibid., 197.

17. See ibid..

18. Sylvia Wynter, "Unsettling the Coloniality of Being/Power/Truth/Freedom: Towards the Human, After Man, Its Overrepresentation—An Argument," *CR: The New Centennial Review* 3, no. 3 (Fall 2003): 329.

19. See Aníbal Quijano, "Coloniality and Modernity/Rationality," *Cultural Studies* 21, nos. 2–3 (March/May 2007): 175–76.

20. See ibid., 177.

21. Walter D. Mignolo, "The Geopolitics of Knowledge and the Colonial Difference," *South Atlantic Quarterly* 101, no. 1 (Winter 2002): 61.

22. Ibid., 66.

23. Ibid., 67.

24. Walter D. Mignolo, *Local Histories/Global Designs: Coloniality, Subaltern Knowledges, and Border Thinking* (Princeton, NJ: Princeton University Press, 2000), 23; see also Linda Martín Alcoff, "Mignolo's Epistemology of Coloniality," *CR: The New Centennial Review* 7, no. 3 (2007); and Alcoff, "Mignolo's Epistemology of Coloniality," 93.

25. See Alcoff, "Mignolo's Epistemology of Coloniality"; and Mignolo, *Local Histories/Global Designs*, 12.

26. Dussel, "World-System and 'Trans'-Modernity," 234.

27. See Linda Martín Alcoff, "Enrique Dussel's Transmodernism," *TRANSMODERNITY: Journal of Peripheral Cultural Production of the Luso-Hispanic World* 1, no. 3 (2012): 65–67.

28. See Walter D. Mignolo, *The Darker Side of Western Modernity: Global Futures, Decolonial Options* (Durham, NC: Duke University Press, 2011), 92.

29. See Mignolo, *Local Histories/Global Designs*, 12, 23.

30. See ibid., 72.

31. See for example, David Alvarez, "Of Border Crossing Nomads and Planetary Epistemologies," *CR: The New Centennial Review* 1, no. 3 (2001): 332, 335.

32. See Mignolo, "The Geopolitics of Knowledge," 71.

33. See Aníbal Quijano, "The Return of the Future and Questions about Knowledge," *Current Sociology* 50, no. 1 (January 2002): 75–87.

34. Chela Sandoval, *Methodology of the Oppressed* (Minneapolis: University of Minnesota Press, 2000), 140.

35. Paula M. L. Moya has critically engaged Sandoval's work in a similar way. See Moya, *Learning from Experience: Minority Identities, Multicultural Struggles* (Berkeley, CA: University of California Press, 2002), 78-85.

36. See Sandoval, *Methodology of the Oppressed*, 54-59; and Chela Sandoval, "US Third World Feminism: The Theory and Method of Oppositional Consciousness in the Postmodern World," *GENDERS* 10 (Spring 1991): 1–24.

37. Sandoval defines "US third world feminism" as referring to "a deliberate politics organized to point out the so-called third world *in* the first world. The very effort of this 1970s naming by US feminists of color was meant to signal a *conflagration* of geographic, economic, and cultural borders in the interest of creating a new feminist and internationalist consciousness and *location*: not just the third world *in* the first world, but a new global consciousness and terrain that challenges the distinctions of nation-state. This usage also prepared the way for the contemporary phase of US feminist of color politics that is called 'third *space* feminism.'" (Sandoval, *Methodology of the Oppressed*, 192, n1).

38. See ibid., 31.

39. Ibid., 58.

40. See ibid., 59.

41. Ibid., 140.

42. Ibid., 144.

43. Moya defines postmodernism as a diffuse cultural phenomenon characterized primarily on the following commonalities she draws out: "a strong epistemological skepticism, a valorization of flux and mobility, and a general suspicion of, or hostility toward, all normative and/or universalist claims." (Moya, *Learning from Experience*, 8, n9).

44. See Jorge A. Aquino, "Revolutionary Ambivalence: A Dialogue Between US Third World Feminism and Liberation Theology on the Limits of 'Love' as an Axis of Radical Social Change," *Critical Sense* XX (Fall 2002): 11–46.

45. See ibid., 16.

46. In reference to Althusser's understanding of interpellation as ideology forming subjectivity, Aquino refers to this implicit move in Sandoval's work as "reverse-interpellation." See ibid., 24.

47. Ibid., 24.

48. Ibid., 25.

49. See ibid., 25.

50. See Walter D. Mignolo, *The Idea of Latin America* (Malden, MA: Blackwell Publishing, 2005), xi.

51. Chela Sandoval identifies this tendency of an "apartheid of academic knowledges" in her observation that that white male poststructuralist theory, queer theory, white feminism, subaltern studies, US third world feminism, etc., are divided along lines of race, gender, and sexuality. "In spite of the profoundly similar theoretical and methodological foundation that underlies such seemingly separate domains, there is a prohibitive and restricted flow of exchange that connects them, and their terminologies are continuing to develop in a dangerous state of theoretical apartheid that insists on their differences." (Sandoval, *Methodology of the Oppressed*, 70).

52. See Mignolo, *The Idea of Latin America*, xv.

53. Ibid., 3–4. Mignolo calls decoloniality a "double-faced concept," as it implies an analysis of coloniality and a building of decolonial futures. Walter D. Mignolo, "Decolonizing Western Epistemology/Building Decolonial Epistemologies," in *Decolonizing Epistemologies: Latina/o Theology and Philosophy*, ed. Ada María Isasi-Díaz and Eduardo Mendieta (New York: Fordham University Press, 2012), 20.

54. See Mignolo, "Decolonizing Western Epistemology," 22.

55. Mignolo, "Decolonizing Western Epistemology," 39.

56. Mignolo, *The Darker Side of Western Modernity*, 92.

57. Here I follow the terminology that William R. Jones uses. In *Is God a White Racist?* (1973), Jones applies the method of internal criticism, whereas I am primarily using external criticism by using black liberation theology's

principles—and, I would aver, the core principles of Christian theology as such—to demonstrate a problem with black theology. Jones's basic thesis it that when the particular nature of ethnic suffering—its maldistribution (why it afflicts some people and not others), negative quality (a suffering without value for the person's well-being or salvation), enormity (its numbers in relation to the total class, and in reference to its quality), and its non-catastrophic character (its extension over historical eras)—is held together with the claim of divine benevolence, the result is a charge of divine racism. Black theology, Jones argues, never deals with this issue. Black theologians' theological systems prompt a question to which they fail to adequately respond. Jones's question: "Is God a white racist?" is a threshold question for black theology because it is a question to which black theologians have to provide an adequate response before moving on to other theological concepts, such as liberation and salvation. See William R. Jones, *Is God a White Racist? A Preamble to Black Theology* (Boston: Beacon Press, 1998).

58. Gustavo Gutiérrez, *A Theology of Liberation: History: Politics, and Salvation*, rev. ed., trans. Sister Caridad Inda and John Eagleson (Maryknoll, NY: Orbis Books, 1973), 11.

59. Gustavo Gutiérrez, "The Option for the Poor Arises from Faith in Christ," trans. Robert Lassalle-Klein, James Nickoloff, and Susan Sullivan, *Theological Studies* 70 (2009): 318.

60. Gutiérrez, *A Theology of Liberation*, xxix.

61. Ibid., xxxiv.

3. DECOLONIAL OPENINGS IN THEOLOGIES OF LIBERATION

1. Ignacio Ellacuría, *Escritos teológicos, tomo II* (San Salvador, UCA Editores, 2000), 134–35.

2. Althaus-Reid, *Indecent Theology: Theological Perversions in Sex, Gender and Politics* (London: Routledge, 2000), 31.

3. See ibid., 133–34.

4. See Marcella Althaus-Reid, *From Feminist Theology to Indecent Theology: Readings on Poverty, Sexual Identity and God* (London: SCM Press, 2004), 139.

5. See Vine Deloria Jr., *God is Red: A Native View of Religion* (Golden, CO: North American Press, 1994); Althaus-Reid, *Indecent Theology* and Althaus-Reid, *From Feminist Theology to Indecent Theology*; Ivan Petrella, *The Future of Liberation Theology: An Argument and Manifesto* (Aldershot: Ashgate, 2004); Delores S. Williams, *Sisters in the Wilderness: The Challenge of Womanist God-Talk* (Maryknoll, NY: Orbis, 1993); Ivone Gebara, *Longing for Running Water: Ecofeminism and Liberation*, trans. David Molineaux (Minneapolis: Fortress Press, 1999); James A. Noel, *Black Religion and the Imagination of Matter in the Atlantic World* (New York: Palgrave MacMillan, 2009); Noel Leo Erskine, *Decolonizing Theology: A Caribbean Perspective* (Maryknoll, NY:

Orbis Books, 1981); Jawanza Eric Clark, *Indigenous Black Theology: Toward an African-Centered Theology of the African American Religious Experience* (New York: Palgrave Macmillan, 2012); Ada María Isasi-Díaz, *La Lucha Continues: Mujerista Theology* (Maryknoll, NY: Orbis Books, 2004); Mayra Rivera, *Poetics of the Flesh* (Durham, NC: Duke University Press, 2015); An Yountae, *The Decolonial Abyss: Mysticism and Cosmopolitics from the Ruins* (New York: Fordham University Press, 2017); and Josiah Ulysses Young, III, *A Pan-African Theology: Providence and the Legacies of the Ancestors* (Trenton, NJ: Africa World Press, 1992).

6. See Enrique Dussel, "Sobre la Historia de la Teología en América Latina," in *Liberación y Cautiverio: Debates en Torno al Método de la Teología en América Latina*, ed. Enrique Ruiz Maldonado (Mexico City: Venecia, 1975), 20.

7. See Gustavo Gutiérrez, *A Theology of Liberation: History, Politics, and Salvation* rev. ed., trans. Sister Caridad Inda and John Eagleson (Maryknoll, NY: Orbis Books, 1999), xx.

8. See ibid., xx–xxxvii.

9. Gustavo Gutiérrez, "The Irruption of the Poor in Latin America and the Christian Communities of the Common People," in *The Challenge of Basic Christian Communities*, ed. Sergio Torres and John Eagleson (Maryknoll, NY: Orbis, 1981), 108.

10. Gustavo Gutiérrez, "Option for the Poor," in *Mysterium Liberationis: Fundamental Concepts of Liberation Theology*, trans. Robert R. Barr, ed. Ignacio Ellacuría and Jon Sobrino (Maryknoll, NY: Orbis Books, 1993), 240.

11. This tension is especially evident in Gustavo Gutiérrez, *On Job: God-Talk and the Suffering of the Innocent*, trans. Matthew J. O'Connell (Maryknoll, NY: Orbis Books, 2009), especially in the conclusion.

12. Ada María Isasi-Díaz, "Living Into the Future—*A Mujerista Proyecto Histórico*," in *Capital, Poverty, Development*, ed. Raúl Fornet-Betancourt (Wissenschaftsverlag Mainz, 2012), 108–9.

13. See Clodovis Boff, *Theology and Praxis: Epistemological Foundations*, trans. Robert Barr (Maryknoll, NY: Orbis, 1987). The Vatican's International Theological Commission began studying and evaluating liberation theology in 1974, and issued several cautions that would be repeated by Joseph Ratzinger's 1984 and 1986 instructions on liberation theology. Criticisms from academics in the United States came as early as 1973, when Thomas G. Sanders critiqued liberation theology for subscribing to a socialist utopian hope, a hope he described as failing to provide a strong basis for social change; see Thomas G. Sanders, "The Theology of Liberation: Christian Utopianism," *Christianity and Crisis* 33, no. 15 (1973): 167–73. Cardinal Alfonso López Trujillo, the former president of CELAM, is the most notable Latin American critic. López Trujillo distinguishes between the acceptable theology of

Medellín, which emphasizes reconciliation and the unacceptable theology of
Gutiérrez, Juan Luis Segundo, and others, which emphasizes the conflictive
nature of society; see Alfonso López Trujillo, *De Medellín a Puebla* (Madrid:
Biblioteca de Autores Cristianos, 1980); and López Trujillo, *Liberation or Revolution?* (Huntington, IN: Our Sunday Visitor, 1977). For an overview of the
theological and political critics of liberation theology, to which the preceding
references are indebted, see Arthur F. McGovern, *Liberation Theology and its
Critics: Towards an Assessment* (Maryknoll, NY: Orbis Books, 1989), 47–61.

14. See McGovern, *Liberation Theology*, 58–61.

15. Lewis R. Gordon, "Shifting the Geography of Reason in an Age of
Disciplinary Decadence," *TRANSMODERNITY: Journal of Peripheral Cultural Production of the Luso-Hispanic World* 1, no. 2 (Fall 2011): 98.

16. See Lewis R. Gordon, *Disciplinary Decadence: Living Thought in Trying
Times* (Boulder, CO: Paradigm Publishers, 2006), 8.

17. See Boff, *Theology and Praxis*, 42.

18. See ibid.

19. See Louis Althusser, *For Marx*, trans. Ben Brewster (London:
Verso, 1990), 182–93. Daniel Franklin Pilario argues that Boff's reliance
on Althusser (1) helps him to address the charge of an ideological basis to
(liberation) theology, but (2) disallows Boff from adequately accounting for
how people's actual praxis can make a theological contribution; see Pilario,
Back to the Rough Grounds of Praxis (Leuven, Belgium: Leuven University
Press, 2005), 279.

20. See Boff, *Theology and Praxis*, 71.

21. See ibid., 72.

22. Clodovis Boff, "Epistemology and Method of the Theology of Liberation," in *Mysterium Liberationis: Fundamental Concepts of Liberation Theology*,
ed. Ignacio Ellacuría and Jon Sobrino, trans. Robert R. Barr (Maryknoll, NY:
Orbis Books, 2004), 74.

23. In its initial stages, liberation theology drew on Andre Gunder Frank's
Marxist version of dependency theory. This is apparent in a talk given by
Gonzalo Arroyo at an early conference on liberation theology in 1972. Gon-
zalo Arroyo, "Pensamiento latinoamericano sobre sub-desarrollo y depen-
dencia externa," in *Fe cristiana y cambio social en América latina: Encuentro de El
Escorial, 1972* (Salamanca: Ediciones Sígueme, 1973), 305–21.

24. See Boff, *Theology and Praxis*, 7. Likewise, Gustavo Gutiérrez sees
the social sciences as allowing theology "to gain a more accurate knowledge
of society as it really is and so to articulate with greater precision the challenges [poverty and suffering] poses for the proclamation of the gospel and
thus for theological reflection as well." Gutiérrez, *The Truth Shall Set You
Free: Confrontations*, trans. Matthew O'Connell (Maryknoll, NY: Orbis Books,
1990), 55.

25. See Boff, *Theology and Praxis*, 11.

26. Ibid., 15; see Pilario, *Back to the Rough Grounds*, 299.

27. Boff, *Theology and Praxis*, 31.

28. Boff provides a helpful diagram in *Theology and Praxis*, 83. Elsewhere, he describes the constructive aspect of second theology: "Armed with the mediations they require, and with all of the material accumulated through these mediations, liberation theologians now address the construction of genuinely new syntheses of faith and the production of new theoretical significations, with a view to meeting the great challenges of today. Liberation theologians are never mere accumulators of theological materials. They are authentic architects of theology. Thus, they arm themselves with the necessary theoretical daring and a good dose of creative fantasy, in order to be in a position to deal with the unprecedented problems they find on the oppressed continents. Extracting and creatively developing the liberative content of the faith, they attempt to realize a new codification of the Christian mystery, in order thereby to help the church fulfill its mission of liberative evangelization in history." Boff, "Epistemology and Method of the Theology of Liberation," 83.

29. In a footnote, Boff cites Ellacuría as one of those theologians who problematically "imply or even state" that "second theology excludes or replaces first theology." This footnote in Boff's work reveals differences between the two thinkers on a fundamental level. Rather than limiting theology to working on the irruption of the poor, Ellacuría elevates the historical appearance of the poor to a formal object of theology. Boff's passing critique of Ellacuría indicates his sacrifice of the radical nature of this basis of liberation theology; Boff, *Theology and Praxis*, 272, n61.

30. "For that theology must be considered 'ideological' that is content with a philosophico-anthropological discourse, and remains mute vis-à-vis the social relationships of human beings—for example, their class situation, political situation, and the like—reducing itself to the detection of the common traits of all human beings in their transcendentality." Ibid., 11.

31. This question is, of course, rhetorical. Boff prioritizes categories from first theology because of the nature of the critiques to which he is responding.

32. Boff, *Theology and Praxis*, 166.

33. See ibid., 175.

34. Pilario makes a similar point: "in [Boff's] framework, *praxis* only features as a passive 'raw material' which can only be 'processed' theologically. It has neither the power to question nor to enhance theology's 'scientific' discourse. To put it differently, in its conscientious care not to admit 'ideology' into theology, Boff's theoreticism has denied access to the concrete, fleshly, vibrant elements of the people's *praxis*"; see Pilario, *Back to the Rough Grounds*, 329.

35. Audre Lorde, *Sister Outsider: Essays and Speeches by Audre Lorde* (New York: Crossing Press, 2007), 111.

36. See Ada María Isasi-Díaz, "Living into the Future," 108–9.

37. See Isasi-Díaz, *La Lucha Continues*, 95.

38. Ignacio Ellacuría, "Laying the Philosophical Foundations of Latin American Theological Method," in *Ignacio Ellacuría: Essays on History, Liberation, and Salvation*, ed. Michael E. Lee, trans. J. Matthew Ashley and Kevin F. Burke (Maryknoll, NY: Orbis, 2013), 84–85.

39. For a summary of Ellacuría's method of historicization, see Sajid Alfredo Herrera, "Aproximación al método de historización de Ignacio Ellacuría," in *Para una filosofía liberadora* (San Salvador, UCA Editores, 1995), 31–39.

40. See ibid., 35.

41. Ibid.

42. Ibid., 36.

43. Maldonado-Torres develops this idea in two articles: "Post-Continental Philosophy: Its Definition, Contours, and Fundamental Sources," *Review of Contemporary Philosophy* 9 (2010): 40–86; and Nelson Maldonado-Torres, "The Topology of Being and the Geopolitics of Knowledge: Modernity, Empire, and Coloniality," *City* 8, no. 1 (April 2004): 29–56.

44. Maldonado-Torres, "Post-Continental Philosophy," 40.

45. See ibid., 48.

46. Ibid., 58.

47. Ibid., 56.

48. See Andrew Prevot, *Thinking Prayer: Theology and Spirituality Amid the Crises of Modernity* (Notre Dame, IN: University of Notre Dame Press, 2015), 251.

49. Ignacio Ellacuría, *Filosofía de la realidad histórica* (San Salvador: UCA Editores, 1980), 42.

50. See ibid., 43–44.

51. J. Matthew Ashley defines this term in a translator's footnote of an essay from Jon Sobrino: "*Theologal* is a technical term used by both Ellacuría and Sobrino (coming ultimately from Zubiri), not to be confused with *theological*. A first approximation of what it means can be reached by means of an analogy with other disciplines and what they study. For example, just as the relevance and relative autonomy of sociology are premised on the existence and relative autonomy of a social dimension to reality that is not reducible to other dimensions (to the realms studied by biology and psychology, for instance), so too the relevance and relative autonomy of *theology* presume the reality of a 'theologal' dimension to all reality, which is most definitely related to all the other dimensions in the most intimate way imaginable, but cannot

be reduced to them without distortion. Just as sociology must determine the appropriate tools and loci to gain access to the social dimension of reality it wishes to understand, so too must theology find the tools and loci to gain access to the 'theologal dimension,' which ultimately has to do with the whole Trinitarian sweep of God's relationship to reality in creation, redemption, sanctification, and ultimate consummation." Jon Sobrino, "Monseñor Romero's Impact on Ignacio Ellacuría," in *A Grammar of Justice: The Legacy of Ignacio Ellacuría*, ed. J. Matthew Ashley, Kevin F. Burke, and Rodolfo Cardena, trans. J. Matthew Ashley (Maryknoll, NY: Orbis, 2014), 60–61, n7.

52. See Xavier Zubiri, "El problema teologal del hombre," in *Teologia y mundo contemporaneo: Homenaje a K. Rahner*, ed. Antonio Vargas Machuca (Madrid: Ediciones Cristianidad, 1975), 57.

53. Xavier Zubiri, *El hombre y Dios* (Madrid: Alianza Editorial, Sociedad de Estudios y Publicaciones, 1984), 12.

54. Prevot, *Thinking Prayer*, 257.

55. See Zubiri, "El problema teologal," 58.

56. See Robert Lassalle-Klein, *Blood and Ink: Ignacio Ellacuría, Jon Sobrino, and the Jesuit Martyrs of the UCA* (Maryknoll, NY: Orbis Books, 2014), 218.

57. Michael E. Lee, *Bearing the Weight of Salvation: The Soteriology of Ignacio Ellacuría* (New York: Herder & Herder, 2009), 54.

58. Zubiri, "El problema teologal," 58.

59. Ibid.

60. Ibid., 56.

61. Ellacuría develops the thesis that "Salvation history is a salvation in history" in *Freedom Made Flesh: The Mission of Christ and His Church*, trans. John Drury (Maryknoll, NY: Orbis Books, 1976), 15–18.

62. Ignacio Ellacuría, "The Historicity of Christian Salvation," in *Mysterium Libertionis: Fundamental Concepts of Liberation Theology*, trans. Margaret D. Wilde, ed. Ignacio Ellacuría and Jon Sobrino (Maryknoll, NY: Orbis Books, 1993), 253; translation modified.

63. Ignacio Ellacuría, "The Christian Challenge of Liberation Theology," trans. Michael E. Lee, in *Ignacio Ellacuría: Essays on History, Liberation, and Salvation*, ed. Michael E. Lee (Maryknoll, NY: Orbis Books, 2013), 129.

64. Ibid., my emphasis.

65. See Ignacio Ellacuría, "The Crucified People: An Essay in Historical Soteriology," (1978), trans. Phillip Berryman and Robert R. Barr, in *Ignacio Ellacuría: Essays on History, Liberation, and Salvation*, ed. Michael E. Lee (Maryknoll, NY: Orbis Books, 2013), 196.

66. Ellacuría, *Escritos teológicos, tomo II*, 134. In reference to this claim made by Ellacuría, Sobrino states: "In my opinion, in this paragraph Ellacuría is using the concept of 'sign' (of the times) not only in its historical-pastoral meaning as that which characterizes an epoch (cf. GS 4), but also in

its historical-theologal meaning as a place of the presence of God and God's plans. With this we want to say, theologically, that God is really present in the crucified people, and to make use of this radical theologization is to also affirm the ultimacy of its historical tragedy." Jon Sobrino, "Ignacio Ellacuría: el hombre y el cristiano," in Ignacio Ellacuría, *Fe y justicia* (Bilbao, Spain: Editorial Desclée, 1999), 22, n12.

67. See Ignacio Ellacuría, *Escritos teológicos, tomo II*, 177.

68. He defines the crucified people as such: "that collective body that, being the majority of humanity, owes its situation of crucifixion to a social order organized and maintained by a minority that exercises its dominion through a series of factors, which, taken together and given their concrete impact within history, must be regarded as sin. This is not a purely individual way of looking at every person who suffers due to unjust actions by others or even because such a person is sacrificed in the struggle against prevailing injustice. Although looking collectively at the crucified people does not exclude such an individual perspective, the latter is subsumed in the former, since the collective is the historical location of the individual's realization. Nor is the viewpoint here one of looking at purely natural misfortunes, although natural evils play a role, albeit derivatively, insofar as they take place in a particular historical order." Ellacuría, "The Crucified People," 208.

69. Jon Sobrino, *Jesus the Liberator: A Historical-Theological Reading of Jesus of Nazareth*, trans. Paul Burns and Francis McDonagh (Maryknoll, NY: Orbis Books, 1993), 255.

70. Sobrino defines the poor as such: "The poor are those close to the slow death poverty brings, those for whom surviving is a heavy burden and their chief task, and those who are also deprived of social dignity and sometimes also of religious dignity for not complying with church legislation." Ibid., 81.

71. Ibid., 3.

72. Jon Sobrino, *Christ the Liberator: A View from the Victims*, trans. Paul Burns (Maryknoll, NY: Orbis Books, 2001), 8.

73. See Sobrino, *Jesus the Liberator*, 70–79.

74. See ibid., 87–104.

75. Ibid., 79.

76. Ibid., 33.

77. "Modern theology, even in its progressive wings, generally uses what I have called the notional way, sometimes adding the way of practice, *but generally ignores the way of the addressee, on which liberation theology insists. And the resulting conclusions are very different.*" Ibid., 70, my emphasis.

78. Jon Sobrino, *The Principle of Mercy: Taking the Crucified People from the Cross* (Maryknoll, NY: Orbis Books, 1994), 30, 34.

79. Sobrino, *Jesus the Liberator*, 36.

80. See ibid., 37.
81. Ibid., 39. See also Sobrino, *The True Church and the Poor*, trans. Matthew J. O'Connell (London: SCM Press, 1985), 7–38.
82. Sobrino, *Principle of Mercy*, 28.
83. Sobrino, *Jesus the Liberator*, 41.
84. Ibid., 42–44.
85. Enrique Dussel, "Sobre la historia," 20.
86. "It is said of the Servant of Yahweh that God has set him up as the light of the nations. Pauline theology says that the *crucified* Christ is wisdom, and John's theology says that we must fix our eyes on this man who was *crucified*. If these expressions are not understood as purely rhetorical, they are saying that there is something in this crucified man that gives our intellect a light it does not obtain in other places. This is exactly what I am trying to say about the world of the poor, and I might add that this is why it is so surprising that 'Christian' christologies, which are confronted of necessity with a crucified man and have to admit that in him there is a 'revelation' of God, are not able to integrate into their method, or even to understand, the option for the poor." Sobrino, *Jesus the Liberator*, 33.

4. FRANTZ FANON'S DECOLONIAL LOVE: A NEW HUMANISM IN HISTORICAL STRUGGLE

1. Rufus Burnett, Jr. and Steven Battin, "Indigeneity and Theological Discourse," *Newsletter CLT* 7 (February, 2014): 8.
2. Fanon makes the following claim: "The interesting thing about this evolution [toward a 'verbal mystification' of enslavement] is that racism was taken as a topic of meditation, sometimes even as a publicity technique. Thus the blues—'the black slave lament'—was offered up for the admiration of the oppressors. This modicum of stylized oppression is the exploiter's and the racist's rightful due. Without oppression and without racism, you have no blues. The end of racism would sound the knell of the great Negro music." Frantz Fanon, *Toward the African Revolution: Political Essays: Political Essays* (New York: Grove Press, 1967), 37. Lewis R. Gordon argues that here Fanon erroneously holds to "the fallacy of causal permanence." It is not because racism provokes the appearance of the blues that the blues must continuously be linked to a context that is necessarily racist. Gordon argues: "Many people . . . not only enjoy music that is not intimately linked to their personal experience but also attach their own experience to music born of a different one." Lewis R. Gordon, *What Fanon Said: A Philosophical Introduction to His Life and Thought* (New York: Fordham University Press, 2015), 88.
3. Frantz Fanon, *Black Skin, White Masks*, trans. Richard Philcox (New York: Grove Press, 2008), xi.

4. Ibid., 202.

5. Henry Louis Gates observes, "It may be a matter of judgment whether his writings are rife with contradiction or richly dialectical, polyvocal, and multivalent; they are in any event highly porous, that is, wide open to interpretation, and the readings they elicit are, as a result, of unfailing *symptomatic* interest: Frantz Fanon, not to put too fine a point on it, is a Rorschach blot with legs." Henry Louis Gates, "Critical Fanonism," *Critical Enquiry* 17, no. 3 (Spring 1991): 458.

6. Fanon, *Black Skin*, xi.

7. Fanon, *Toward the African Revolution*, 18.

8. Ibid., 21.

9. Ibid., 22, emphasis in original.

10. Ibid., 22.

11. Ibid., 23.

12. Ibid., 24.

13. See Peter Hudis, *Frantz Fanon: Philosopher of the Barricades* (London: Pluto Press, 2015), 17.

14. See ibid., 18–19; and David Macey, *Frantz Fanon: A Biography* (New York: Picador, 2001), 93–108.

15. Fanon, *Black Skin*, xii, translation modified.

16. Ibid.

17. Ibid., xv, my emphasis.

18. Ibid., 90.

19. Ibid., xv.

20. See Maldonado-Torres, "On the Coloniality of Being: Contributions to the Development of a Concept," *Cultural Studies* 21, no. 2–3 (2007): 240–70.

21. See Marilyn Nissim-Sabat, "Fanonian Musings: Decolonizing/Philosophy/Psychiatry," in *Fanon and the Decolonization of Philosophy*, ed. Elizabeth A. Hoppe and Tracey Nicholls (Lanham, MD: Lexington Books, 2010), 43.

22. See, for example, Hudis, *Frantz Fanon: Philosopher of the Barricades*, 37.

23. G. W. F. Hegel, *Phenomenology of Spirit*, trans. A.V. Miller (New York: Oxford University Press, 1977), 110.

24. See ibid., 110–11.

25. Ibid., 113.

26. See ibid., 114.

27. Fanon, *Black Skin*, 191.

28. Ibid., 193; see also George Ciccariello-Maher, *Decolonizing Dialectics* (Durham, NC: Duke University Press, 2017), 54–55.

29. See Hegel, *Phenomenology*, 115.

30. Ibid., 117.

31. See ibid.

32. Ibid., 118–19.

33. Charles Taylor emphasizes the first of these two links the slave has to the universal— fear or the activity of the master. See Charles Taylor, *Hegel* (New York: Cambridge University Press, 1975), 155–57. As Maldonado-Torres has pointed out, Taylor's appropriation of Hegel is more concerned with Hegel's achievement of a harmonic vision of subjectivity than with Hegel's engagement with the question of the struggle for recognition in the master-slave dialectic. A focus on the latter would open up an awareness of power relationships, something that Maldonado-Torres argues is not adequately presented in Taylor's work. See Nelson Maldonado-Torres, *Against War: Views from the Underside of Modernity* (Durham, NC: Duke University Press, 2008), 123–24. See Taylor's essay on recognition, where Maldonado-Torres points out that he (strangely) lacks any substantial references to Hegel: Charles Taylor, "The Politics of Recognition," in *Multiculturalism*, ed. Amy Gutman (Princeton, NJ: Princeton University Press, 1994), 3–24.

34. Frantz Fanon, *The Wretched of the Earth*, trans. Richard Philcox (New York: Grove Press, 2004), 44.

35. In the *Elements of the Philosophy of Right*, Hegel argues that the totality of a state's structures is what is actual and rational. It is not necessary for philosophy to leave its historical situation; it is only necessary that philosophy comprehend its particular reality: "To comprehend *what is* is the task of philosophy, for *what is* is reason. As far as the individual is concerned, each individual is in any case a *child of his time*; thus philosophy, too, is *its own time comprehended in thoughts*. It is just as foolish to imagine that any philosophy can transcend its contemporary world as that an individual can overleap his own time or leap over Rhodes. If this theory does indeed transcend his own time, if it builds itself a world *as it ought to be*, then it certainly has an existence, but only within his opinions—a pliant medium in which the imagination can construct anything it pleases." G. W. F. Hegel, *Elements of the Philosophy of Right*, ed. Allen W. Wood, trans. H. B. Nisbet, (Cambridge: Cambridge University Press, 1991), 21–22. Marx will take issue with Hegel here, because Marx wants to respond to this totality.

36. See Ciccariello-Maher, *Decolonizing Dialectics*, 53–54.

37. See Fanon, *Black Skin*, 89.

38. Ibid., 94.

39. Ibid.

40. Ibid., 94–95, last emphasis mine.

41. Ibid., 101–2.

42. See ibid., 102.

43. George Ciccariello-Maher understands this to be a pivotal point in *Black Skin*: "For equality to be contemplated, for the obligation to recognize

the other to have any traction at all, racialized subjects must first seize access to ontology, storming the fortified heaven of *being itself*." George Ciccariello-Maher, "Jumpstarting the Decolonial Engine: Symbolic Violence from Fanon to Chávez," *Theory & Event* 13, no. 1 (2010). This is why Ciccariello-Maher sees Fanon's later engagement with the Hegelian master-slave dialectic to be crucial: "for the racialized subject, self-consciousness *as human* requires symbolic violence, it requires the assertion of reciprocity within a historical situation marked by the denial of such reciprocity, and if necessary, the provocation of conflict through the assertion of alterity." Ibid.

44. Ciccariello-Maher, *Decolonizing Dialectics*, 58.
45. Fanon, *Black Skin*, 102.
46. See Ciccariello-Maher, "Jumpstarting the Decolonial Engine."
47. Cited in Fanon, *Black Skin*, 111–12.
48. See Ciccariello-Maher, *Decolonizing Dialectics*, 69.
49. Fanon, *Black Skin*, 114.
50. Ibid., xii, translation modified.
51. Ibid., 63.
52. Ibid., xv.
53. Ibid., 191, translation modified.
54. Ibid., 193.
55. See Ciccariello-Maher, *Decolonizing Dialectics*, 66.
56. Fanon, *Black Skin*, 199.
57. See Ciccariello-Maher, *Decolonizing Dialectics*, 72.
58. See Alice Cherki, *Frantz Fanon: A Portrait*, trans. Nadia Benabid (Ithaca, NY: Cornell University Press, 2006), 67–73; David Macey, *Frantz Fanon: A Biography* (New York: Picador, 2000), 199–240; Hussein Abdilahi Bulhan, *Frantz Fanon and the Psychology of Oppression* (New York: Plenum Press, 1985), 227–78; and Hudis, *Frantz Fanon: Philosopher of the Barricades*, 59–62.
59. See Hudis, *Frantz Fanon: Philosopher of the Barricades*, 62.
60. See ibid., 73.
61. Fanon, *Toward the African Revolution*, 32.
62. Ibid., 33.
63. See ibid. 34.
64. Ibid., 38.
65. Ibid., 41.
66. Ibid., 43.
67. Ibid.
68. See Hudis, *Frantz Fanon: Philosopher of the Barricades*, 79.
69. See Cherki, *Frantz Fanon: A Portrait*, 90.
70. See ibid.
71. Fanon, *Toward the African Revolution*, 53.

72. Ibid.
73. Many of these articles are collected in *Toward the African Revolution* (published in French in 1964, after Fanon's death).
74. Fanon, *Toward the African Revolution*, 146.
75. Fanon, *The Wretched*, 156.
76. Ibid., 159.
77. See ibid., 148.
78. Ibid., 150.
79. Ibid., 152.
80. Ibid., 154.
81. Ibid., 155.
82. Ibid., 159, my emphasis.
83. Ibid., 160.
84. See ibid.
85. Ibid., 178.
86. Frantz Fanon, *A Dying Colonialism*, trans. Haakon Chevalier (New York: Grove Press, 1965), 27–28.
87. Ibid., 31.
88. Ibid., 119–20, my emphasis.
89. Peter Hudis, *Frantz Fanon: Philosopher of the Barricades*, 88.
90. Fanon, *The Wretched*, 1.
91. Ibid., 3, 1.
92. Ibid., 2.
93. Ibid.
94. Ibid., 4.
95. Ibid., 6, translation modified.
96. See Ciccariello-Maher, *Decolonizing Dialectics*, 39.
97. Ibid., 6–7.
98. See ibid., 10–11.
99. See ibid., 78–81.
100. Fanon, *The Wretched*, 11.
101. Ibid., 15.
102. Ibid., 67.
103. Ibid., 79.
104. Ibid., 93.
105. Ibid., 95.
106. Ibid., 141.
107. Ibid., 16.
108. See ibid., 17–19.
109. Ibid., 18.
110. Ibid., 18–19.

111. See Sylvester A. Johnson, *African American Religions, 1500–2000: Colonialism, Democracy, and Freedom* (New York: Cambridge University Press, 2015), 56–106.

112. Fanon, *The Wretched*, 19.

113. Ibid., 20.

114. Although she is ultimately critical of Fanon, Anne McClintock admires Fanon's pseudo-feminist sensibility. McClintock comments, "Fanon understands brilliantly how colonialism inflicts itself as a domestication of the colony, a reordering of the labor and sexual economy of the people, so as to divert female power into colonial hands and disrupt the patriarchal power of colonized men." Anne McClintock, "Fanon and Gender Agency," in *Rethinking Fanon: The Continuing Dialogue*, ed. Nigel C. Gibson (Amherst, NY: Humanity Books, 1999), 289. T. Denean Sharpley-Whiting, in a constructive reading of Fanon for a feminist project, stops short of speaking of Fanon as a feminist but does argue for "Fanon's radically humanist profeminist consciousness." T. Denean Sharpley-Whiting, *Frantz Fanon: Conflicts and Feminisms* (Lanham, MD: Rowan and Littlefield, 1998), 24.

115. See Fanon, *Dying Colonialism*, 39.

116. Ibid., 47.

117. At the same time, it's important to note that Fanon also makes important statements about women consistent with his other claims against assimilation; for example: "Involved in the struggle, the husband or father learns to look upon the relations between the sexes in a new light. The militant man discovers the militant woman, and *jointly* they create new dimensions for Algerian society." Ibid., 60, n14, my emphasis.

118. Ibid., 48.

119. Saba Mahmood, "Feminist Theory, Embodiment, and the Docile Agent: Some Reflections on the Egyptian Islamic Revival," *Cultural Anthropology*, 16, no. 2 (May 2001): 203.

120. Ibid., 209.

121. "My argument simply is that in order for us to be able to judge, in a morally and politically informed way, even those practices we consider objectionable, it is important to take into consideration the desires, motivations, commitments, and aspirations of the people to whom these practices are important. . . . This is not simply an analytic point, but reflects, I would contend, a political imperative born out of a realization that we can no longer presume that secular reason and morality exhaust the forms of valuable human flourishings." Ibid., 225.

122. Fanon, *The Wretched*, 237.

123. Ibid., 237, translation modified.

5. JAMES BALDWIN'S DECOLONIAL LOVE:
UNCOVERING THE REVELATION OF THE BEAT

1. James Baldwin, *Go Tell It on the Mountain* (New York: Random House, 1981), 32. See 1 Cor 4:5; and 1 Tim 6:15.

2. Baldwin, *Go Tell It on the Mountain*, 32.

3. James Baldwin, *Collected Essays*, ed. Toni Morrison (New York: The Library of America, 1998), 503.

4. Baldwin, *Go Tell It on the Mountain*, 33.

5. Ibid.

6. Ibid., 34.

7. Ibid.

8. This prompts Clarence E. Hardy III to name the first chapter of his book on James Baldwin and religion, "But the City Was Real." See Clarence E. Hardy, *James Baldwin's God: Sex, Hope, and Crisis in Black Holiness Culture* (Knoxville, TN: University of Tennessee Press, 2003), 1–16.

9. Jonathan S. Kahn develops this point much more fully. See Kahn, "Conclusion: James Baldwin and a Theology of Justice in a Secular Age," in *Race and Secularism in America*, ed. Jonathan S. Kahn and Vincent W. Lloyd (New York: Columbia University Press, 2016), 239–56.

10. Baldwin, *Collected Essays*, 13.

11. James Baldwin, *The Price of the Ticket: Collected Nonfiction, 1948–1985* (New York: St. Martin's Press, 1985), 647.

12. There have been a number of publications on Baldwin's understanding of religion, which occupies a central place in his work. See Hardy, *James Baldwin's God*; and Josiah Ulysses Young III, *James Baldwin's Understanding of God: Overwhelming Desire and Joy* (New York: Palgrave Macmillan, 2014). In an article that appeared between these two monographs, Douglas Field argues that Baldwin's Pentecostal background is central to his work, particularly the connection between music and church that permeates his fiction and nonfiction. Field considers Baldwin's concept of love to be crucial to Baldwin's exploration of religion and his understanding of salvation. See Douglas Field, "Pentecostalism and All That Jazz: Tracing James Baldwin's Religion," *Literature & Theology*, 22, no. 4 (December 2008): 436–57.

13. See Baldwin, *Collected Essays*, 501–04.

14. Baldwin, *Collected Essays*, 566.

15. Ibid.

16. See James Baldwin, *The Fire Next Time* (New York: Vintage International, 1993), 86.

17. Ibid., 95.

18. Ibid.

19. Baldwin, *The Price of the Ticket*, 646.

20. Baldwin, *The Fire Next Time*, 9–10.

21. See Charles H. Long, *Significations: Signs, Symbols, and Images in the Interpretation of Religion* (Aurora, CO: Davies Group, 1995), 1–2.

22. See ibid,, 4–5.

23. See ibid., 114.

24. See ibid., 116.

25. Long, *Significations*, 65–66, my emphasis.

26. Fanon, *Black Skin, White Masks*, trans. Richard Philcox (New York: Grove Press, 2008), 89–90.

27. See Baldwin, *Collected Essays*, 14–15.

28. Baldwin, *Collected Essays*, 23.

29. James Baldwin and Nikki Giovanni, *A Dialogue* (Philadelphia: J. B. Lippincott, 1973), 35–36.

30. Baldwin, *Collected Essays*, 841.

31. Ibid., 842.

32. Ibid.

33. The Christian concept of redemptive suffering has a difficult history, especially as Christianity has functioned vis-à-vis black communities in the United States. Delores S. Williams has demonstrated the painful historical consequences of the Christian notion of redemptive suffering by showing how an emphasis on Jesus' suffering on the cross has legitimized suffering, particularly of black women, giving it divine sanction. Rather than focus on Jesus' cross, and thus suffering, as salvific, Williams turns to Jesus' life and to his "ministerial vision." Delores S. Williams, *Sisters in the Wilderness: The Challenge of Womanist God-Talk* (Maryknoll, NY: Orbis Books, 1993), 167.

34. Victor Anderson, *Creative Exchange: A Constructive Theology of African American Religious Experience* (Minneapolis: Fortress Press, 2008), 99.

35. See Anderson, *Creative Exchange*, 108.

36. Baldwin describes such a context of suffering in his 1957 short story, "Sonny's Blues." See James Baldwin, *Going to Meet the Man* (New York: Penguin Books, 1991), 101–42. In this sense, although I do not follow Douglas Field's reading of Baldwin as effecting a return to the early church because of his Pentecostalism, I do agree with Field's interpretation of the significance of suffering in Baldwin's work: "Baldwin's most radical rewriting of Christian— or at least spiritual identity—is to place emphasis on salvation and redemption, not through God, but through a love that is founded on the sharing of pain. . . . Baldwin offers salvation through support and love of another." Field, "Pentecostalism and All That Jazz," 450.

37. James Baldwin, *Going to Meet the Man* (New York: Penguin Books, 1991), 139.

38. See James Baldwin, *The Cross of Redemption: Uncollected Writings*, ed. Randall Kenan (New York: Vintage International, 2011), 145–53.

39. See James Lincoln Collier, *The Making of Jazz: A Comprehensive History* (New York: Dell, 1979). Collier presents a "comprehensive history" of jazz without much recourse to jazz scholarship. He relies, rather, on a personal approach in which, for example, he focuses on the personal inadequacies of jazz musicians without describing the musicians in their contexts. See Tom Hennessey, review of *The Making of Jazz: A Comprehensive History*, by James Lincoln Collier, *Ethnomusicology* 25, no. 2 (May, 1981): 335–36.

40. James Baldwin, *The Cross of Redemption: Uncollected Writings*, ed. Randall Kenan (New York: Vintage International, 2011), 146.

41. Ibid., 147.

42. Ibid., 149.

43. Ibid., 149–50.

44. Ibid., 151.

45. Ibid., 151–52.

46. Ibid., 152.

47. Ibid.

48. Ibid.,153.

49. Baldwin, *Cross of Redemption*, 153.

50. Ibid.

51. Baldwin, *Collected Essays*, 749.

52. Ibid., 750.

53. Ibid.

54. Ibid., 755.

55. Ibid., 754.

56. Ibid., 220–21.

57. Ibid., 782.

6. THE THEOLOGICAL PEDAGOGY OF
FRANTZ FANON AND JAMES BALDWIN

1. Marcella Althaus-Reid writes, for example, about the "pedagogic role" that Queer Holiness should "play in church and in society," Marcella Althaus-Reid, *The Queer God* (London: Routledge, 2003), 169, or how "Indecent love becomes pedagogic because it teaches the difference between the church as a heterosexual colony (or neo-colony) and the church as the Queer *Kingdom* where the love which exceeds institutions (as God exceeds Godself in Christ and in the Trinity) knows more and knows better about alternative projects for justice and peace." Ibid., 171.

2. Here I bring together the way Gustavo Gutiérrez and Jon Sobrino define theology. Gustavo Gutiérrez, *A Theology of Liberation: History, Politics, and Salvation*, rev. ed., trans. Sister Caridad Inda and John Eagleson (Maryknoll, NY: Orbis Books, 1973), xxix; and Jon Sobrino, *The True Church and the Poor*, trans. Matthew J. O'Connell (London: SCM Press, 1985), 7–38.

3. Phillip J. Linden Jr., "Interview," in *Newsletter CLT* 4 (January 2013): 8.

4. See Vincent Lloyd, *Religion of the Field Negro* (New York: Fordham University Press, 2017), 6.

5. Frantz Fanon, *The Wretched of the Earth*, trans. Richard Philcox (New York: Grove Press, 2004), 6.

6. Ibid., 7.

7. Ibid.

8. Lloyd, *Religion of the Field Negro*, 4.

9. Fanon, *The Wretched*, 11.

10. James Baldwin, *James Baldwin: Collected Essays*, ed. Toni Morrison (New York: The Library of America, 1998), 471; cited in Lloyd, *Religion of the Field Negro*, 40.

11. Lloyd, *Religion of the Field Negro*, 43.

12. See ibid., 59.

13. Lloyd, *Religion of the Field Negro*, 40.

14. See Ibid., 27. Lloyd draws on James Cone's articulation of blackness here.

15. Lloyd, *Religion of the Field Negro*, 49.

16. Ibid., 55.

17. James Baldwin, *The Cross of Redemption: Uncollected Writings*, ed. Randall Kenan (New York: Vintage International, 2011), 70.

18. Ibid., 73.

19. See ibid.

20. Ibid., 74; my emphasis.

21. Ibid., 79.

22. Ibid.

23. Ibid., 81.

24. Baldwin, *Collected Essays*, 754–55, my emphasis.

25. Phillip J. Linden Jr., "Letting Go of Race: Reflections from a Historical Theological View," *Voices* 35, no. 1 (2013): 77.

26. See Fernand Braudel, *On History*, trans. Sarah Matthews (Chicago: University of Chicago Press, 1980), 27; and Linden, "Interview," 9.

27. See Braudel, *On History*, 33.

28. Linden, "Letting Go of Race," 76.

29. See ibid., 80–81.

30. Fanon, *The Wretched*, 12.

31. Linden, "Interview," 8.

32. See, for example, Paul's use of "time" (as "*kairós*") in Rom 8:18–23.

33. Braudel, *On History*, 10–11.

34. Ignacio Ellacuría, "Laying the Philosophical Foundations of Latin American Theological Method," trans. J. Matthew Ashley and Kevin F.

Burke, ed. Michael E. Lee in *Ignacio Ellacuría: Essays on History, Liberation, and Salvation* (Maryknoll, NY: Orbis Books), 80. I follow the translation of Ellacuría's three stages of the apprehension of reality, which are difficult to translate, that Jon Sobrino and Robert Lassalle-Klein offer. See Jon Sobrino, "Jesus of Galilee from the Salvadoran Context: Compassion, Hope, and Following the Light of the Cross," trans. Robert Lassalle-Klein and J. Matthew Ashley, *Theological Studies* 70 (2009): 449.

35. See Kevin F. Burke, *The Ground Beneath the Cross: The Theology of Ignacio Ellacuría* (Washington, DC: Georgetown University Press, 2000), 102.

36. Jon Sobrino, "The Kingdom of God and the Theologal Dimension of the Poor: The Jesuanic Principle," in *Who Do You Say That I Am? Confessing the Mystery of Christ*, ed. John C. Cavadini and Laura Holt (Notre Dame, IN: University of Notre Dame Press, 2004), 112.

37. Roger Haight develops an understanding of the experience of revelation that would more adequately account for how Sobrino understands revelation in *Dynamics of Theology* (Maryknoll, NY: Orbis Books, 2001), 75–77.

38. See Ellacuría, "Laying the Philosophical Foundations," 82–83.

39. See Burke, *The Ground Beneath the Cross*, 105.

40. See Ellacuría, "Laying the Philosophical Foundations," 83.

41. Jon Sobrino, *Christ the Liberator: A View from the Victims*, trans. Paul Burns (Maryknoll, NY: Orbis Books, 2001), 17.

42. See ibid., 19.

43. Sobrino, *Christ the Liberator*, 19.

44. Ibid., 59.

45. Ibid., 45.

46. From a biblical perspective, Elsa Tamez concretizes this with respect to the Pauline image of living "in the Spirit," "in Christ" or "as resurrected (cf. Romans 6 and 8)." See Elsa Tamez, "The Challenge to Live as Resurrected: Reflections on Romans Six and Eight," *Spiritus* 3 (2003): 86–95.

47. Sobrino, *Christ the Liberator*, 70.

48. Sobrino draws on Zubiri to make this point. See Sobrino, *Christ the Liberator*, 35.

7. DECOLONIZING SALVATION

1. Ignacio Ellacuría, "The Historicity of Christian Salvation," in *Mysterium Libertionis: Fundamental concepts of Liberation Theology*, trans. Margaret D. Wilde, ed. Ignacio Ellacuría and Jon Sobrino (Maryknoll, NY: Orbis Books, 1993), 254.

2. See ibid., 253.

3. See José Sols Lucia, *La teología histórica de Ignacio Ellacuría* (Valladolid, Spain: Editorial Trotta, 1999), 106–7.

4. Ellacuría, "The Historicity of Christian Salvation," 277; translation modified.

5. Ibid.

6. Ibid.

7. Frantz Fanon, *The Wretched of the Earth*, trans. Richard Philcox (New York: Grove Press, 2004), 6; translation modified.

8. See Lucia, *La teología histórica*, 119.

9. Ignacio Ellacuría, "Salvation History," in *Ignacio Ellacuría: Essays on History, Liberation, and Salvation*, ed. Michael E. Lee, trans. Margaret D. Wilde (Maryknoll, NY: Orbis, 2013), 193.

10. See Lucia, *La teología histórica*, 120; and Ellacuría, *Essays on History, Liberation, and Salvation*, 193.

11. See Ellacuría, "Salvation History," 173.

12. Ibid., 175–76.

13. Ellacuría, "The Historicity of Christian Salvation," 286.

14. Ibid., 287.

15. Ellacuría, "Salvation History," 189, my emphasis.

16. See Ivone Gebara, *Out of the Depths: Women's Experience of Evil and Salvation*, trans. Ann Patrick Ware (Minneapolis: Fortress Press, 2002), 52.

17. See Ivone Gebara, *Longing for Running Water: Ecofeminism and Liberation*, trans. David Molineaux (Minneapolis: Fortress Press, 1999), 45.

18. Ibid., 47.

19. "My analysis is not particularly biblical, although I do make reference to Scripture from time to time. I prefer to work from the perspective of theological anthropology, which I see as essential if we are to establish relationships of justice and solidarity." Gebara, *Out of the Depths*, 8; see also ibid., 4, 121).

20. See Gebara, *Longing for Running Water*, 76–82.

21. Ibid., 83.

22. See ibid., 86–87.

23. Ibid., 89.

24. See ibid., 94–95.

25. Ibid., 70.

26. Ibid., 85.

27. See ibid., 95.

28. Christopher D. Tirres similarly develops a tension between relatedness as a metaphysical and epistemological category. See Christopher D. Tirres, *The Aesthetics and Ethics of Faith: A Dialogue between Liberationist and Pragmatic Thought* (New York: Oxford University Press, 2014), 117.

29. Gebara, *Longing for Running Water*, 84, my emphasis.

30. See ibid., 83.

31. Ibid., 90.
32. See Gebara, *Out of the Depths*, 121.
33. Gebara, *Longing for Running Water*, 180.
34. Ibid.,183.
35. Ibid., 184.
36. Ibid., 185.
37. Ibid., 184–85.
38. See Marcella Althaus-Reid, *Indecent Theology: Theological Perversions in Sex, Gender and Politics* (London: Routledge, 2000), 18.
39. Ibid., 53.
40. Ibid., 25.
41. Ibid., 31.
42. Ibid., 40–44.
43. Ibid., 21, 27–28.
44. Ibid., 22.
45. See ibid., 22–23.
46. See ibid., 25.
47. See ibid., 30.
48. Marcella Althaus-Reid, *The Queer God* (London: Routledge, 2003), 133–34.
49. See ibid.,134.
50. Ibid., 135–37.
51. See ibid.,138–39.
52. See ibid., 152–53.
53. See ibid., 154–66.
54. Ibid., 167.
55. "This Christ [in the image of liberator] and this faith . . . provoke *conflict*. Jesus is *for* some, the oppressed, and *against* other, the oppressors. The poor proclaim him as the true Christ, while their oppressors warn against him, attack him, or at the very least seek to introduce other, alienating images of Christ. Following Jesus essentially involves conflict because it means reproducing a way of acting in favour of one group of people and against another, and this gives rise to attacks and persecution." Jon Sobrino, *Jesus the Liberator: A Historical-Theological Reading of Jesus of Nazareth*, trans. Paul Burns and Francis McDonagh (Maryknoll, NY: Orbis Books), 13.
56. See ibid., 95.
57. Ibid., 126. For a counter-example, see William T. Cavanaugh, *Torture and Eucharist: Theology, Politics, and the Body of Christ* (Oxford: Blackwell, 1998).
58. "History contains the true God (of life), God's mediation (the Kingdom) and its mediator (Jesus) as well as the idols (of death), their mediation

(the anti-Kingdom) and mediators (oppressors). The two types of reality are not only distinct, but conflictually disjunctive, so mutually exclusive, not complementary, and work against each other." Sobrino, *Jesus the Liberator*, 162.

59. Sobrino, *Jesus the Liberator*, 163.

60. Ibid., 27.

61. See ibid., 33.

62. "For christology this means using the light of the poor to penetrate better the totality of Christ. . . . Pauline theology says that the *crucified* Christ is wisdom, and John's theology says that we must fix our eyes on this man who was *crucified*. If these expressions are not understood as purely rhetorical, they are saying that there is something in this crucified man that gives our intellect a light it does not obtain in other places. This is exactly what I am trying to say about the world of the poor, and I might add that this is why it is so surprising that 'Christian' christologies, which are confronted of necessity with a crucified man and have to admit that in him there is a 'revelation' of God, are not able to integrate into their method, or even to understand, the option for the poor." (Sobrino, *Jesus the Liberator*, 33).

63. See Sobrino, *Jesus the Liberator*, 196.

64. Cf. John 3:16; and 1 John 4:9. See Sobrino, *Jesus the Liberator*, 230.

65. Sobrino, *Jesus the Liberator*, 261.

66. John Sobrino, *Christ the Liberator: A View from the Victims*, trans. Paul Burns (Maryknoll, NY: Orbis Books, 2001), 45.

67. Sobrino argues, "while it is important to realize who the *addressees* (victims) are if we are to understand God's action as liberating, it is equally important to realize who the *agents* (executioners) are if we are to understand God's action as being part of a struggle. This struggle is a way in which to express the antagonistic theologal structure of history, which contains the God of life and the idols of death, locked in struggle against one another." He goes on: "There is in history a mutually exclusive and antagonistic opposition between both the *mediations* of divinity (in Jesus' time, the Kingdom of God, on the one hand, and the *pax romana* and the circles that gathered around the Temple, on the other) and between the *mediators* (Jesus, on the one hand, and the high priest and Pilate, on the other), and this dialectic is introduced in the way God is revealed. According to this, God does not show himself in a history that is a *tabula rasa* with respect to his revelation, in which he could just as well reveal whatever he chose about himself, but God has to manifest himself actively against other divinities." Sobrino, *Christ the Liberator*, 85.

68. Sobrino, *Christ the Liberator*, 85.

69. Gebara, *Out of the Depths*, 122–23.

70. See Gebara, *Longing for Running Water*, 103.

71. Ibid.

72. Ibid., 104.

73. See ibid., 105.

74. See Gebara, *Longing for Running Water*, 129. Gutiérrez argues for the former title in his *The God of Life*, trans. Matthew J. O'Connell (Maryknoll, NY: Orbis Books, 1991).

75. See Frantz Fanon, *A Dying Colonialism*, trans. Haakon Chevalier (New York: Grove Press, 1965), 119–20.

76. See James Baldwin, *The Fire Next Time* (New York: Vintage International, 1993), 9–10.

77. See James Baldwin, *James Baldwin: Collected Essays*, ed. Toni Morrison (New York: The Library of America, 1998), 782; and Baldwin, *The Fire Next Time*, 95.

78. Baldwin, *The Fire Next Time*, 95.

79. See Aimé Césaire, *Discourse on Colonialism*, trans. John Pinkham (New York: Monthly Review Press, 2000), 54–55.

80. Gebara, *Out of the Depths*, 69.

81. Frantz Fanon, *Black Skin, White Masks*, trans. Richard Philcox (New York: Grove Press, 2008), 191.

82. Fanon, *Black Skin*, xv.

83. For example, she sees sites of social exclusion as sites "where important reflections on forms of love-knowing and theology may enlighten our Queer quest *for the face of God in human relationships.*" Marcella Althaus-Reid, *From Feminist Theology to Indecent Theology: Readings on Poverty, Sexual Identity and God* (London: SCM Press, 2004]), 148, my emphasis.

84. Althaus-Reid, *Queer God*, 38, my emphasis.

85. Althaus-Reid, *Queer God*, 171.

86. See ibid., 21. Althaus-Reid is specifically setting up a critique of Latin American liberation theology.

87. Althaus-Reid, *From Feminist Theology to Indecent Theology*, 92.

88. Althaus-Reid, *Indecent Theology*, 27.

89. Ibid.

90. See ibid., 27–28. Althaus-Reid refers to this theological process as "straightening" (Althaus-Reid, *Queer God*, 82–85).

91. Althaus-Reid, *Indecent Theology*, 148.

92. Mark 7:24-30.

93. Althaus-Reid, *From Feminist Theology to Indecent Theology*, 48.

94. See ibid., 51–52.

95. Kristien Justaert, "Liberation Theology: Deleuze and Althaus-Reid," *SubStance* 39, no. 1 (2010): 160.

96. Sobrino, *Christ the Liberator*, 125.

97. Jorge A. Aquino, "Revolutionary Ambivalence: A Dialogue between US Third World Feminism and Liberation Theology on the Limits of 'Love' as an Axis of Radical Change," *Critical Sense* 11, no. 1 (Fall 2002): 11.

98. See ibid., 11–48.

99. Ibid., 26–27.

100. Ibid., 11–12.

101. See ibid., 22.

102. Ibid., 36.

103. In this respect, James H. Cone's theological understanding of love would be much closer to that of Fanon and Baldwin. See James H. Cone, *Black Theology and Black Power* (Maryknoll, NY: Orbis Books, 1999), 47–56.

104. In a revolutionary struggle, the "artificial sentinel" guarding "the Greco-Roman pedestal" in the back of the minds of colonized intellectuals "is smashed to smithereens." Frantz Fanon, *The Wretched of the Earth*, trans. Richard Philcox (New York: Grove Press, 2004), 11.

105. Fanon perceives this signification within the context of the French colonization of Algeria: "This man whom you thingify by calling him systematically Mohammed, whom you reconstruct, or rather whom you dissolve, on the basis of an idea, an idea you know to be repulsive (you know perfectly well you rob him of something, that something for which not so long ago you were ready to give up everything, even your life) well, don't you have the impression that you are emptying him of his substance?," Frantz Fanon, *Toward the African Revolution*, trans. Haakon Chevalier (New York: Grove Press, 1967), 14.

106. Baldwin, *The Fire Next Time*, 9.

107. Ibid., 9–10, my emphasis.

CONCLUSION: SHARPENING DECOLONIAL
OPTIONS IN THE PRESENT MOMENT

1. On the "forced" character of theology, see Gerald M. Boodoo, "De Schrijver's Wager, Theology and Dehumanization: The Meaning of Liberation in a Forced Theological Context," in *Liberation Theologies on Shifting Grounds: A Clash of Socio-Economic and Cultural Paradigms*, ed. Georges De Schrijver (Louvain, Belgium: Peeters Publishers, 1998): 138–43.

2. Michelle A. Gonzalez argues that this theology of God is the novel contribution of Latin American liberation theology. See *A Critical Introduction to Religion in the Americas: Bridging the Liberation Theology and Religious Studies Divide* (New York: New York University Press, 2014), 50.

Alcoff, Linda Martín. "Enrique Dussel's Transmodernism." *TRANSMODER-NITY: Journal of Peripheral Cultural Production of the Luso-Hispanic World* 1, no. 3 (2012): 60–68.

———. "Mignolo's Epistemology of Coloniality," *CR: The New Centennial Review* 7, no. 3 (Winter, 2007): 79–101.

Althusser, Louis. *For Marx*. Translated by Ben Brewster. London: Verso, 2005.

Alvarez, David. "Of Border Crossing Nomads and Planetary Epistemologies." *CR: The New Centennial Review* 1, no. 3 (2001): 325–43.

Anderson, Victor. *Creative Exchange: A Constructive Theology of African American Religious Experience*. Minneapolis: Fortress Press, 2008.

Aquino, Jorge. "Revolutionary Ambivalence: A Dialogue between US Third World Feminism and Liberation Theology on the Limits of 'Love' as an Axis of Radical Social Change." *Critical Sense* 11, no. 1 (Fall 2002): 11–46.

Althaus-Reid, Marcella. *From Feminist Theology to Indecent Theology: Readings on Poverty, Sexual Identity and God*. London: SCM Press, 2004.

———. *Indecent Theology: Theological Perversions in Sex, Gender and Politics*. London: Routledge, 2000.

———. *The Queer God*. London: Routledge, 2003.

Baldwin, James. *The Cross of Redemption: Uncollected Writings*. Edited by Randall Kenan. New York: Vintage International, 2011.

———. *The Fire Next Time*. New York: Vintage International, 1993.

———. *Go Tell It on the Mountain*. New York: Random House, 1981.

———. *Going to Meet the Man*. New York: Penguin Books, 1991.

———. *James Baldwin: Collected Essays*. Edited by Toni Morrison. New York: The Library of America, 1998.

———. "James Baldwin's National Press Club Speech 1986." *YouTube*, December 22, 2014. https://www.youtube.com/watch?v=CTjY4rZFY5c&t=1657s.

———. *The Price of a Ticket: Collected Nonfiction, 1948–1985*. New York: St. Martin's Press, 1985.

Baldwin, James and Nikki Giovanni. *A Dialogue*. Philadephia: J. B. Lippincott, 1973.

Boff, Clodovis. "Epistemology and Method of the Theology of Liberation."
Translated by Robert R. Barr. In *Mysterium Liberationis: Fundamental
Concepts of Liberation Theology*, edited by Ignacio Ellacuría and Jon Sobrino,
57–84. Maryknoll, NY: Orbis Books, 2004.

———. *Theology and Praxis: Epistemological Foundations*. Translated by Robert
Barr. Maryknoll, NY: Orbis Books, 1987.

Boodoo, Gerald M. "De Schrijver's Wager, Theology and Dehumanization:
The Meaning of Liberation in a Forced Theological Context." In *Libera-
tion Theologies on Shifting Grounds: A Clash of Socio-Economic and Cultural
Paradigms*, edited by Georges De Schrijver, 131–51. Louvain, Belgium:
Peeters Publishers, 1998.

Braudel, Fernand. *On History*, Translated by Sarah Matthews. Chicago: University of Chicago Press, 1980.

Bulhan, Hussein Abdilahi. *Frantz Fanon and the Psychology of Oppression*.
New York: Plenum Press, 1985.

Burke, Kevin F. *The Ground Beneath the Cross: The Theology of Ignacio Ellacuría*.
Washington, DC: Georgetown University Press, 2000.

Burnett, Rufus Jr. and Steven Battin. "Indigeneity and Theological Discourse." *Newsletter CLT* 7 (February 2014): 8–9.

Cavanaugh, William T. *Torture and Eucharist: Theology, Politics, and the Body of
Christ*. Oxford: Blackwell, 1998.

Césaire, Aimé. *Discourse on Colonialism*. Translated by John Pinkham. New
York: Monthly Review Press, 2000.

Cherki, Alice. *Frantz Fanon: A Portrait*. Translated by Nadia Benabid. Ithaca,
NY: Cornell University Press, 2006.

Ciccariello-Maher, George. *Decolonizing Dialectics*. Durham, NC: Duke University Press, 2017.

———. "Jumpstarting the Decolonial Engine: Symbolic Violence from
Fanon to Chávez." *Theory and Event* 13 (2010). https://muse.jhu.edu/
article/377395.

Clark, Eric Jawanza. *Indigenous Black Theology: Toward an African-Centered
Theology of the African American Religious Experience*. New York: Palgrave
Macmillan, 2012.

Collier, James Lincoln. *The Making of Jazz: A Comprehensive History*.
New York: Dell, 1979.

Cone, James H. *Black Theology and Black Power*. Maryknoll, NY: Orbis Books,
1997.

Deloria, Vine Jr. *God is Red: A Native View of Religion*. Golden, CO: North
American Press, 1994.

Dussel, Enrique. "Europe, Modernity, and Eurocentrism," *Nepantla: Views
from South* 1, no. 3 (2000): 465–78.

———. "Sobre la historia de la teología en América Latina." In *Liberación y Cautiverio: Debates en torno al método de la teología en América Latina*, edited by Enrique Ruiz Maldonado, 19–68. Mexico City: Imprenta Venecia, 1976.

———. *The Underside of Modernity: Apel, Ricoeur, Rorty, Taylor, and the Philosophy of Liberation.* Translated by Eduardo Mendieta. Atlantic Highlands, NJ: Humanities Press: 1996.

———. "World System and 'Trans'-Modernity." Translated by Alessandro Fornazzari. *Nepantla: Views from South* 3, no. 2 (2002): 221–44.

Ellacuría, Ignacio. "The Christian Challenge of Liberation Theology" (1987). Translated by Michael E. Lee. In *Ignacio Ellacuría: Essays on History, Liberation, and Salvation*, edited by Michael E. Lee, 123–36. Maryknoll, NY: Orbis Books, 2013.

———. "The Crucified People: An Essay in Historical Soteriology" (1978). Translated by Phillip Berryman and Robert R. Barr. In *Ignacio Ellacuría: Essays on History, Liberation, and Salvation*, edited by Michael E. Lee, 195–224. Maryknoll, NY: Orbis Books, 2013.

———. *Escritos teológicos, tomo II.* San Salvador, UCA Editores, 2000.

———. *Filosofía de la realidad histórica.* San Salvador: UCA Editores, 1980.

———. *Freedom Made Flesh: The Mission of Christ and His Church.* Translated by John Drury. Maryknoll, NY: Orbis Books, 1976.

———. "The Historicity of Christian Salvation." Translated by Margaret D. Wilde. In *Mysterium Libertionis: Fundamental concepts of Liberation Theology*, edited by Ignacio Ellacuría and Jon Sobrino, 251–88. Maryknoll, NY: Orbis Books, 1993.

———. "Laying the Philosophical Foundations of Latin American Theological Method (1975)." Translated by J. Matthew Ashley and Kevin F. Burke. In *Ignacio Ellacuría: Essays on History, Liberation, and Salvation*, edited by Michael E. Lee, 63–92. Maryknoll, NY: Orbis Books, 2013.

———. "Salvation History." Translated by Margaret D. Wilde. In *Ignacio Ellacuría: Essays on History, Liberation, and Salvation*, edited by Michael E. Lee, 169–94. Maryknoll, NY: Orbis Books, 2013.

Erskine, Noel Leo. *Decolonizing Theology: A Caribbean Perspective.* Maryknoll, NY: Orbis Books, 1981.

Escobar, Arturo. "Latin America At a Crossroads: Alternative Modernizations, Post-Liberalism, or Post-Development." *Cultural Studies* 24, no. 1 (2010): 1–65.

Fanon, Frantz. *Black Skin, White Masks.* Translated by Richard Philcox. New York: Grove Press, 2008.

———. *A Dying Colonialism.* Translated by Haakon Chevalier. New York: Grove Press, 1965.

———. *Toward the African Revolution: Political Essays*. Translated by Haakon Chevalier. New York: Grove Press, 1967.

———. *The Wretched of the Earth*. Translated by Richard Philcox. New York: Grove Press, 2004.

Field, Douglass. "Pentecostalism and All That Jazz: Tracing James Baldwin's Religion." *Literature & Theology*, 22, no. 4 (December 2008): 436–57.

Fricker, Miranda. *Epistemic Injustice: Power and the Ethics of Knowing*. Oxford: Oxford University Press, 2007.

Gates, Henry Louis. "Critical Fanonism," *Critical Enquiry* 17, no. 3 (Spring 1991): 457–70.

Gebara, Ivone. *Longing for Running Water: Ecofeminism and Liberation*. Translated by David Molineaux. Minneapolis: Fortress Press, 1999.

———. *Out of the Depths: Women's Experience of Evil and Salvation*. Translated by Ann Patrick Ware. Minneapolis: Fortress Press, 2002.

Gonzalez, Michelle A. *A Critical Introduction to Religion in the Americas: Bridging the Liberation and Religious Studies Divide*. New York: New York University Press, 2014.

Gordon, Lewis R. *Disciplinary Decadence: Living Thought in Trying Times*. Boulder, CO: Paradigm, 2006.

———. "Shifting the Geography of Reason in an Age of Disciplinary Decadence." *TRANSMODERNITY: Journal of Peripheral Cultural Production of the Luso-Hispanic World* 1, no. 2 (Fall 2011): 95–103.

———. *What Fanon Said: A Philosophical Introduction to His Life and Thought*. New York: Fordham University Press, 2015.

Gutiérrez, Gustavo. *The God of Life*. Translated by Matthew J. O'Connell. Maryknoll, NY: Orbis Books, 1991.

———. "The Irruption of the Poor in Latin America and the Christian Communities." In *The Challenge of Basic Christian Communities*, edited by Sergio Torres and John Eagleson, 107–23. Maryknoll, NY: Orbis, 1981.

———. *On Job: God-Talk and the Suffering of the Innocent*. Translated by Matthew J. O'Connell Maryknoll, NY: Orbis Books, 2009.

———. "Option for the Poor." In *Mysterium Liberationis: Fundamental Concepts of Liberation Theology*. Translated by Robert R. Barr and edited by Ignacio Ellacuría and Jon Sobrino, 235-50. Maryknoll, NY: Orbis Books, 1993.

———. "The Option for the Poor Arises from Faith in Christ." Translated by Robert Lassalle-Klein, James Nickoloff, and Susan Sullivan. *Theological Studies* 70 (2009): 317–26.

———. *A Theology of Liberation: History, Politics, and Salvation*. Revised Edition. Translated by Sister Caridad Inda and John Eagleson. Maryknoll, NY: Orbis Books, 1973.

———. *The Truth Shall Set You Free: Confrontations*. Translated by Matthew J. O'Connell. Maryknoll, NY: Orbis Books, 1990.

———. *We Drink from Our Own Wells: The Spiritual Journey of a People*. Translated by Matthew J. O'Connell. Maryknoll, NY: Orbis Books, 1984.

Haight, Roger. *Dynamics of Theology*. Maryknoll, NY: Orbis Books, 2001.

Hardy Clarence E. III. *James Baldwin's God: Sex, Hope, and Crisis in Black Holiness Culture*. Knoxville, TN: University of Tennessee Press, 2003.

Harvey, David. *A Companion to Marx's Capital*. London: Verso, 2010.

Hegel, G. W. F. *Elements of the Philosophy of Right*. Translated by H. B. Nisbet. Edited by Allen W. Wood. Cambridge: Cambridge University Press, 1991.

———. *Phenomenology of Spirit*. Translated by A. V. Miller. New York: Oxford University Press, 1977.

Hudis, Peter. *Frantz Fanon: Philosopher of the Barricades*. London: Pluto Press, 2015.

Isasi-Díaz, Ada María. "Living Into the Future—*A Mujerista Proyecto Histórico*." In *Capital, Poverty, Development*, edited by Raúl Fornet-Betancourt, 107–19. Aachen, Germany: Wissenschaftsverlag Mainz, 2012.

———. *La Lucha Continues: Mujerista Theology*. Maryknoll, NY: Orbis Books, 2004.

———. "Mujerista Discourse: A Platform for Latinas' Subjugated Knowledge." In *Decolonizing Epistemologies: Latina/o Theology and Philosophy*, edited by Ada María Isasi-Díaz and Eduardo Mendieta, 44–67. New York: Fordham University Press, 2012.

Jennings, Willie James. *The Christian Imagination: Theology and the Origins of Race*. New Haven, CT: Yale University Press, 2010.

Johnson, Cedric. *Revolutionaries to Race Leaders: Black Power and the Making of African American Politics*. Minneapolis: University of Minnesota Press, 2007.

Johnson, Sylvester A. *African American Religions, 1500–2000: Colonialism, Democracy, and Freedom*. New York: Cambridge University Press, 2015.

Jones, William R. *Is God a White Racist? A Preamble to Black Theology*. Boston: Beacon Press, 1998.

Justaert, Kristien. "Liberation Theology: Deleuze and Althaus-Reid." *SubStance* 39, no. 1 (2010): 154–64.

Kahn, Jonathan S. "Conclusion: James Baldwin and a Theology of Justice in a Secular Age." In *Race and Secularism in America*, edited by Jonathan S. Kahn and Vincent W. Lloyd, 239–56. New York: Columbia University Press, 2016.

Lassalle-Klein, Robert. *Blood and Ink: Ignacio Ellacuría, Jon Sobrino, and the Jesuit Martyrs of the UCA*. Maryknoll, NY: Orbis Books, 2014.

Lee, Michael E. *Bearing the Weight of Salvation: The Soteriology of Ignacio Ellacuría*. New York: Herder and Herder, 2009.

Linden, Phillip J. Jr. "God in History: Reflections on the Theological and Historical Roots of the Religious Reality in the Americas." Unpublished manuscript, 1–13.

———. "Interview." *Newsletter CLT* 4 (January 2013): 5–9.

———. "Letting Go of Race: Reflections from Historical Theological View." *Voices* 35, no. 1 (2013): 75–88.

Lloyd, Vincent. *Religion of the Field Negro*. New York: Fordham University Press, 2017.

Long, Charles H. *Significations: Signs, Symbols, and Images in the Interpretation of Religion*. Aurora, CO: Davies Group, 1995.

Lorde, Audre. *Sister Outsider: Essays and Speeches by Audre Lorde*. New York: Crossing Press, 2007.

Lucia, José Sols. *La teología histórica de Ignacio Ellacuría*. Madrid: Editorial Trotta, 1999.

Lugones, María. "Heterosexualism and the Colonial/Modern Gender System." *Hypatia* 22, no. 1 (Winter 2007): 186–209.

Macey, David. *Frantz Fanon: A Biography*. New York: Picador, 2001.

Mahmood, Saba. "Feminist Theory, Embodiment, and the Docile Agent: Some Reflections on the Egyptian Islamic Revival." *Cultural Anthropology* 16, no. 2 (May 2001): 202–36.

Maldonado-Torres, Nelson. "AAR Centennial Roundtable: Religion, Conquest, and Race in the Foundations of the Modern/Colonial World." *Journal of the American Academy of Religion* 82, no. 3 (September 2014): 636–65.

———. *Against War: Views from the Underside of Modernity*. Durham, NC: Duke University Press, 2008.

———. "Frantz Fanon and C. L. R. James on Intellectualism and Enlightened Rationality." *Caribbean Studies* 33, No. 2 (2005): 149–94.

———. "On the Coloniality of Being: Contributions to the Development of a Concept." *Cultural Studies* 21, no. 2–3 (2007): 240–70.

———. "Post-Continental Philosophy: Its Definition, Contours, and Fundamental Sources." *Review of Contemporary Philosophy* 9 (2010): 40–86.

———. "Race, Religion, and Ethics in the Modern/Colonial World." *Journal of Religious Ethics* 42, no. 4 (2014): 691–711.

———. "The Topology of Being and the Geopolitics of Knowledge." *City* 8, no. 1 (April 2004): 29–56.

Mariátegui, José Carlos. *Seven Interpretive Essays on the Peruvian Reality*. Translated by Marjory Urquidi. Austin, TX: University of Texas Press, 1971.

Marx, Karl. *Capital: A Critique of Political Economy, Volume I*. Translated by Ben Fowkes. London: Penguin Books, 1990.

Massad, Joseph A. *Islam in Liberalism*. Chicago: University of Chicago Press, 2015.

McGovern, Arthur F. *Liberation Theology and its Critics: Towards an Assessment*. Maryknoll, NY: Orbis Books, 1989.

Mendieta, Eduardo. "Ethics of (not) Knowing: Take Care of Ethics and Knowledge will Come of its own Accord." In *Decolonizing Epistemology: Latina/o Philosophy and Theology*, edited by Ada María Isasi-Díaz and Eduardo Mendieta, 247–64. New York: Fordham University Press, 2011.

Mignolo, Walter D. *The Darker Side of Western Modernity: Global Futures, Decolonial Options*. Durham, NC: Duke University Press, 2011.

———. "Decolonizing Western Epistemology/Building Decolonial Epistemologies." In *Decolonizing Epistemologies: Latina/o Theology and Philosophy*, edited by Ada María Isasi-Díaz and Eduardo Mendieta. New York: Fordham University Press, 2012.

———. "Delinking: The Rhetoric of Modernity, the Logic of Coloniality and the Grammar of De-Coloniality." *Cultural Studies* 21, no. 2–3 (2007): 449–514.

———. "Epistemic Disobedience and the Decolonial Option: A Manifesto." *TRANSMODERNITY: Journal of Peripheral Cultural Production of the Luso-Hispanic World* 1, no. 2 (2012): 44–66.

———. "The Geopolitics of Knowledge and the Colonial Difference." *South Atlantic Quarterly* 101, no. 1 (2002): 57–96.

———. *The Idea of Latin America*. Malden, MA: Blackwell Publishing, 2005.

———. *Local Histories/Global Designs: Coloniality, Subaltern Knowledges, and Border Thinking*. Princeton, NJ: Princeton University Press, 2000.

———. "The Many Faces of Cosmo-polis: Border Thinking and Critical Cosmopolitanism." *Public Culture* 12, no. 3 (2000): 721–48.

Mills, Charles W. *The Racial Contract*. Ithaca, NY: Cornell University Press, 1997.

Morrison, Toni. "Unspeakable Things Unspoken: The Afro-American Presence in American Literature." In *The Black Feminist Reader*, edited by Joy James and T. Denean Sharpley-Whiting, 24–56. Malden, MA: Blackwell Publishers, 2000.

Mossman, James. "Race, Hate, Sex, and Colour: A Conversation with James Baldwin and Colin MacInnes." In *Conversations with James Baldwin*, edited by Fred L. Standley and Louis H. Pratt, 46–58. Jackson, MS: University Press of Mississippi, 1989.

Moya, Paula M. L. *Learning from Experience: Minority Identities, Multicultural Struggles*. Berkeley, CA: University of California Press, 2002.

Nissim-Sabat, Marilyn. "Fanonian Musings: Decolonizing/Philosophy/Psychiatry." In *Fanon and the Decolonization of Philosophy*, edited by

Elizabeth A. Hoppe and Tracey Nicholls, 39–54. Lanham, MD: Lexington Books, 2010.

Noel, James A. *Black Religion and the Imagination of Matter in the Atlantic World*. New York: Palgrave Macmillan, 2009.

Pavlić, Ed. *Who Can Afford to Improvise? James Baldwin and Black Music, the Lyric and the Listeners*. New York: Fordham University Press, 2016.

Petrella, Ivan. *The Future of Liberation Theology: An Argument and Manifesto*. Aldershot: Ashgate, 2004.

Pilario, Daniel F. *Back to the Rough Grounds of Praxis: Exploring Theological Method with Pierre Bordieu*. Leuven, Belgium: Peeters Press, 2006.

Quijano, Aníbal. "Colonialidad del poder y clasificación social." *Journal of World-Systems Research* 6, no. 2 (Summer/Fall 2000): 342–86.

———. "Coloniality and Modernity/Rationality." *Cultural Studies* 21, nos. 2–3 (March/May 2007): 168–78.

———. "Coloniality of Power, Eurocentrism, and Latin America," *Nepantla: Views from South* 1, no. 3 (2000): 533–80.

———. "The Return of the Future and Questions about Knowledge." *Current Sociology* 50, no. 1 (January 2002): 75–87.

Reuther, Rosemary Radford and Marion Grau, eds. *Interpreting the Postmodern: Responses to "Radical Orthodoxy."* New York: T&T Clark, 2006.

Rivera, Mayra. *Poetics of the Flesh*. Durham, NC: Duke University Press, 2015.

———. *The Touch of Transcendence: A Postcolonial Theology of God*. Louisville: Westminster John Knox Press, 2007.

Robinson, Cedric J. *Black Marxism: The Making of the Black Radical Tradition*. Chapel Hill, NC: University of North Carolina Press, 2000.

Sandoval, Chela. *Methodology of the Oppressed*. Minneapolis: University of Minnesota Press, 2000.

———. "U.S. Third World Feminism: The Theory and Method of Oppositional Consciousness in the Postmodern World," *GENDERS* 10 (Spring 1991): 1–24.

Sekyi-Otu. Ato. *Fanon's Dialectic of Experience*. Cambridge, MA: Harvard University Press, 1996.

Sharpley-Whiting, T. Denean. *Frantz Fanon: Conflicts and Feminisms*. Lanham, MD: Rowan and Littlefield, 1998.

Sobrino, Jon. *Christ the Liberator: A View from the Victims*. Translated by Paul Burns. Maryknoll, NY: Orbis Books, 2001.

———. "Ignacio Ellacuría: el hombre y el cristiano." In Ignacio Ellacuría, *Fe y justicia*, 11–114. Bilbao, Spain: Editorial Desclée, 1999.

———. "Jesus of Galilee from the Salvadoran Context: Compassion, Hope, and Following the Light of the Cross." Translated by Robert Lassalle-Klein and J. Matthew Ashley. *Theological Studies* 70 (2009): 437–60.

———. *Jesus the Liberator: A Historical-Theological Reading of Jesus of Nazareth*. Translated by Paul Burns and Francis McDonagh. Maryknoll, NY: Orbis Books, 1993.

———. "The Kingdom of God and the Theologal Dimension of the Poor: The Jesuanic Principle." In *Who Do You Say That I Am? Confessing the Mystery of Christ*, edited by John C. Cavadini and Laura Holt, 109–45. Notre Dame, IN: University of Notre Dame Press, 2004.

———. "Monseñor Romero's Impact on Ignacio Ellacuría." In *A Grammar of Justice: The Legacy of Ignacio Ellacuría*, edited by J. Matthew Ashley, Kevin F. Burke, and Rodolfo Cardenal, 57–76, translated by J. Matthew Ashley. Maryknoll, NY: Orbis Books, 2014.

———. *The Principle of Mercy: Taking the Crucified People from the Cross*. Translated by Dimas Planas. Maryknoll, NY: Orbis Books, 1994.

———. *The True Church and the Poor*. Translated by Matthew J. O'Connell. London: SCM Press, 1985.

Sullivan, Shannon, and Nancy Tuana, eds. *Race and Epistemologies of Ignorance*. Albany, NY: SUNY Press, 2007.

Tamez, Elsa. "The Challenge to Live as Resurrected: Reflections on Romans Six and Eight." *Spiritus* 3 (2003): 86–95.

Taylor, Charles. *Hegel*. New York: Cambridge University Press, 1975.

Tirres, Christopher D. *The Aesthetics and Ethics of Faith: A Dialogue between Liberationist and Pragmatic Thought*. New York: Oxford University Press, 2014.

Vigil, José M. "The Option for the Poor is an Option for Justice—And not Preferential." *Voices from the Third World* 27, no. 1 (June 2004): 7–21.

Walker, Malik J. M. "Just Sit: Liberation Theology as Abiding in an Urban Future." *Newsletter CLT* 11 (June 2015): 5–7.

Wallerstein, Immanuel. *World-Systems Analysis: An Introduction*. Durham, NC: Duke University Press, 2004.

Wayne White, Carol. *Black Lives and Sacred Humanity*. New York: Fordham University Press, 2016.

Williams, Delores S. *Sisters in the Wilderness: The Challenge of Womanist God-Talk*. Maryknoll, NY: Orbis Books, 1993.

Wright, Richard. *The Color Curtain*. Jackson, MS: University of Mississippi Press, 1995.

Wynter, Sylvia. "1492: A New World View." In *Race, Discourse, and the Origin of the Americas: A New World View*, edited by Vera Lawrence Hyatt and Rex Nettleford, 5–57. Washington, DC: Smithsonian Institution Press, 1995.

———. "Unsettling the Coloniality of Being/Power/Truth/Freedom: Towards the Human, After Man, Its Overrepresentation—An Argument," *CR: The New Centennial Review* 3, no. 3 (Fall 2003): 257–337.

Wynter Sylvia and David Scott. "The Re-Enchantment of Humanism: An
    Interview with Sylvia Wynter." *Small Axe: A Caribbean Journal of Criticism*
    4, no. 2 (September 2000): 119–207.
Young, Josiah Ulysses III. *James Baldwin's Understanding of God: Overwhelming
    Desire and Joy*. New York: Palgrave Macmillan, 2014.
———. *A Pan-African Theology: Providence and the Legacies of the Ancestors*.
    Trenton, NJ: Africa World Press, 1992.
Zubiri, Xavier. "El problema teologal del hombre." In *Teologia y mundo
    contemporaneo: Homenaje a K. Rahner*, edited by Antonio Vargas Machuca,
    55–64. Madrid: Ediciones Cristianidad, 1975.